THE SOCIAL PROTECTION INDICATOR FOR ASIA

TRACKING DEVELOPMENTS IN SOCIAL PROTECTION

DECEMBER 2022

ASIAN DEVELOPMENT BANK

Contents

Tables, Figures, and Boxes

Tables

Figures

Foreword

In the last decade, social protection has taken a prominent role in national development agendas and policies as a tool for addressing poverty, inequality, and social exclusion in Asia. Strengthening social protection systems and service delivery is an important priority in most countries in the region. The Asian Development Bank (ADB) has long recognized social protection as one of the key strategic areas for promoting inclusive development in the Asia and Pacific region. Our most recent corporate strategy, Strategy 2030, considers social protection as one of the key areas for support in pursuing the operational priority of addressing remaining poverty and reducing inequalities in the region.

This report analyzes 2018 data on social protection programs implemented by governments in 26 countries in Asia. It uses the Social Protection Indicator (SPI) to assess the level of resources invested in social protection as well as the value of the benefits, coverage, and distribution of expenditures in terms of poverty, gender, and disability. It also reviews progress on social protection at the individual country and regional levels between 2009 and 2018. The report continues the effort to systematically monitor and assess the developments in social protection begun by ADB and its development partners in 2005. The SPI initiative contributes to building evidence-based knowledge to support the development of social protection systems in the region.

The report suggests that average social protection expenditure per intended beneficiary (or SPI) in 24 countries with complete data in Asia increased from 3.3% of gross domestic product per capita in 2009 to 4.1% in 2018. Over the years, many countries have achieved remarkable success in promoting universal pension and health coverage. The gender gap in access to social protection has also been steadily decreasing. For the first time, this report offers an assessment of government social protection expenditure for people with disabilities. It suggests that average spending for programs supporting people with disabilities in Asia increased over 2009-2018.

The report's findings also underline the need for deepening and accelerating social protection investments to address remaining coverage gaps, improve benefit value, promote gender and disability inclusive programs, and develop comprehensive systems. The coronavirus disease (COVID-19) pandemic has demonstrated the importance of social protection in dealing with the effects of large, covariate shocks. It highlighted the urgent need to develop inclusive social protection systems and invest in human capital to promote people's resilience to shocks. Availability of robust, consistent, and comparable data is key to development of social protection, and the report offers an insightful assessment of constraints on data production and compilation in the region.

We hope that the SPI continues to be a useful resource to our partners and stakeholders. We thank everyone who contributed to this report, and we look forward to further engagement with social protection practitioners, advocates, and decision-makers in our efforts to promote inclusive, equitable, and sustainable development.

Bruno Carrasco
Director General concurrently Chief Compliance Officer
Sustainable Development and Climate Change Department
Asian Development Bank

Acknowledgments

This publication, *The Social Protection Indicator for Asia: Tracking Developments in Social Protection*, has been a collaborative effort among various social protection experts within and outside ADB, with particular recognition of the various government line agencies that provided the data used for this report. Special thanks to colleagues from the International Labour Organization (ILO)—Nuno Cunha, senior social protection specialist, Decent Work Technical Support Team for East and South-East Asia, and Valeria Nesterenko, data officer on social protection, Social Protection Department—for writing a chapter on social protection data and statistics in Asia and the Pacific.

The main chapters on the social protection indicator were written by Terry McKinley, professor at School of Oriental and African Studies in London, and Babken Babajanian, associate professorial lecturer at the London School of Economics. Additional special features were added to this report: a chapter on the social protection response to the coronavirus disease (COVID-19) in Asia written by Anand Ramesh Kumar, ADB consultant on social protection; a chapter on addressing disability through social protection written by Joanna Rogers, ADB consultant on disability inclusion; and a chapter on the future of social protection in Asia penned by Michael Samson, director of research at the Economic Policy and Research Institute. Ludovico Carraro, ADB consultant, provided valuable inputs. Flordeliza C. Huelgas, ADB consultant on statistics and social protection, did the data review and consolidation of 26 country calculations and reports prepared by national researchers. These were prepared by Mohammad Asif Mukhtar (Afghanistan), Diana Ghazaryan (Armenia), Ilkin Nazarov (Azerbaijan), Mohammad Yunus (Bangladesh), Chimmi Dolkar (Bhutan), Chey Tech (Cambodia), Xinping Guan (People's Republic of China), David Jijelava (Georgia), Mayang Rizky (Indonesia), Yoko Komatsubara (Japan), Orynbassar Abeldinova (Kazakhstan), Sangmi Han (Republic of Korea), Temir Burzhubaev (Kyrgyz Republic), Inthasone Phetsiriseng (Lao People's Democratic Republic), Suman Sharma (Malaysia and Singapore), Sofoora Usman (Maldives), Enkhtsetseg Byambaa (Mongolia), Sailesh Bhandary (Nepal), Hina Shaikh (Pakistan), Ahmid Bualan (Philippines), Ganga Tilakaratna (Sri Lanka), Ganjina Zardodkhonova (Tajikistan), Vichelle Roaring-Arunsuwannakorn (Thailand), Hamidulla Hamdamov (Uzbekistan), and Nguyen Thi Lan Huong (Viet Nam). These country reports are available on request from ADB.

The preparation of this report was led by Michiel Van Der Auwera, former senior social development specialist, under the overall guidance of Wendy Walker, chief of the Social Development Thematic Group, Sustainable Development and Climate Change Department.

The report benefited from comments received from relevant resident missions and regional departments, and from members of the social protection technical working group. Imelda Marquez provided administrative support.

Kimberly Fullerton copyedited the report, Lumina Datamatics did the layout, and Tuesday Soriano did the proofreading.

Abbreviations

4Ps	Pantawid Pamilyang Pilipino Program
ADB	Asian Development Bank
BISP	Benazir Income Support Programme
CHT	Chittagong Hill Tracts
COVID-19	coronavirus disease
CPF	Central Provident Fund
CRPD	Convention on the Rights of People with Disabilities
GBD	Global Burden of Disease
GDP	gross domestic product
GNI	gross national income
ILO	International Labour Organization
ILO/SSI	International Labour Organization Social Security Inquiry
IMF	International Monetary Fund
Lao PDR	Lao People's Democratic Republic
LMPs	labor market programs
NADRA	National Database Registration Authority
NGO	nongovernment organization
NSF	National Savings Fund
OECD	Organisation for International Co-operation and Development
PES	Public Employees Scheme
PKH	Program Keluarga Harapan
PPP	purchasing power parity
PRC	People's Republic of China
ROK	Republic of Korea
SDG	Sustainable Development Goal
SPI	Social Protection Indicator
UEEPS	Urban Enterprise Employees Pension Scheme
UNESCAP	United Nations Economic and Social Commission for Asia and the Pacific
UNICEF	United Nations Children's Fund
URRPS	Urban and Rural Residents Pension Scheme
WGQs	Washington Group questions
WHO	World Health Organization
WHO DAS 2	World Health Organization Disability Assessment Schedule 2
WHS	World Health Survey
VRG	Village Representative Group Member

Executive Summary

This report presents the results from 26 national reports[1] that are based on the compilation of individual country and regional level-data for social protection programs implemented by governments in 2018. It uses the Social Protection Indicator (SPI) to assess the level of resources invested in social protection as well as benefits, coverage, and distribution of expenditures in terms of poverty, gender, and disability status. The report also provides information on the historical trends in social protection expenditures and beneficiaries in the region.

The Asian Development Bank (ADB) developed the SPI in 2005 as a tool for monitoring and analyzing social protection at the individual country and regional levels. This is the fourth in the series of SPI publications prepared by ADB and follows reports produced for 2009, 2012, and 2015.

In addition to presenting the SPI trends, this report contains thematic chapters focusing on the social protection response to the coronavirus disease (COVID-19) pandemic; constraints and opportunities in producing and analyzing social protection data and statistics at the national and regional levels; challenges in identifying people with disabilities and measuring disability prevalence for effective monitoring of disability-focused social protection measures; and anticipating the future of social protection in Asia.

Social Protection Expenditure in Asia Is Increasing Modestly

Across 26 countries in Asia, the average social protection expenditure per intended beneficiary—the SPI—was 4.0% of the gross domestic product (GDP) per capita, and the average social protection expenditure amounted to 5.2% of GDP in 2018. Expenditure at the individual country's level varied widely, ranging from a 0.9 SPI in the Lao People's Democratic Republic (Lao PDR) to an 11.7 SPI in Japan.

Social protection spending is associated with an individual country's income, demographic structure, and extent of inequality; it is also influenced by its policy vision and institutional context. The level of social protection expenditure is most affected by the share of people aged 60 and over, followed by the country's income level, and level of income equality. The larger the share of people aged 60 and over and the higher the country's income, the higher

---

[1] These include Afghanistan, Armenia, Azerbaijan, Bangladesh, Bhutan, Cambodia, the People's Republic of China (PRC), Georgia, Indonesia, Japan, Kazakhstan, the Republic of Korea (ROK), the Kyrgyz Republic, the Lao People's Democratic Republic (Lao PDR), Malaysia, Maldives, Mongolia, Nepal, Pakistan, the Philippines, Singapore, Sri Lanka, Tajikistan, Thailand, Uzbekistan, and Viet Nam.

social protection expenditure is likely to be. Countries with low income inequality are likely to have higher levels of social protection spending.

Social protection has come to be seen as a key public policy instrument in most countries in Asia; however, progress in social protection spending in the past decade has been modest. The SPI in Asia for 24 countries with complete data for 2009 to 2018 increased from 3.3 in 2009 to 4.1 in 2018, driven mainly by the expansion of social insurance. Similarly, social protection expenditure increased from 4.6% of GDP in 2009 to 5.4% of GDP in 2018. Social protection spending in most countries in the region, however, did not outpace growth in GDP and remained lower than what may have been possible given their average income levels. In fact, social protection in Asia has been primarily responsive to large crises. Thus, the 1997 Asian financial crisis, the 2008 global financial crisis, and the COVID-19 pandemic were key triggers that spiked social protection expenditure in the region.

Developing and strengthening effective and inclusive social protection requires sustained financial commitment and higher levels of investment. Countries must develop and sustain comprehensive social protection systems that provide broad-based support and address different vulnerabilities across the life cycle. Such systems can help poor and disadvantaged people be more resilient to the effects of the life cycle and covariate shocks. Comprehensive systems develop close complementarity among different social protection programs—social insurance, social assistance, and labor market programs (LMPs)—to ensure basic income security and access to essential health care for all. Greater investments in system preparedness can help deal with shocks effectively. Given the presence and high visibility of social protection in national agendas during the COVID-19 crisis, governments currently have a unique opportunity to increase investment in social protection and to develop shock-responsive systems to support their populations more effectively.

Social Insurance Dominates Social Protection Expenditure, but Coverage Gaps Remain

Social insurance dominated spending across income groups, with an average SPI of 3.0 (3.9% of GDP). On average, pensions and health insurance comprised the largest share of social insurance as well as overall social protection expenditure in Asia—accounting for 2.5% and 0.9% of GDP and about 50.3% and 13.5% of total social protection expenditure, respectively. The social insurance SPI increased from 2.3 in 2009 to 3.1 in 2018. Among the three social protection categories, social insurance had the highest share of benefits at 28.2% of GDP per capita and the widest coverage, reaching 38.5% of intended beneficiaries.

These indicators reflect remarkable success in achieving universal or near-universal pension and health coverage in many countries in Asia. However, large pockets of the population in at least half of the countries in this study remain uncovered by pensions and health insurance. People who are employed in the informal economy are the least likely to benefit from social insurance schemes; inadequate social insurance coverage leaves women particularly vulnerable. Women comprise a disproportionate share of workers in the informal sector, tend to have lower incomes than men, and are less likely to be covered by social insurance. The key policy prerogative is thus to extend social insurance coverage to those excluded from protection. This entails removing the barriers that prevent workers in some forms of employment from accessing social insurance and utilizing noncontributory mechanisms to support those unable to make individual contributions.

Only a Few Countries Combine Generous Benefits with Wide Coverage

The depth of social insurance benefits was particularly substantial in high-income Japan, the Republic of Korea (ROK), and Singapore. Social insurance coverage in these countries was high, especially in Japan and ROK, which have universal pensions and health insurance coverage. However, they did not combine large social assistance benefits with high coverage. Social assistance in these countries is deployed as a last resort to support vulnerable society members who face particular social risks and require more targeted assistance.

Majority of Countries in Asia Offer Small Benefits but Have Achieved High Coverage

The prevailing trends in both social insurance and social assistance were to keep the depth of benefits low and to expand the breadth of coverage. The majority of countries in Asia fell into this category. Social insurance coverage increased from 22.5% in 2009 to 41.0% in 2018. The progress in coverage was driven by the expansion of health insurance in Japan, the ROK, Maldives, the Philippines, Thailand, and Viet Nam, largely due to progressive universalization of health insurance coverage. Equally, it was propelled by the expansion in pension coverage, which is especially evident in Armenia, the People's Republic of China (PRC), Indonesia, Japan, the Kyrgyz Republic, and Tajikistan. A similar picture is observed in social assistance, where coverage increased from 16.8% in 2009 to 25.7% in 2018. Several countries, such as Armenia, Bangladesh, Georgia, Indonesia, Mongolia, Pakistan, Sri Lanka, and Viet Nam, offered small benefits but have achieved substantial coverage.

These countries chose to extend social protection coverage but to retain low benefits, with the prospect of raising benefit levels incrementally. Prioritizing coverage over the value of benefits can be a practical trade-off to enable countries to reduce the coverage gap initially. However, it is imperative that social protection programs provide adequate protection; therefore, national strategies and fiscal policies need to explicitly incorporate the goal of an incremental increase in the value of benefits and to mandate that policy makers identify strategies to mobilize resources and to expand fiscal space.

The SPI data suggest that not all countries in Asia followed this pattern, however. A handful of countries provided generous benefits to a small share of the eligible population under social insurance (e.g., Bangladesh, Bhutan, Malaysia, and Pakistan) and social assistance (e.g., Japan, the ROK, Maldives, and Singapore). Finally, several countries provided low benefits and low coverage regarding social insurance (e.g., Cambodia, Maldives, and Nepal) and social assistance (e.g., Bhutan, the Lao PDR, Tajikistan, and Uzbekistan).

Contributory and Noncontributory Pensions Have Been Extended

Old-age pensions in this report are defined as contributory benefits to persons aged 60 and over. Pensions took up a large share of social insurance spending—2.5% of GDP—in Asia. Spending on pensions was above the regional average in the PRC, Japan, Mongolia, Viet Nam, and most post-Soviet Union transition countries. Several countries in the region have achieved universal or near-universal coverage of pensions, including the PRC, Japan, the ROK, Maldives, Mongolia, Nepal, and Thailand. Similarly, all post-Soviet Union transition countries considered in this study, except Armenia and Azerbaijan, have universal pension coverage.

The progress in pension coverage has been possible partly due to strengthening and extending contributory schemes to workers in the informal economy. This expansion was supported by parallel efforts to establish and to extend noncontributory tax-financed schemes (social pensions) to support the poor and near-poor who are unable to make social insurance contributions. Notable are institutional arrangements to extend pension coverage using these two avenues in the PRC and Thailand. Both countries established universal coverage by extending contributory pensions to include all employed and a share of self-employed workers and by providing tax-financed pension benefits for those not eligible for contributory pensions.

Social pensions, categorized in this report under social assistance, took up 0.3% of GDP on average across Asia. Social pensions were instrumental in promoting universal coverage in several countries in the region. Social pensions in Maldives, Nepal, and Thailand are offered to all citizens without access to existing contributory schemes. Georgia's universal pension, the country's main pension scheme, replaced the existing contributory pension and offers basic flat-rate pensions to the entire population that reaches retirement age. Other countries in the region, such as Bangladesh, the Philippines, and Viet Nam, offer means-tested social pensions, which have more limited coverage. They offer much-needed support to their target groups but leave a significant share of older people without coverage.

Health Insurance Is Expanding, as Many Countries Have Established Universal Health Insurance Programs

Health insurance refers to contributory programs that enable access to health care. Health insurance constituted 0.9% of GDP on average across Asia. Legal frameworks in many countries in Asia guarantee entitlements to health care for the entire population. In several of these countries, such as the PRC, Japan, the ROK, the Lao PDR, Thailand, and Viet Nam, health protection extends to more than 90% of the respective populations. Indonesia and the Philippines have also achieved substantial progress, reaching 70%-90% coverage of their populations. There are ongoing efforts in the region to extend social insurance and to enhance equitable access to health care.

Like old-age pensions, the extension of health insurance coverage in Asia tended to be driven by the expansion of both contributory and noncontributory financing arrangements. Several countries, such as the PRC, Indonesia, the Philippines, Thailand, and Viet Nam, extended their contributory schemes with noncontributory, tax-funded provision of health coverage for groups deemed poor or near-poor. Several countries, such as Armenia, Azerbaijan, Bangladesh, and Cambodia, do not have contributory systems, but they also offer limited health assistance. These countries' systems heavily rely on out-of-pocket payments as the main health care financing mechanism.

Social Assistance Has an Important Role in Reducing Poverty and Vulnerabilities, but It Needs to Be Strengthened

Social assistance expenditure was much smaller than social insurance, with an SPI of 0.9 (1.1% of GDP). Social assistance was driven by welfare assistance, which under the SPI classification includes cash transfers (0.4% of GDP) and assistance to older people (0.3% of GDP). The depth of social assistance benefits was 4.6% of GDP per capita, and social assistance covered 25.1% of all intended beneficiaries. The social assistance SPI remained at 0.9 between 2009 and 2018.

Countries with high social assistance SPIs include the high-income countries of Japan and the ROK; post-Soviet Union transition countries; as well as Indonesia, Maldives, Mongolia, and the Philippines. In high-income Japan and the ROK, social assistance spending translated into relatively generous benefits. High SPI levels in other countries reveals substantial gains in coverage. Especially notable is the expansion in social welfare programs, including the Pantawid Pamilyang Pilipino Program in the Philippines, Program Keluarga Harapan in Indonesia, and Vulnerable Group Development food assistance program in Bangladesh. Countries that enhanced the coverage of noncontributory social pensions include Bangladesh, Georgia, the ROK, Maldives, Nepal, the Philippines, Tajikistan, and Thailand.

Evidence from the region demonstrates the important poverty reduction role of social assistance. However, social assistance remained limited in its coverage and benefit effectiveness. The majority of social assistance programs were patchy, focusing on smaller population subsections and selected geographic areas. They provided small benefits that offered limited means for lifting households out of poverty. Extension in social assistance coverage based on the International Labour Organization's Social Protection Floor approach can ensure minimum income security for all and help protect the "missing middle"—those who are excluded from social insurance coverage but also lack social assistance protection.

Labor Market Programs Are Underutilized

Spending on LMPs was limited, with an SPI of 0.1. Expenditure on LMPs stayed unchanged between 2009 and 2018. The depth of LMP benefits came to 5.9% of GDP per capita, and the breadth of LMP coverage was very low at 1.6% of intended beneficiaries. While LMP coverage declined from 3.7% to 1.8%, LMP benefits showed some progress, from 5.4% to 6.5% of GDP per capita.

Spending on cash- and food-for-work programs slightly outweighed spending on skills development and training as a share of GDP. Bangladesh had the highest expenditure on cash- and food-for-work assistance in Asia, accounting for nearly 18.0% of its social protection spending. Countries that recorded the highest contribution to skills development and training programs include Cambodia (6.3%), Singapore (5.5%), and Bhutan (4.7%).

Overall, LMPs remain the most underfunded area of social protection in Asia, and there is a clear need to strengthen their reach and effectiveness. LMPs have an important role to play in supporting disadvantaged low-skilled workers to obtain adequately paid, decent work and to sustain and to promote their livelihoods. Global evidence suggests that well-designed and contextually appropriate skills training can improve employment chances and incomes among marginalized and disadvantaged groups, including people with disabilities, and contribute to reducing poverty, inequality, and exclusion.

Social Protection Spending Needs to Better Support Poor People

Social protection spending in Asia clearly favored the nonpoor over the poor. Intended nonpoor beneficiaries were allocated a 3.2 SPI and intended poor beneficiaries a 0.8 SPI, a substantial gap of 2.4 percentage points. The gap between spending on the nonpoor and poor persisted across all income groups from 2009 to 2018.

Higher spending on the nonpoor was mainly driven by contributory social insurance. Social insurance was not specifically targeted at the poor and, in most countries of Asia, it tended to favor the nonpoor, mainly those in formal sector employment. The key policy problem, however, is that the poor—including people with disabilities—were the least represented in social insurance across the region. As discussed earlier, coverage gaps persisted despite substantial progress in achieving universal or near-universal coverage. While most social assistance programs in the region have a clear poverty reduction mandate, spending on social assistance was limited in most countries, and this restricted the breadth of coverage and depth of benefits.

The key policy implication is that further investments in social protection are needed to enhance its reach and generosity to better support the poor. A system perspective to policy formulation and programming would allow development of these instruments to complement each other in addressing specific vulnerabilities.

Social Protection Is Becoming More Gender-Sensitive, but More Is Needed to Support Gender Equality

Social protection spending in the 26 countries was equally split between men and women, with the SPI for each accounting for 2.0 of the overall SPI. Social protection expenditure appeared to be more favorable for women in countries with broad-based social insurance coverage, such as high-income Japan and the ROK, and it was more favorable for men in countries with limited social insurance coverage. The gender gap in access to social protection in 24 countries with complete data decreased between 2009 and 2018, as spending on women increased from 1.4 to 2.1, while spending on men hovered around 2.0-2.1 of the overall SPI.

Further expansion of social insurance coverage, including pensions and health insurance, is likely to contribute to greater inclusion of women relative to men in terms of their overall access to social protection. Additionally, an expansion in social assistance programs targeted at women and children can contribute to reducing gender disparities.

Social Protection in Asia Needs to Be More Disability-Inclusive

On average for the 26 countries in 2018, the SPI for people with disabilities was 0.5 of the overall SPI of 4.0. The SPI for disability was generally a small part of the overall SPI for all countries in this study, which is to be expected, as the population of people with disabilities is a small proportion of the overall population. The SPI was calculated using data on disability-targeted programs in which only people with disabilities benefitted and using estimates of the proportion of people with disabilities who may be beneficiaries of general social protection programs such as old-age pensions. The average spending for disability-targeted programs in Asia increased from 0.1% of GDP in 2009 to 0.2% of GDP in 2018.

Most countries in Asia, with a few exceptions, provided at least one main form of cash assistance for people with disabilities, either through contributory social insurance schemes for people who acquire disabilities when they are working or through noncontributory social assistance schemes. However, better administrative and statistical data are needed—disaggregated for people with disabilities by age and ability to function—to be able to better understand the extent to which general social protection expenditure is reaching people with disabilities.

Inclusive access to health care, education, employment services, social care, assistive devices, housing, and transport—as well as income security—is essential to support people with disabilities. Therefore, a key policy priority should be to expand social protection coverage and to ensure the adequacy of benefits considering disability-related extra costs. Enhancing access entails, for example, making social protection programs flexible to cover people with disabilities in the informal economy or outside of the labor market. In addition, special programs are required to address specific needs and circumstances of people with disabilities.

The COVID-19 Pandemic Has Created a Momentum That Should Be Used to Further Expand Social Protection

In Asia, as in other regions of the world, social protection measures formed a critical pillar of the overall government response to the COVID-19 pandemic. On average, COVID-19-related social protection spending across the 26 countries included in this report is estimated at 2.0% of 2020 GDP and 1.2% of GDP for 2020 when excluding high-income countries. However, severe data gaps persist, and due to lack of available data, these figures represent broad estimations rather than verified administrative or program data.

Measures introduced in Asia ranged across social assistance, social insurance, and LMPs, but social assistance dominated the response, comprising 67% of all measures. Sixty-three percent of the measures were reported to be new programs, composed of ad-hoc or temporary measures specifically introduced in the wake of the pandemic.

Many countries additionally invoked vertical expansion (i.e., increasing benefit size) and horizontal expansion (i.e., extension in coverage) of existing social protection programs. Countries adopted a range of innovative means, such as the use of digital technology to identify newly vulnerable populations and digital delivery mechanisms, to quickly extend social protection support through the pandemic period.

The pandemic experience highlights the potential of social protection measures and systems as an effective public policy tool in dealing with a covariate shock. It also demonstrates the importance of inclusive social protection systems; adequate health, income, and livelihood support to build people's resilience before shocks occur; and investing in programs and systems to ensure that they respond to shocks quickly and effectively. This is especially important given the adverse economic and social effects of the pandemic, with an estimated additional 75 million to 80 million people pushed into extreme poverty in 2020 alone.

As countries move toward transition and recovery from the pandemic, the vision for inclusive and resilient social protection needs to be strongly embedded in their respective development strategies and sector plans. Adequate financial resources must be allocated to expand social protection coverage; disadvantaged groups, such as people with disabilities, must be better covered; benefits must be enhanced; and delivery systems must be improved. A key prerequisite in this process is developing adequate national capacity for design and implementation to sustain and to facilitate these goals.

Improving Social Protection Data Can Enhance Monitoring and Evaluation

Monitoring and evaluation systems are key for the development of effective national social protection systems. However, there are substantial gaps in the production and compilation of statistical information in Asia, resulting in the limited availability of up-to-date indicators, disaggregation of data by sex, national/nonnational status and other classifications, and time-series indicators that would allow monitoring progress over time. There are conceptual and methodological challenges in measuring coverage, expenditure, and benefit adequacy as well. Administrative data in many countries are of poor quality and are fragmented, as they originate from various sources. Few countries include questions on social protection in regular household survey instruments, and even fewer systematically analyze and use this information.

Different national agencies collect various types of information, but data are not collected and aggregated through clear and consistent methodology. This makes it challenging to generate internationally comparable data. Furthermore, international organizations are not always in agreement on the conceptual definitions and methodologies used to collect, classify, and analyze social protection data, including disability-disaggregated data.

Several measures can improve the collection and compilation of social protection data, however. These include better coordination and collaboration among different institutions at a national level; standardization of conceptual definitions and methodologies; and collaboration among international and regional organizations to coordinate data production. International and regional organizations should also provide knowledge sharing and capacity development to countries regarding the development of their own statistical definitions and data collection instruments.

Accurate data on disability prevalence at various ages can help ensure more targeted and effective policy responses that promote equity and social inclusion. However, defining the population of people with disabilities—and therefore defining the reference population for social protection programs that are targeting people with disabilities—has been challenging in all countries. Stigma, discrimination, complicated assessment procedures, or other barriers may mean that people are not motivated to register as people with disabilities. Thus, disability prevalence estimates based on registrations can significantly undercount the number of people with disabilities in the population.

It also remains challenging to generate data on disabilities that are comparable across countries. There are often significant variations among prevalence rates in various countries in Asia for the same age groups. The Washington Group questions, based on functioning across different domains, are designed to address the challenges of estimating the population of people with disabilities in censuses and household surveys and were used in almost half of the SPI study countries for estimating disability prevalence. This is a positive step forward, as it is important that governments monitor disability prevalence using function-based questions in surveys and social registers where people are enrolled into poverty alleviation, employment, or other social protection programs.

Anticipating the Future of Social Protection in Asia

Structural drivers, such as demographic changes, globalization, technological advances, and urbanization, together with major shocks, are shaping the future of social protection in the region. Five major trends are likely to impact policy development:

(i)   Social protection systems in the region need to improve the coverage of vulnerable groups, including people with disabilities, and adopt more universal approaches. This reflects the reality of universal shocks, like COVID-19 and disasters induced by climate change.

(ii)   Social protection systems increasingly link to social and infrastructure services. Social protection incorporates a responsibility to ensure that everyone—particularly the most vulnerable, including older people and people with disabilities—can access vital benefits required to sustain well-being and realize opportunities. These include health, education, and livelihoods but also more intensively infrastructure-dependent services including energy, transport, information, and communications.

(iii) In the face of climate risks, social protection systems in Asia are expected to play a strategic role in supporting the social dimension of the transition to a green and sustainable economy and society.

(iv)   These systems support and rely on the development of inclusive digital technologies, which will strengthen shock-responsiveness and build resilience in health, education, livelihoods, and other sectors.

(v)   Policy makers rely on high-quality evidence to drive good practices, raising the demand for improved initiatives for data collection and monitoring. This increases the agency of governments and their development partners to overcome various difficulties and to realize future opportunities.

I. Overview and Methodology

This report is the fourth in a series that examines the state of social protection in Asia. It summarizes the results from 26 national reports that are based on the compilation of the individual country-level data for social protection programs implemented by various governments in 2018. It uses the Social Protection Indicator (SPI) to assess resources invested in social protection as well as the value of benefits, level of coverage, and distribution of expenditures in terms of poverty, gender, and disability status.

This report also provides information on historical trends in social protection expenditures and beneficiaries in Asia. This is based on similar data provided by earlier Asian Development Bank (ADB) publications on the SPI.[2] Hence, one of this report's most important contributions is to document the progress regarding social protection at the individual country and regional levels between 2009 and 2018. This report also introduces an additional dimension by assessing social protection expenditure for people with disabilities.

In addition to presenting the SPI results, this report incorporates three thematic chapters focusing on the social protection response to the coronavirus disease (COVID-19) pandemic; constraints and opportunities in social protection data collection and analysis; and challenges in identifying people with disabilities and measuring disability prevalence rates for effective monitoring of disability-focused social protection measures.

Methodology

This report draws on methodology set out in 2012, which defines the SPI and key data sources.[3] The SPI first compares a country's total social protection expenditures to the number of its total intended beneficiaries, and then divides this ratio by the country's gross domestic product (GDP) per capita. Thus, the magnitude of expenditure per intended beneficiary is judged relative to a country's level of per capita income.

Intended beneficiary population groups are the key unit used to assess social protection effectiveness.[4] This is defined as the share of the population that qualifies for benefits from a particular social protection category and program.

---

[2] ADB. 2012. *The Revised Social Protection Index: Methodology and Handbook.* Manila; ADB. 2016. *The Social Protection Indicator: Assessing Results for the Pacific.* Manila; and ADB. 2019. *The Social Protection Indicator for the Pacific: Assessing Progress.* Manila.

[3] ADB. 2012. *The Revised Social Protection Index: Methodology and Handbook.* Manila.

[4] This report uses the terms "intended" and "target" beneficiaries interchangeably.

The 26 countries included in this analysis are presented in Table 1. This report does not cover several countries in Asia, including Myanmar, Timor-Leste, and notably, India, due to lack of data. The report uses the term "post-Soviet Union transition countries" when referring to Armenia, Azerbaijan, Georgia, Kazakhstan, the Kyrgyz Republic, Tajikistan, and Uzbekistan. Analysis of social protection has been carried out according to individual country's income levels as indicated in Table 1 as well.[5]

Table 1: Countries Involved in the Social Protection Indicator Classified by Income Group, 2022

Category	Countries
High-income countries	Japan, Republic of Korea, Singapore
Upper middle-income countries	Armenia, Azerbaijan, People's Republic of China, Georgia, Kazakhstan, Malaysia, Maldives, Thailand
Lower middle-income countries	Bangladesh, Bhutan, Cambodia, Indonesia, Kyrgyz Republic, Lao People's Democratic Republic, Mongolia, Nepal, Pakistan, Philippines, Sri Lanka, Tajikistan, Uzbekistan, Viet Nam
Low-income countries	Afghanistan[a]

[a] ADB placed on hold its assistance in Afghanistan effective 15 August 2021. ADB Statement on Afghanistan | Asian Development Bank (published on 10 November 2021). Manila. This report was prepared based on the information available for Afghanistan as of 31 July 2021.

Source: World Bank. World Bank Country and Lending Groups. Data. https://datahelpdesk.worldbank.org/knowledgebase/articles/906519 (accessed 4 April 2022).

Throughout this report, countries' group averages are unweighted. In other words, when computing group estimates, each country is counted as one, without considering its relative weight in terms of population or GDP. This helps avoid giving undue weight to countries with higher levels of GDP per capita or larger populations.

As in the past three SPI reports, this report presents, for each country, both the depth of benefits and breadth of coverage of its social protection programs. The depth of benefits indicates the average value of the benefits received by each actual beneficiary as a share of GDP per capita. The breadth of coverage of social protection programs indicates the total number of actual beneficiaries as a ratio to the total intended beneficiaries. The breadth indicator may exceed 100%, as it combines the total number of actual beneficiaries for different programs not adjusted for double counting.

To a limited degree, the disaggregation of the SPI can also be used to reveal the impact of programs on various population groups. This report assesses the impact of social protection with regard to the poor and nonpoor, women and men, and people with and without disabilities. Definitions of poverty differ across countries, and, even within countries, the definition of poverty can change over time. The analysis of the SPI gender dimension in this study draws on sex-disaggregated data.

---

[5]   For fiscal year 2022 (i.e., 1 July 2021 to 30 June 2022), the World Bank classifies countries by income as follows: low-income countries with gross national income (GNI) per capita of $1,045 or less in 2020; lower middle-income countries with a GNI per capita between $1,046 and $4,095; upper middle-income countries with a GNI per capita between $4,096 and $12,695; and high-income countries with a GNI per capita of $12,696 or more. See World Bank. World Bank Country and Lending Groups. Data. https://datahelpdesk.worldbank.org/knowledgebase/articles/906519 (accessed 4 April 2022).

Categories of Social Protection

ADB divides all social protection expenditures and corresponding beneficiaries into three major categories: social insurance, social assistance, and labor market programs (LMPs). Table 2 presents the main social protection categories and subprograms and corresponding intended beneficiary groups used in the analysis.

Table 2: Social Protection Programs and Intended Beneficiary Groups

Program	Intended Beneficiary Group
Social Insurance	
Health insurance	Employed population
Unemployment insurance	Employed population
Pensions	Population aged 60 and above
Social Assistance	
Welfare assistance	Poor and disadvantaged population groups (all ages)
Child welfare	Children, aged 0-14
Assistance to older people	Population aged 60 and above who are not part of contributory pension schemes
Health assistance	Poor and disadvantaged population groups (all ages)
Disability assistance	People with disabilities
Labor Market Programs	
Skills development and training	Unemployed and underemployed
Cash- and food-for-work	Unemployed and underemployed

Source: ADB. 2012. *The Revised Social Protection Index: Methodology and Handbook*. Manila.

Social Insurance

A characteristic of social insurance is that its beneficiaries usually contribute payments to a fund that eventually disburses benefits. The most well-known form of social insurance is old-age pensions. For example, formal sector workers often have deductions made from their salaries or wages to help finance their future pensions when they reach retirement age.

Health insurance, another major form of social insurance, has become more common in recent years in Asia. In fact, several countries have been making such a critical form of insurance universal. Again, beneficiaries often make payments into a fund for such insurance, or some form of co-payment for health services is provided to them.

Where the number of target beneficiaries is close to the entire population of a country, the total population is used as the reference population for the SPI calculation for social insurance, along with older people as the reference population for pensions. Otherwise, the employed population is used as the reference population for health insurance. When health insurance becomes universal—as has happened in some Asian countries—the intended beneficiaries can be expanded to encompass the entire population. This "universalization" of health insurance has been a major factor in significantly changing the social insurance SPI.

When health services are provided free of charge or at a nominal cost, they are usually categorized as health assistance. These are then included in this report as social assistance, and poor and disadvantaged population groups are used as the corresponding reference population.

Social Assistance

In Asia, social assistance is a much smaller portion of social protection than social insurance. It is usually targeted at disadvantaged members of society, such as those living in poverty, children, disadvantaged women, older people, and people with disabilities. It can take several forms, such as cash or in-kind transfers. The biggest of these are assistance to older people, health assistance, and disability assistance. General subsidies and loans, such as microcredit, are not regarded as a form of social assistance by ADB unless they concern temporary subsidies during a crisis period.

Labor Market Programs

LMPs represent the smallest of the three forms of social protection. This report focuses on active LMPs with their two subcategories: skills development and training, and short-term cash- and food-for-work or public works programs.

Structure of the Report

Chapter II presents social protection expenditures in Asia in terms of the SPI value and as a share of GDP, focusing on expenditures by category and program. This analysis continues in Chapter III, which discusses the main trends in the SPI from 2009 to 2018. Chapter IV discusses the depth of benefits and breadth of coverage, while Chapter V provides an assessment of poverty, gender, and disability dimensions of social protection in Asia. Chapter VI examines the social protection responses to the COVID-19 pandemic in Asia. Chapter VII presents an overview of challenges in gathering and monitoring social protection data both at the individual country and regional levels. Chapter VIII discusses challenges in monitoring disability-related social protection. The final chapter discusses the emerging regional trends and outlines the key directions for social protection in Asia. More details on the SPI results are presented in the Appendixes.

II. Social Protection Results for Asia, 2018

- The average SPI in Asia for 2018 was 4.0 of GDP per capita (5.2% of GDP).
- There was a wide variation in SPIs at the individual country level, ranging from 0.9 in the Lao People's Democratic Republic to 11.7 in Japan.
- Social protection spending was associated with a country's income, demographic structure, and extent of inequality; it was also influenced by its policy vision and institutional context.

Social protection continues to be a critical policy area in Asia, albeit accompanied by varying national priorities and expenditure patterns. This chapter examines such expenditure in the 26 countries in Asia included in this report, first in the form of expenditure for intended beneficiaries as a share of GDP per capita—the SPI for 2018—and then as overall expenditure as a share of the aggregate GDP. It then examines the SPI disaggregated by the various categories of social protection as well as by countries' income group.

Social Protection Expenditures

In 2018, the average SPI for Asia was 4.0, with values ranging from as low as 0.9 in the Lao People's Democratic Republic (Lao PDR) to 11.7 in Japan. The average social protection expenditure in the 26 countries was 5.2% of GDP (Figure 1). Usually, the SPI is lower than the social protection expenditure as a percentage of GDP, because the overall sum of intended beneficiaries is higher than the population.[6] As explained in Chapter I, this happens because the same people can be the intended beneficiaries of more than one social protection measure.

---

[6] An exception is Singapore, where the SPI was higher than the social protection expenditure as a percentage of GDP. This was due to the large difference between the resident population and population that includes temporary workers and foreign students. For the calculation of GDP per capita, the total population of 5.6 million was used, whereas for the SPI, the population of 4.0 million was used. This means that the number of intended social protection beneficiaries was lower than the population; hence, the SPI was higher than the expenditure as a percentage of GDP.

Figure 1: Overall Social Protection Indicator and Expenditures, 2018

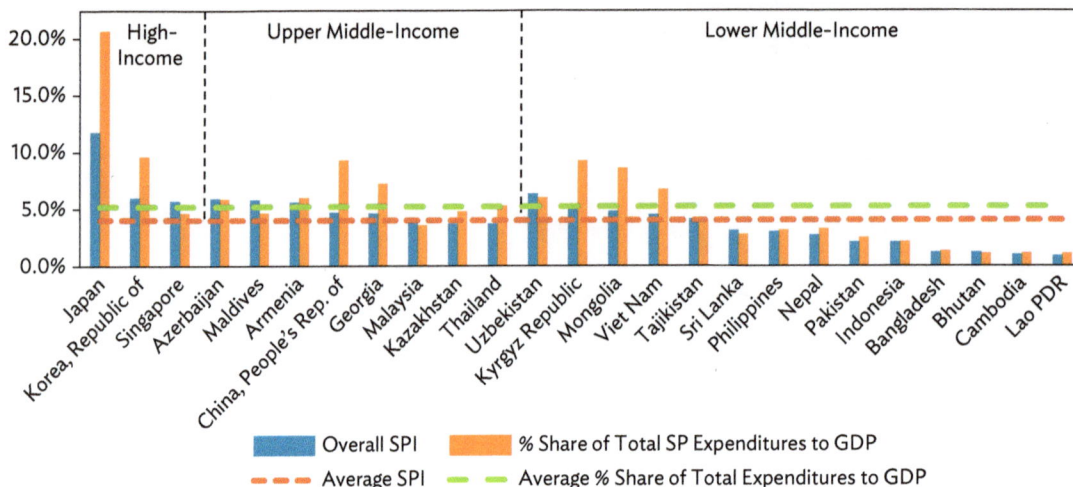

GDP = gross domestic product, Lao PDR = Lao People's Democratic Republic, SP = social protection, SPI = Social Protection Indicator.

Source: ADB estimates based on consultants' reports.

Figure 2: Overall Social Protection Indicator and Expenditures by Income Group, 2018

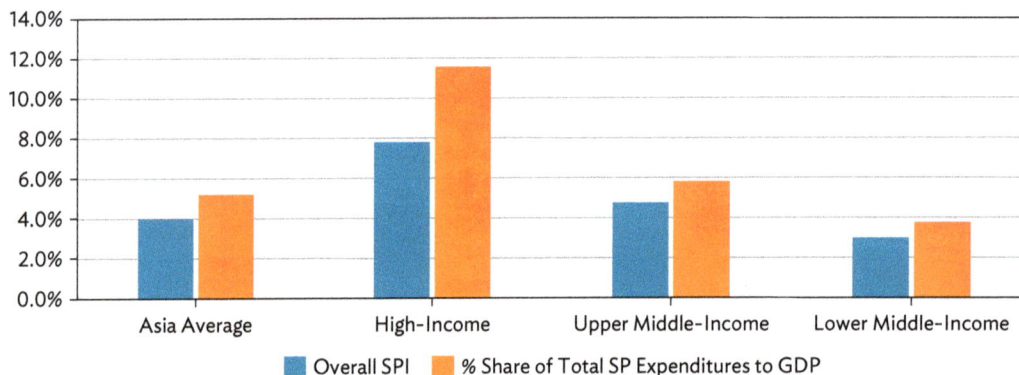

GDP = gross domestic product, SP = social protection, SPI = Social Protection Indicator.

Source: ADB estimates based on consultants' reports.

By income group, social protection spending was the highest in the three high-income countries (i.e., Japan, the Republic of Korea, and Singapore), with an average SPI of 7.8 and an average expenditure of 11.6% of GDP. It was 1.6 times higher than spending in the upper middle-income countries, where the average SPI was 4.8 (5.8% of GDP), and 2.5 times higher than that in the lower middle-income countries, with an average SPI of 3.0 (3.8% of GDP) (Figure 2).

On the other hand, several countries, primarily in the lower middle-income group, registered SPI values and social protection expenditures as a share of GDP that were considerably lower than the unweighted regional averages for Asia as well as for their respective income groups. Countries, such as the Lao PDR (SPI of 0.9 and expenditure of 1.1% of GDP), and Cambodia (SPI of 1.0 and expenditure of 1.1% of GDP), Bangladesh (SPI of 1.2 and expenditure of 1.3% of GDP), and Bhutan (SPI of 1.2 and expenditure of 1.1% of GDP) had values substantially lower in comparison to the regional averages for 2018. However, in these countries, such low expenditure indicators represent greater increments from the previous round of data collection in 2015.

Figure 3 plots the 26 countries based on their social protection expenditure as a percentage of GDP and GDP per capita.[7] The same figure also shows the regression

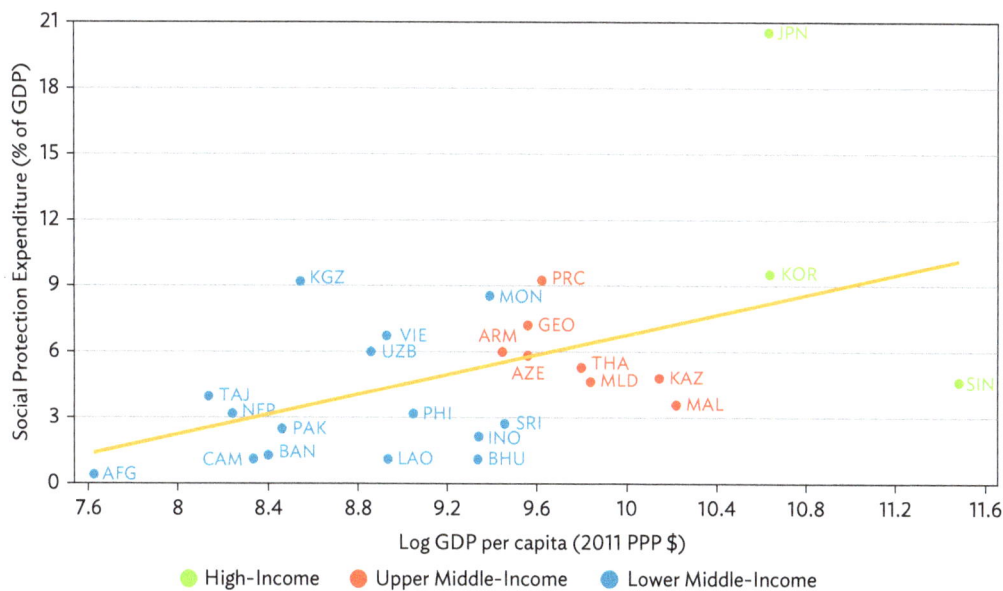

Figure 3: Relationship between Social Protection Expenditure and Gross Domestic Product per Capita

AFG = Afghanistan, ARM = Armenia, AZE = Azerbaijan, BAN = Bangladesh, BHU = Bhutan, CAM = Cambodia, GEO = Georgia, GDP = gross domestic product, INO = Indonesia, JPN = Japan, KAZ = Kazakhstan, KGZ = Kyrgyz Republic, KOR = Republic of Korea, LAO = Lao People's Democratic Republic, MAL = Malaysia, MLD = Maldives, MON = Mongolia, NEP = Nepal, PAK = Pakistan, PHI = Philippines, PPP = purchasing power parity, PRC = People's Republic of China, SIN = Singapore, SRI = Sri Lanka, THA = Thailand, TAJ = Tajikistan, UZB = Uzbekistan, VIE = Viet Nam.

Note: Afghanistan is the only low-income country and is included with lower middle-income countries.

Sources: ADB; and World Bank. World Development Indicators. https://databank.worldbank.org/source/world-development-indicators (accessed 12 February 2022).

7   Expressed in logarithmic terms and constant US dollar purchasing power parity.

line that fits these observations. The slope is positive and statistically significant, meaning that as the GDP per capita increases, the social protection expenditure should also increase. This regression, however, explains only one-quarter of the variation in the social protection expenditure.

As shown in Figure 4, however, a significantly stronger correlation is found between social protection expenditure and the percentage of people who are aged 60 and over, explaining more than 50% of the variation in social protection expenditure. In most of the countries considered, the bulk of social protection expenditure consists of pensions and other expenditures associated with older age. Generally, there is a strong correlation notwithstanding some outliers. This reflects the importance attached to old-age social protection in these countries.

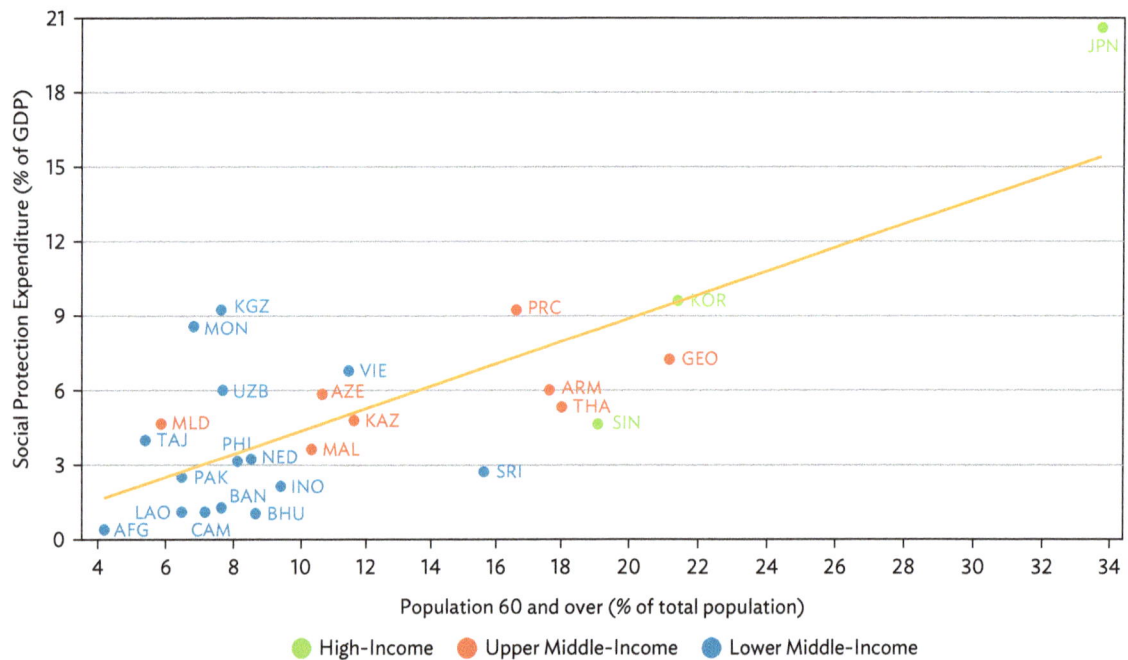

Figure 4: **Social Protection Expenditure and Populations Aged 60 and Over**

AFG = Afghanistan, ARM = Armenia, AZE = Azerbaijan, BAN = Bangladesh, BHU = Bhutan, CAM = Cambodia, GEO = Georgia, GDP = gross domestic product, INO = Indonesia, JPN = Japan, KAZ = Kazakhstan, KGZ = Kyrgyz Republic, KOR = Republic of Korea, LAO = Lao People's Democratic Republic, MAL = Malaysia, MLD = Maldives, MON = Mongolia, NEP = Nepal, PAK = Pakistan, PHI = Philippines, PRC = People's Republic of China, SIN = Singapore, SRI = Sri Lanka, THA = Thailand, TAJ = Tajikistan, UZB = Uzbekistan, VIE = Viet Nam.

Note: Afghanistan is the only low-income country and is included with lower middle-income countries.

Sources: ADB; and World Bank. World Development Indicators. https://databank.worldbank.org/source/world-development-indicators (accessed 12 February 2022).

This analysis considers the level of income inequality as another explanatory variable. GDP per capita and the percentage of the population aged 60 and over are highly correlated, so they cannot be jointly included as explanatory variables. However, the Gini index—a measure of inequality—is independent. In fact, it has a negative and significant effect on the level of social protection expenditure so that, on average, an extra 3 percentage points in the Gini index are associated with a decrease of 1 percentage point in social protection expenditure, everything else being equal.

This shows that, after accounting for the percentage of the population over age 60, high income inequality is associated with a lower expenditure than expected, and, on the contrary, countries with relatively low income inequality have higher expenditures than expected.[8] It suggests that inequality may affect specific configurations for social protection outside of old-age pensions and, in particular, a possibility that inequality lowers support for more broadly redistributive social assistance measures. This model explains two-thirds of the overall social protection expenditure.[9]

These factors need to be considered in conjunction with a country's policy and institutional context that influences social protection spending. In particular, historical legacies and economic development strategies determine the trajectory of the evolution of social protection systems and programs and institutional models that underpin a country's social protection spending.

For example, consider the variation in social protection expenditure in Japan and Singapore. Japan (SPI of 11.7 and expenditure of 20.5% of GDP) has a high level of social protection, while Singapore, another high-income country, has a relatively low level of social protection (SPI of 5.7 and expenditure of 4.6% of GDP). These differences can be explained by their institutional configurations of social protection systems, which have been influenced by each country's history and economic development strategy.[10]

The public sector in Japan tends to have a greater role in financing and providing social protection. National pension schemes and health insurance in Japan cover the entire population. In contrast, Singapore, despite its high level of economic development, maintains limited state involvement in social protection; social protection there is primarily delivered through the Central Provident Fund (CPF), which places the responsibility to provide for one's own retirement needs on individuals and their families. CPF savings schemes are financed almost entirely through the contribution of employees and employers and can also be used to finance other needs such as education, health, and housing.

---

[8]　A similar model that includes nine Pacific countries produces very similar results on coefficient levels and their significance.

[9]　This analysis does not consider three countries for which there is no information on inequality: Afghanistan, Cambodia, and Singapore. The Gini index used in the regression is not necessarily for the year of social protection expenditure, but as close as possible to the year of reported social protection expenditure.

[10]　I. Holliday. 2000. Productivist Welfare Capitalism: Social Policy in East Asia. *Political Studies.* 48 (4). pp. 706-723; C. Park, and D. Jung. 2007. The Asian Welfare Regimes Revisited: The Preliminary Typologies Based on Welfare Legislation and Expenditure. http://www.welfareasia.org/4thconference/papers/Park_The%20Asian%20Welfare%20Regimes%20Revisited.pdf.

Similarly, the policy and institutional context explain the relatively high level of spending in lower middle-income Nepal and the Kyrgyz Republic. Nepal's Constitution and legal framework guarantee a citizen's rights to social security, employment, education, health, food, and housing as well as special rights for marginalized and vulnerable citizens, including Dalits, women, and older people.[11] Government investment in both social insurance and social assistance in Nepal has steadily expanded in the past 10 years.[12]

Social protection in the Kyrgyz Republic is also regarded as a right enshrined in the Constitution.[13] In fact, the 2010 Constitution explicitly specifies the responsibility of the state to provide pensions and social assistance to maintain people's living standards at an acceptable level. The country's social protection system has contracted since the breakup of the Soviet Union, but social protection spending still dominates government expenditure. Social insurance took up the bulk of social protection expenditure, as the country has achieved near-universal pension coverage of older people.

Social Protection by Category and by Program

- Social insurance dominated spending across country income groups, with an average SPI of 3.0 (3.9% of GDP).
- Contributory pensions took up a large share of social insurance spending (2.5% of GDP), followed by health insurance (0.9% of GDP).
- Social assistance expenditure was significantly smaller, with an SPI of 0.9 (1.1% of GDP).
- Social assistance was driven by welfare assistance, which included cash transfers (0.4% of GDP) and assistance to older people (0.3% of GDP).
- Spending on LMPs was limited, at an SPI of 0.1, with cash- and food-for-work programs somewhat exceeding skills development and training.

Figure 5 presents different categories of social protection as a share of GDP and SPI values across different income groups in Asia. To assess the relative share of these categories, it is also helpful to visualize them as a share of overall government social protection expenditure across country income groups in Asia.

---

[11]   NITI. 2019. Policy Landscape of Social Protection in Nepal. *NITI Notes*. Kathmandu. https://spcsnnepal. org/wp-content/uploads/2021/11/Policy-Landscape-of-Social-Protection-in-Nepal-Web.pdf.

[12]   World Bank. 2020. *Nepal—Social Protection: Review of Public Expenditure and Assessment of Social Assistance Programs*. Kathmandu. https://openknowledge.worldbank.org/bitstream/handle/10986/36329/ Main-Report-FY11-FY20.pdf?sequence=1&isAllowed=y.

[13]   OECD. 2018. *Social Protection System Review of Kyrgyzstan*. Paris. https://www.oecd-ilibrary.org/ docserver/9789264302273-6-en.pdf?expires=1649341278&id=id&accname=guest&checksum=0BACC A494EB14B12DECE0151DBC55F5E.

Figure 5: Social Protection Indicator by Category, Income Group, and Expenditure, 2018

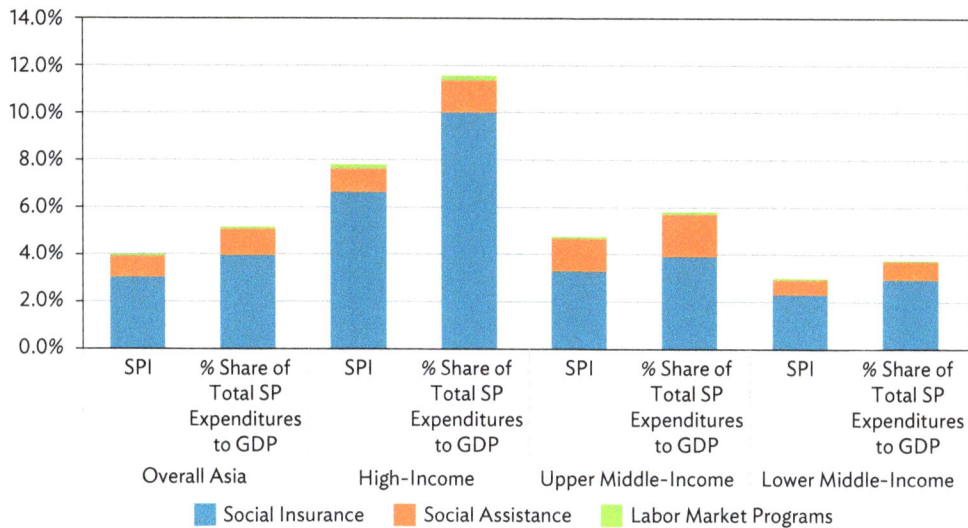

GDP = gross domestic product, SP = social protection, SPI = Social Protection Indicator.

Source: ADB estimates based on consultants' reports.

The social insurance SPI dominated social protection systems in Asia, accounting for 3.0 out of the 4.0 total. Equally, social insurance dictated the largest share of overall social protection expenditure in Asia at 3.9% of GDP or 73.0% of overall social protection expenditure. Social assistance registered an average SPI of 0.9 (1.1% of GDP), and LMPs had an SPI of 0.1 (and an equal share of GDP).

On average, pensions and health insurance were the largest contributors to the overall social protection expenditure in Asia, accounting for 2.5% and 0.9% of GDP and about 50.3% and 13.5% of overall social protection expenditure, respectively. Among social assistance measures, welfare assistance (0.4% of GDP and 8.9% of overall expenditure) and assistance to older people (0.3% of GDP and 5.4% of overall expenditure) were the largest contributors to overall social protection expenditure. Spending on LMPs was negligible, with food- and cash-for-work programs only slightly outweighing skills development and training programs as a share of GDP.

The income groups largely reflect the overall expenditure pattern for Asia, with social insurance contributing the largest shares, followed by social assistance and LMPs. In high-income countries, social insurance accounted for over 80% of the SPI and of the overall social protection expenditure. Moving down the country income ladder, social insurance continued to be the largest contributor to social protection expenditure with smaller shares, and higher shares of social assistance. The largest share of social assistance was observed in upper middle-income countries, comprising one-third of SPI and social protection expenditure. The share of LMPs remained low in all income groups, with high-income countries registering the largest share at a 0.1 SPI and 2.8% of social protection expenditure (Figure 6).

Figure 6: **Categories of Social Protection as Shares of Overall Social Protection Expenditure across Income Groups, 2018**

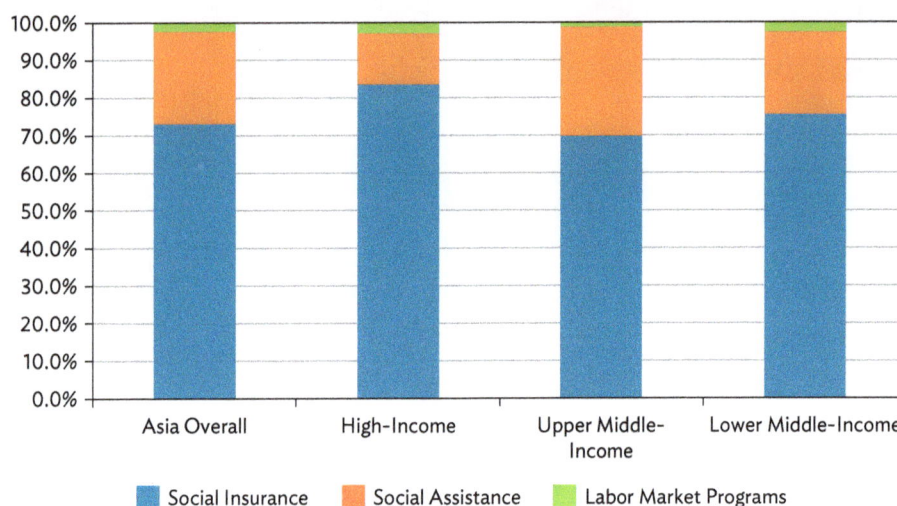

Source: ADB estimates based on consultants' reports.

At the individual country level, social protection expenditure in terms of its main categories exhibited a similar pattern across most of Asia (Figures 7 and 8). In most countries, social insurance expenditure prevailed. It was especially high in high-income countries such as Japan, where the SPI for social insurance made up more than 90% of overall SPI as well as of total social protection expenditure. This was driven primarily by the country's well-developed old-age pension and health insurance provisions. In the People's Republic of China (PRC), Malaysia, Singapore, and Viet Nam, the SPI for social insurance made up over 80% of the overall SPI and of total social protection expenditure.

In comparison, the SPIs for social assistance in Georgia and Bangladesh were close to 95% and 47%, respectively, of overall SPI and overall social protection expenditure. In Georgia, this was driven by the state-funded universal pension and universal health care assistance, which were the largest social assistance programs in the country. In Bangladesh, it can be explained by the sheer variety of social assistance programs on offer, accounting for 22 of the 30 social protection programs reported. Similarly, Cambodia and Bangladesh were the only countries where the SPI for LMPs register a share greater than 10% of the total SPI.

Many countries in the region had significantly enhanced their spending on social insurance and have had remarkable success in achieving universal or near-universal pension and health coverage. However, large pockets of the population in at least half of the countries remained uncovered by pensions and health insurance. The majority of people who were employed in the informal economy typically did not benefit from social insurance schemes. Women are less likely to be covered by contributory schemes, as they make up a disproportionate share of workers in the informal sector and tend to have less income than men. This leaves them particularly vulnerable to shocks, especially in the absence of any guaranteed minimum income support.

Figure 7: Social Protection Indicator by Category and by Country, 2018

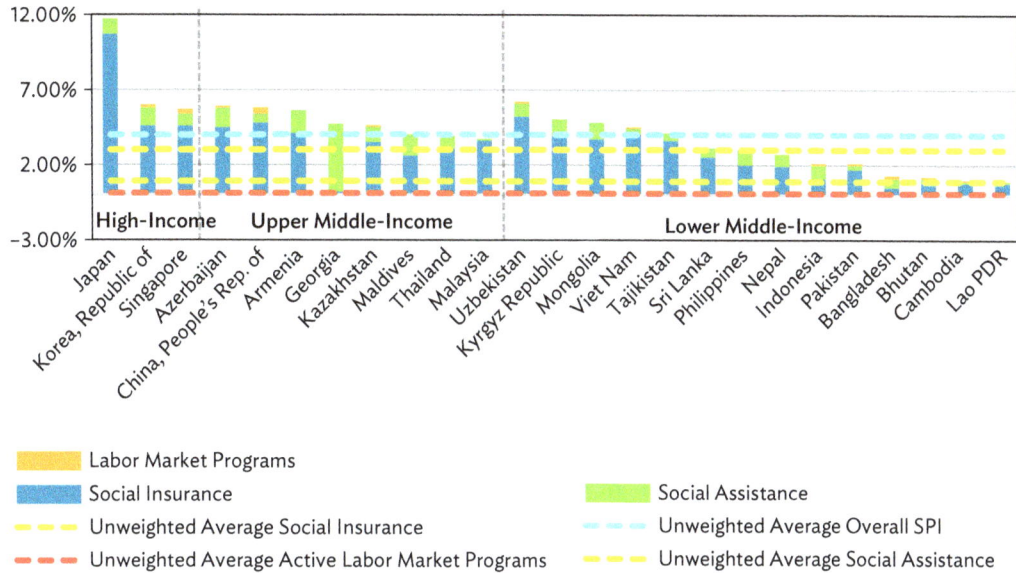

Legend:
- Labor Market Programs
- Social Insurance
- Social Assistance
- Unweighted Average Social Insurance
- Unweighted Average Overall SPI
- Unweighted Average Active Labor Market Programs
- Unweighted Average Social Assistance

GDP = gross domestic product, Lao PDR = Lao People's Democratic Republic, SPI = Social Protection Indicator.

Source: ADB estimates based on consultants' reports.

Figure 8: Social Protection Expenditures by Category and Income Group, 2018 (% of GDP)

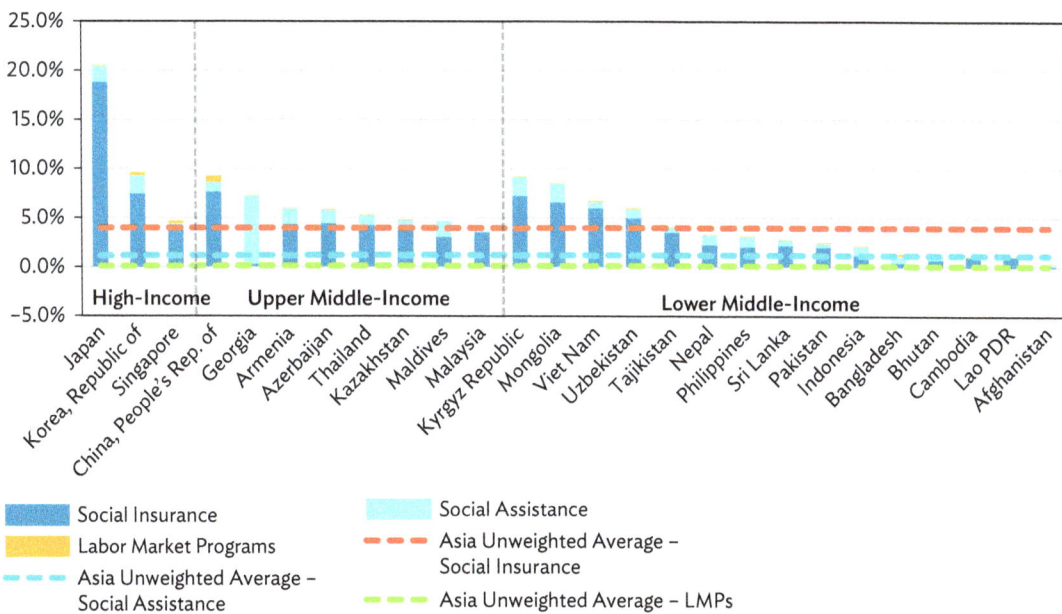

Legend:
- Social Insurance
- Social Assistance
- Labor Market Programs
- Asia Unweighted Average – Social Insurance
- Asia Unweighted Average – Social Assistance
- Asia Unweighted Average – LMPs

GDP = gross domestic product, Lao PDR = Lao People's Democratic Republic.

Source: ADB estimates based on consultants' reports.

Social assistance programs generally target poor and vulnerable people and tend to be the primary instrument for poverty reduction in the region. However, social assistance remained limited in its coverage and benefit adequacy. Most social assistance programs were patchy, focusing on smaller population subsections and select geographic areas. They provided small benefits that offered limited means for lifting households and individuals out of poverty.

To enhance the effectiveness of social protection, most countries need to develop and to sustain comprehensive social protection systems that provide universal coverage and address different vulnerabilities across the life cycle. Such systems would develop close complementarity among different schemes and programs to provide basic income security and access to essential health care for all. This poses the need to extend social insurance coverage to those excluded from coverage. It also necessitates extending social assistance coverage based on the Social Protection Floor approach. This would ensure minimum income security for all and help protect the "missing middle," i.e., those who are excluded from social insurance coverage but who also lack social assistance protection as they are missed by narrowly targeted programs.[14] In addition, a key policy task is to enhance the adequacy of both social insurance and social assistance to ensure effective protection against risks.

The remainder of this chapter offers in-depth analysis on social protection spending by category, specifically focusing on the programs that dominated social insurance and social assistance expenditure in the region. It highlights successful experiences in extending coverage and developing comprehensive systems.

Social Insurance

In terms of the SPI value, social insurance spending was above the Asia average SPI of 3.0 in 13 countries. As a share of GDP, social insurance spending in 2018 was higher than the region's average of 3.9% of GDP in 10 countries. These include high-income countries such as Japan, the Republic of Korea (ROK), and Singapore as well as the PRC and all post-Soviet Union transition countries considered in this report.

As presented earlier, the share of social insurance in the total expenditure was largest in high-income countries, with an SPI of 6.6 and accounting for 10.0% of GDP and close to 84.0% of the overall social protection expenditure. Social insurance expenditures in these countries were driven, on average, by pension expenditures (4.2% of GDP) followed by health insurance (4.0% of GDP). This was largely due to high spending in Japan, including 10.1% of GDP on pensions and 8.1% on health insurance. A high level of social insurance expenditure in Japan has translated into broad-based coverage and generous benefits under both programs. Similarly, in upper and lower middle-income countries, social insurance spending was driven primarily by pension expenditures, accounting for 2.7% of GDP and 2.3% of GDP, respectively.

---

[14]   ILO. 2019. *Extending Social Security Coverage to Workers in the Informal Economy: Lessons from International Experience.* Geneva. p. 4.

Pensions

Old-age pensions in this report are defined as contributory benefits to persons aged 60 and over. In the past decade, their financing structure has changed to incorporate noncontributory elements or social pensions.

Pensions took up 2.5% of GDP, on average, across Asia. Spending on pensions was above the regional average in Japan, the PRC, Mongolia, Viet Nam, and most post-Soviet Union transition countries. Several countries in the region have achieved universal or near-universal pension coverage, including Japan, the ROK, the PRC, Mongolia, Thailand, Nepal, and Maldives.[15] Similarly, all post-Soviet Union transition countries considered in this study, except Armenia and Azerbaijan, have universal pension coverage.

The progress in pension coverage in Asia was possible partly due to strengthening and extending contributory schemes to workers in the informal economy. This expansion was supported by parallel efforts to establish and to gradually extend noncontributory tax-financed schemes (i.e., social pensions) to support older people who are unable to make social insurance contributions (Box 1).

Box 1: Extending Old-Age Pensions in the People's Republic of China and Thailand

People's Republic of China. The pension system in the People's Republic of China (PRC) consists of three schemes: the Public Employees Scheme (PES), Urban Enterprise Employees Pension Scheme (UEEPS), and Urban and Rural Residents Pension Scheme (URRPS).

The PES was established in 2015 by merging the previously existing pension schemes for civil servants and public institution employees (e.g., those working in schools, hospitals, and other public institutions). This reform suspended the generous—and rather costly—state pension financing for civil servants and public sector employees and currently requires contributions from both employees and employers. This scheme is envisaged to be integrated into the UEEPS in the future.

The UEEPS was established in 1997 to cover urban employees and was gradually extended to self-employed urban residents. This is considered the main national pension scheme and is mandatory for all formal sector employees. However, it does not cover a large share of informal sector workers, mainly migrants. This program is financed through contributions from employers (initially at 20% of payroll and reduced to 16% in 2019) and employees (8% of salaries from employees and 20% from the self-employed). In 2018, there were 419.02 million participants.

The URRPS was established in 2014 by merging the 2009 New Rural Pension Scheme and the 2011 Urban Residents Pension Scheme. It seeks to provide coverage to workers in the informal economy, including those residing in rural areas and migrant workers not covered by the UEEPS. Today, it covers most adults outside of the formal sector, including agriculture workers in rural areas, nonagriculture workers in the informal sector, and those not working. This is the largest of the three schemes and covered 523.92 million people in 2018.

continued on next page

---

[15]   Universal coverage can be achieved through different means, i.e., reliance on a single social protection scheme/program or a combination of different schemes and programs. ILO. 2021. *ILO World Social Protection Report 2020-22: Social Protection at the Crossroads—In Pursuit of a Better Future.* Geneva.

Box 1: *continued*

The URRPS is financed through individual contributions and government subsidies. Considering the large income difference among members, a multiple-level contribution system has been developed, and participants can choose any level of payment. The minimum contribution to join is CNY100 per year. This system includes a basic pension payable to all persons without individual accounts. The basic pension is subsidized by the central government for the central and western provinces and cofinanced with local governments in the more affluent eastern provinces.

Thailand. Thailand has a three-pillar pension system.[17] The first pillar seeks to help older people address their basic needs and protect them from falling into poverty. The main instrument is the noncontributory Old-Age Allowance. It was established in 1992 as a means-tested program and expanded to the entire population in 2009. This enabled all individuals aged 60 and over outside of institutional care to become eligible for the benefit. Before the reform, only 20% of older people had access to some form of social protection. The second pillar is represented by the Civil Service Pension System, Social Security Fund, and Government Pension Fund and is an occupational pension system for workers in the formal sector. The third voluntary pillar enables members to increase their retirement savings and draw some tax benefits. This includes the Provident Fund, Retirement Mutual Fund, and National Savings Fund (NSF).

The NSF was established in 2015 to solicit contributions from self-employed, typically low-income workers aged 15-60 who are not covered by other public pension schemes. Most NSF members are farmers and self-employed freelance workers. The required minimum contribution is very low, set at B50 per year to ensure affordability; members' contributions are matched by the government as long they stay in the informal sector. The number of NSF members has grown significantly, from around 400,000 in 2016 to 610,600 in 2018, reaching 2.4 million at the end of 2020.

Sources: OECD and Korea Institute of Public Finance. 2020. Managing across Levels of Government: The Challenge of Pension Reform in China. In J. Kim and S. Dougherty, eds. *Ageing and Fiscal Challenges across Levels of Government.* Paris: OECD; R. Ratanabanchuen. 2019. The Pension System in Thailand. *Nomura Journal of Asian Capital Markets.* 3 (2). https://www.nomurafoundation.or.jp/wordpress/wp-content/uploads/2019/03/NJACM3-2SP19-07.pdf; ADB. 2022. *People's Republic of China: Social Protection Indicator.* Manila; and ADB. 2022. *Thailand: Social Protection Indicator.* Manila.

Over the study period, several countries improved financing for contributory pensions for formal sector workers, mainly public sector employees, including under the PRC's urban employees pension insurance, Thailand's Social Security Fund and Government Pension Fund, Cambodia's National Social Security Fund for Civil Servants and National Fund for Veterans of Cambodia, the government employee pension scheme in Pakistan, and Nepal's public sector pension scheme. Government spending during this period also sought to strengthen pension benefits for formal sector workers, as in Nepal and Mongolia.

Health Insurance
Health insurance refers to contributory programs that enable access to health care. Health insurance constituted 0.9% of GDP on average across Asia. Japan and the ROK had the highest spending on health insurance. Spending on health insurance was above the regional average in upper middle-income PRC and Maldives and lower middle-income Mongolia and Viet Nam.

16   R. Ratanabanchuen. 2019. The Pension System in Thailand. *Nomura Journal of Asian Capital Markets.* 3 (2). https://www.nomurafoundation.or.jp/wordpress/wp-content/uploads/2019/03/NJACM3-2SP19-07.pdf.

Legal frameworks in many countries in Asia guarantee entitlements to health care for the whole population. In several of these countries, such as Japan, the ROK, the PRC, Viet Nam, Thailand, and the Lao PDR, health protection has been extended to more than 90% of their respective populations.[17] Indonesia and the Philippines achieved substantial progress, covering 70%–90% of their populations.

As with old-age pensions, the extension of health insurance coverage in developing Asia tended to be driven by the expansion of both contributory and noncontributory financing arrangements. Several countries extended their contributory schemes with noncontributory, tax-funded provision of health coverage for groups deemed poor or near-poor:[18]

(i)   **People's Republic of China.** Health insurance in the PRC was provided through Basic Medical Care Insurance for Urban Employees, and Basic Medical Care Insurance for Urban and Rural Residents. Basic Medical Care Insurance for Urban Employees covered most urban employees, including all in the formal sector. In total, there were 316.8 million participants in 2018. It was funded through contributions by employers (6.0% of payroll) and employees (2.0% of salaries). Basic Medical Care Insurance for Urban and Rural Residents was established in 2016 through merging the 2005 New Rural Cooperative Medical Scheme and 2007 Medical Insurance for Urban Residents. This program covered workers in the informal economy, nonworking adults, and students. In 2018, total participants numbered 897.4 million. The consolidation process was ongoing, and 130.4 million members remained under the former New Rural Cooperative Medical Scheme. This scheme was financed through individual contributions and central and local governments.[19]

(ii) **Lao People's Democratic Republic.** The Lao PDR achieved remarkable success by extending its health insurance coverage from 31% in 2016 to 91% in 2017.[20] This was possible mainly due to the introduction of a tax-based financing model complemented by direct co-payments under the flagship National Health Insurance scheme. This allowed a rapid scale-up of the scheme and extended its coverage to support workers in the informal economy. In 2017, the scheme covered 74% of the population. The remaining coverage was provided through the State Authority of Social Security and the Lao Social Security Organisation through schemes that were established to cover public and private sector employees.[21]

---

[17]   ILO. 2021. *Extending Social Health Protection: Accelerating Progress towards Universal Health Coverage in Asia and the Pacific.* Bangkok. https://www.ilo.org/wcmsp5/groups/public/---asia/---ro-bangkok/documents/publication/wcms_831137.pdf.

[18]   UNESCAP and ILO. 2021. *The Protection We Want: Social Outlook for Asia and the Pacific.* Bangkok. https://www.unescap.org/sites/default/d8files/knowledge-products/Social_Outlook_Report_v10.pdf.

[19]   ADB. 2022. *People's Republic of China: Social Protection Indicator.* Manila.

[20]   ILO. 2021. *Extending Social Health Protection: Accelerating Progress towards Universal Health Coverage in Asia and the Pacific.* Bangkok. https://www.ilo.org/wcmsp5/groups/public/---asia/---ro-bangkok/documents/publication/wcms_831137.pdf.

[21]   ILO. 2019. Lao People's Democratic Republic. *Moving towards Universal Social Health Protection.* Volume 6. https://www.social-protection.org/gimi/RessourcePDF.action;jsessionid=70g8jIPl28IsPx7SqNOUQ5Ke7JabxYxPqdmj0vu0p-iQ40e-CD5t!539423187?id=55648.

(iii) **Mongolia.** The government has been committed to promoting universal health care coverage. Health insurance in Mongolia is mandatory for all public and private sector employees and voluntary for self-employed and unemployed people. The government subsidizes access to services for children (i.e., ages 0–18), older people with only pension incomes, mothers on maternity leave, people with disabilities, members of the armed forces, as well as those in critical need of social assistance. Coverage was around 76% in 2016.[22] There are specific challenges to ensuring adequate coverage in Mongolia, especially among the self-employed and unemployed populations, due to the remoteness of rural population groups, their frequent internal migration across the country, and their often-precarious economic conditions.

Several countries, such as Armenia, Azerbaijan, Bangladesh, and Cambodia, did not have contributory health insurance systems, but they offered limited health assistance.[23] These countries' systems heavily relied on out-of-pocket payments as the main health care financing mechanism, which can result in catastrophic health expenditures, creating a financial burden for households and exacerbating inequalities.

There were ongoing efforts in the region to extend social insurance and to enhance equitable access to health care. For example, Cambodia's National Social Security Fund introduced mandatory contributory health insurance in 2016 for workers employed in the formal sector. Its Health Equity Fund subsidized health costs for the poorest one-fifth of the country's population as well.[24]

Nepal established its first contributory national health insurance program in 2016 to lay the foundation for universal health coverage. This was subsequently scaled up to all 77 districts of the country and aimed to eventually cover all households nationwide. A family of five members, for example, had to pay an annual premium of NRs3,500 for coverage up to NRs100,000. An additional family member must pay an annual premium of NRs700. While the scheme was contributory, the government planned to subsidize the premiums of individuals aged 70 and older and poor households. Expenditures in 2018 amounted to NRs2.1 billion, benefiting 600,000 individuals, compared with 238,000 individuals in 2017.

Social Assistance

The social assistance SPI in 12 countries was equal to or above the Asia average SPI of 0.9. As a share of GDP, social assistance expenditures in eight countries were above the Asia average of 1.2% of GDP. Countries with high social assistance SPI include high-income Japan and the ROK; post-Soviet Union transition countries; as well as Indonesia, Maldives, Mongolia, and the Philippines.

---

[22] ILO. 2021. *Extending Social Health Protection: Accelerating Progress towards Universal Health Coverage in Asia and the Pacific.* Bangkok. https://www.ilo.org/wcmsp5/groups/public/---asia/---ro-bangkok/documents/publication/wcms_831137.pdf.

[23] A contributory health scheme was introduced in Azerbaijan starting 1 January 2021.

[24] ADB. 2022. *Cambodia: Social Protection Indicator.* Manila.

Social assistance expenditure was highest in upper middle-income countries, with an SPI of 1.4, accounting for 1.8% of GDP and close to 30.0% of overall social protection expenditure. Social assistance expenditures in these countries were led by programs assisting older people, accounting for 0.7% of GDP. Spending on these programs was especially prominent in Georgia and Maldives. Upper middle-income countries spent 0.5% of GDP on welfare assistance programs, which was higher than the average spending on these programs in the other two income groups.

High-income countries had a social assistance SPI of 1.0, spending 1.4% of GDP and 14.0% of overall social protection expenditure, which was substantially less than their social insurance spending of 10.0% of GDP. These were mainly Japan and the ROK, while Singapore had more limited social assistance spending. The highest expenditure in this group was on welfare assistance (0.4% of GDP). In lower middle-income countries, the highest spending was on welfare assistance programs, accounting for 0.3% of GDP. Spending was especially high in the Philippines and Mongolia.

Welfare Assistance

Welfare assistance programs include cash transfers, in-kind assistance, voucher schemes, and stipends intended to reduce poverty and vulnerability among specific population groups. The expenditure on welfare assistance was equal to or above the regional average of 0.4% of GDP in 10 countries, with spending twice exceeding the regional average in Armenia, Azerbaijan, Mongolia, and the Philippines. Below are examples of social welfare programs in the region that used different instruments to support their target populations: conditional cash transfers, unconditional cash transfers, food stamps, and food assistance:

(i) **Philippines.** The Pantawid Pamilyang Pilipino Program (4Ps) is the largest social welfare program in the Philippines and is implemented by the Department of Social Welfare and Development. It provides conditional cash transfers to the poorest families and aims to improve the health, nutrition, and education of all poor children up to age 18. For this purpose, beneficiaries received a health grant of P500 per household every month, or a total of P6,000 every year; and an education grant of P300 per child every month for 10 months, or a total of P3,000 every year. A household can register a maximum of three children for the program. In 2018, the program was implemented in 144 cities and 1,483 municipalities in 80 provinces.[25] The number of the program's registered households increased from 3.8 million in 2013 to 4.9 million in 2018. As of June 2018, 4.3 million households remained active and eligible to receive cash grants.[26]

(ii) **Indonesia.** Notable progress in social welfare spending was also observed in Indonesia. Indonesia's Program Keluarga Harapan (PKH), which became a national program in 2013, offers conditional cash transfers to the poorest families supporting prenatal care, growth and nutrition, and school attendance. Coverage sharply increased from 3.5 million households in 2015 to 10.0 million in 2018.[27]

25 ADB. 2022. *Philippines: Social Protection Indicator*. Manila.
26 Government of the Philippines, DSWD. 2018. *Pantawid Pamilyang Pilipino Program Implementation Status Report: 2nd Quarter of 2018*. https://pantawid.dswd.gov.ph/wp-content/uploads/2018/09/Pantawid-Pamilya-2nd-Quarter-Report-2018.pdf.
27 ADB. 2018. *Summary of the Program Keluarga Harapan and Its Technical Assistance Framework*. Manila. https://www.adb.org/sites/default/files/linked-documents/51313-001-sd-02.pdf.

(iii)   **Armenia.** Family Living Standards Enhancement Benefits is the largest social assistance program in that country, providing unconditional cash transfers to the poorest households scoring above a defined vulnerability threshold. The program reached 346,500 persons in 2018, with expenditures amounting to around AMD34.5 million or 2.4% of total state expenditure. It covered 12% of families living in the country, or half the share of those in poverty.[28]

(iv)   **Mongolia.** The Food Stamp Program aims to support the consumption of basic foodstuffs by extremely poor families to reduce vulnerability to food insecurity. It was piloted in 2008 with financial and technical support from ADB and was fully introduced in 2012. It distributes stamps to households that meet the threshold score from a household livelihood assessment. These food stamps can be redeemed for 10 high-protein foods and staples at specified shops. The program budget was increased to MNT42.1 billion in 2018 from MNT18.0 billion in 2016; the transfer value went from MNT13,000 to MNT16,000 per adult and from MNT6,500 to MNT8,000 per child, while coverage increased twofold from 26,000 households to 52,000 households. As of 2018, 263,400 individuals benefited, with funding of MNT36.2 billion.[29]

(v)   **Bangladesh.** The Vulnerable Group Development program is the country's largest social assistance program. It offers food assistance to women from poor households aged 18-49. Between 2015 and 2018, the number of beneficiaries increased by 14.2% per year, from 9.1 million to 14 million, and the total monetary value of the amount of rice distributed increased by 19.8% per year, from Tk8.9 billion to Tk16.1 billion. Therefore, the per capita increase in benefits was more than 5% per year during this period.[30]

Social welfare programs are instrumental for supporting the needs of poor and vulnerable groups; however, they do not fully cover people who struggle to meet their basic needs. Most social welfare programs, including the programs that had national reach, had partial coverage, due to exclusion of certain geographic areas and restrictive eligibility requirements.[31] Additionally, most welfare assistance programs were income-targeted; therefore, they were prone to significant targeting errors, excluding a notable share of their intended beneficiaries. They were not adequately funded and suffered from various implementation bottlenecks due to limited service delivery capacity. Efforts to enhance resource mobilization and financing mechanisms are key to strengthening the reach and delivery of social assistance in the region.[32]

Developing integrated social protection systems can help enhance inclusiveness, effectiveness, and efficiency of social protection programs. For instance, Bangladesh had a plethora of social protection programs implemented by different agencies, often resulting in fragmentation, coverage gaps, and inefficiencies. The government's 2015 National Social Security Strategy seeks to improve social inclusiveness and responsiveness of social protection by streamlining and strengthening the country's

[28]   ADB. 2022. *Armenia: Social Protection Indicator*. Manila.
[29]   ADB. 2022. *Mongolia: Social Protection Indicator*. Manila.
[30]   ADB. 2022. *Bangladesh: Social Protection Indicator*. Manila.
[31]   S. Kidd. 2017. Social Exclusion and Access to Social Protection Schemes. *Journal of Development Effectiveness*. 9 (2). pp. 212-244.
[32]   A. Barrientos. 2019. The Role of Social Assistance in Reducing Poverty and Inequality in Asia and the Pacific. *ADB Sustainable Development Working Papers*. No. 62. Manila: ADB.

social protection system. It intends to expand coverage under existing programs, extend social protection to support previously uncovered vulnerable groups (e.g., people with disabilities and the urban poor), and consolidate the main social protection programs using a life cycle approach. In 2021, ADB developed a program to support policy and institutional reforms underlying this strategy.[33]

Assistance to Older People

Assistance to older people refers to noncontributory transfers or social pensions. This category constituted 0.3% of GDP across Asia, with six countries spending above the regional average—Georgia, the ROK, Maldives, Nepal, Tajikistan, and Thailand. Georgia had the highest spending on such assistance, accounting for 3.6% of GDP and nearly 50.0% of social protection spending.

As mentioned earlier, noncontributory, tax-funded social pensions were instrumental in expanding pension coverage in the region. Social pensions in Asia proliferated in the past decade and have been key to extending pension coverage to workers in the informal economy who are unable to make social insurance contributions. They especially benefited women, who are particularly disadvantaged because of their low and irregular income, and who make up a higher share of pensioners due to their longer life expectancy.[34]

Several countries in the region succeeded in establishing universal pension coverage through the introduction of social pensions. Social pensions in Maldives, Nepal, and Thailand are offered to all citizens who do not have access to existing contributory schemes. Notably, Georgia's Universal Pension is the country's main pension scheme that replaced the existing contributory pension and offers basic flat-rate pensions to the entire population that reaches retirement age (Box 2). In 2018, Georgia approved the contributory Accumulated Pension System with a mandatory individual account to supplement the existing tax-funded pension. The new system enables participants to draw higher-value earnings-related benefits.

Other countries in the region, such as Bangladesh, the Philippines, and Viet Nam, offered means-tested social pensions, which had more limited coverage. These countries increased their spending on social pensions and extended pension coverage during the study period. However, a significant share of older people in these countries did not receive social protection, given that the main social insurance schemes in these countries focused on formal sector workers.

The Old Age Allowance in Bangladesh covers people living below a poverty line who reach age 65; they comprised 40.0% of the population in this age group. Some 7.6% of the population received government retirement pensions, and a further 10.0%—mainly private sector employees—drew on some kind of gratuity or provident fund. This left more than 40.0% of older people not covered by any pension.[35]

[33] ADB. 2021. *Technical Assistance to Bangladesh for the Strengthening Social Resilience Program.* Manila.
[34] HelpAge International. 2020. *Why Social Pensions? Achieving Income Security for All in Older Age.* London.
[35] M. Rahman, T. I. Khan and M. A. Sabbih. 2019. *Introducing a Universal Pension Scheme in Bangladesh: In Search of a Framework.* Dhaka: Centre for Policy Dialogue and Oxfam. https://cpd.org.bd/wp-content/uploads/2019/11/Introducing-a-Universal-Pension-Scheme-UPS-in-Bangladesh.pdf.

Box 2: Universal Pensions in Georgia

Georgia's pension system is different from that of other post-Soviet Union transition countries, which combine mandatory contributory pensions with tax-funded basic pensions. The latter are not earnings-related and seek to offer minimum protection to persons who have not accrued any other pension rights (e.g., have no history of contribution). In Georgia, the existing tax-funded universal old-age pension is the main statutory instrument and only source of income for most retired people.

Georgia's universal old-age pension covers all citizens, permanent residents with at least 10 years of residency, as well as stateless persons. It covers 100% of people above the eligibility age threshold, which is age 60 for women and 65 for men. In 2018, Georgia established a supplementary accumulated pension, which is only mandatory for formal sector employees and voluntary for those registered as self-employed.

The universal pension offers a flat-rate grant and is instrumental for preventing a large part of the population from falling into poverty. The flat rate has been increased periodically since 2006, but it remained modest by international standards. In 2015, it provided a monthly pension equal to 18% of the average wage, marginally above the subsistence level. The pension favors women, as the majority of pension recipients are women. This is mainly due to their higher longevity as well as their entry into retirement 5 years ahead of men, owing to the lower retirement eligibility threshold.

Sources: ILO. 2020. *Assessment of the Social Protection System in Georgia.* Geneva. https://www.developmentpathways. co.uk/wp-content/uploads/2021/02/ILO-Georgia.pdf; and ADB. 2017. *Technical Assistance Completion Report: Improving Domestic Resource Mobilization for Inclusive Growth Program in Georgia.* Manila. https://www.adb.org/sites/default/files/ project-documents/48044/48044-004-pcr-en.pdf.

The social pension in the Philippines is targeted at "indigent" senior citizens, i.e., those who live in extreme poverty and have an illness or disability and receive no family support. The country reduced the age eligibility threshold from 77 to 60 in 2016, covering less than one-third of older people aged 60 and over.[36] Given that only less than 30% of older people received some kind of contributory pension, this still left one-third of the country's older people without coverage.

Viet Nam combines means-tested social pensions to those aged 60-79 living alone and in poverty with universal pensions to everyone aged 80 and above who do not receive the social insurance pension. Thus, 16% of people aged 65 and above received a social pension, including 46% of those aged 80 and above.[37] One-third (33%) of people aged 65 and above were able to access a pension, rising to 58% of those aged 80 and above.

---

[36] C. Knox-Vydmanov, D. Horn, and A. Sevilla. 2017. *The Feasibility of a Universal Pension in the Philippines.* Manila: HelpAge International and COSE. https://www.helpage.org/silo/files/the-feasibility-of-a-universal-social-pension-in-the-philippines.pdf.

[37] S. Kidd, B. Gelders, and A. Tran. 2019. Potential Impacts of Social Pension in Viet Nam. Ha Noi: ILO. https://www.developmentpathways.co.uk/wp-content/uploads/2019/11/Potential-impacts-of-social-pensions-in-Viet-Nam.pdf.

Labor Market Programs

The SPI for LMPs in 12 countries was equal to or above the Asia average of 0.1, with a similar pattern for the expenditure as a share of GDP. Countries with a relatively high overall SPI for LMPs include the high-income countries of Singapore and the ROK as well as the PRC and Bangladesh. Spending on cash- and food-for-work programs slightly outweighed that on skills development and training as a share of GDP.

LMPs made a relatively low contribution to the overall expenditure in all income groups, with the highest in high-income countries, accounting for an average SPI of 0.2. LMP expenditures in these countries were led by skills development and training programs in Singapore, accounting for 0.3% of GDP and 5.5% of social protection spending. More specifically, Singapore's "workfare" schemes were designed to supplement the earnings of low-wage workers and to offer grants for training courses to encourage them to upgrade their skills.

Among the lower middle-income countries, Bangladesh had the highest expenditure on cash- and food-for-work assistance in Asia, accounting for nearly 18% of its social protection spending. Bangladesh had five major cash- and food-for-work programs (Box 3).

In addition to Singapore, Bhutan and Cambodia had the highest contributions—4.7% and 6.3%, respectively—to skills development and training programs as a share of their social protection expenditure in Asia. These programs varied in their objectives and target beneficiaries. Bhutan had four training programs, of which the Overseas Employment Program provided the largest coverage. It arranges placement of jobseekers overseas in direct collaboration with government agencies and overseas companies. Since its launch in 2013, it has supported 8,213 Bhutanese citizens to find overseas employment.[38]

Cambodia's vocational training scheme, with a $17.2 million budget, offered free vocational training to low-skilled workers to improve their employability and to facilitate access to better-paid jobs and livelihoods. The Ministry of Social Affairs, Veterans and Youth Rehabilitation supports vocational training for vulnerable groups, including people with disabilities, women and children who are victims of human trafficking, unhoused people, and children and teenagers who are delinquents or drug addicts.[39]

Overall, LMPs remained the most underfunded area of social protection in Asia, and there is a clear need to strengthen their reach and effectiveness. LMPs have an important role to play in supporting disadvantaged low-skilled workers to sustain and to promote their family livelihoods and help them obtain adequately paid, decent work. They can be especially beneficial for improving labor market opportunities for women who tend to have lower labor force participation rates and who occupy lower-paid and less senior jobs than men. Global evidence suggests that well-designed

---

[38] ADB. 2022. *Bhutan: Social Protection Indicator*. Manila.
[39] ADB. 2022. *Cambodia: Social Protection Indicator*. Manila.

Box 3: Food- and Cash-for-Work Programs in Bangladesh

Food for Work and Work for Money programs. The Food for Work Program was established in 1975. The Ministry of Disaster Management and Relief implemented various projects to maintain and to develop rural infrastructure under renovation programs in post-disaster periods, as well as during normal times, involving mainly earthwork. Due to the growing prominence of cash payments to avoid leakages, a substitute program, the Work for Money Program, was introduced in the 2014 financial year. The relative shares of these programs depend on the stock of rice available under the government's Public Food Distribution System. The daily allowance involves 8 kilograms of rice for 7 hours of work or the cash equivalent. The eligibility criteria involve landlessness due to climate-related shocks and ownership of less than 0.2 hectare of land. Due to the physically demanding nature of the projects, male applicants tended to get preference. Between 2015 and 2018, the number of beneficiaries increased by 4.7% per year from 2.3 million to 2.7 million, and the total amount of payments disbursed increased by 10.3% per year from Tk12.5 billion to Tk17.0 billion. Therefore, the per capita increase in the payment was more than 5.0% per year during this period.

Test Relief Program. The Ministry of Disaster Management and Relief also implements the Test Relief Program in rural areas during lean periods of the year and after natural calamities, such as floods and cyclones. Its objective is to create employment opportunities that enhance food security for the rural poor, wage laborers, and the unemployed through the implementation of small rehabilitation projects, including the development of educational and public welfare institutions. The program beneficiaries receive 8 kg of rice or wheat for working 7 hours per day for specific project activities and standardized volumes of work. The Test Relief Program, along with the Food for Work Program—even after discounting for possible leakages—has succeeded in creating millions of person-days of temporary employment every year in the country, mainly benefiting those in poverty. Between 2015 and 2018, the number of beneficiaries increased by 15.6% per year from 1.1 million to 1.8 million, and the total allocations increased by 17.6% per year from Tk7.7 billion to Tk13.0 billion. Therefore, the per capita benefits increased marginally by about 2.0% per year during the period.

Food Assistance in Chittagong Hill Tracts Area. The Food Assistance Program was initiated by the government in 2007 in response to the livelihood crisis induced by bamboo flowering in the northeastern Indian state of Mizoram and the Chittagong Hill Tracts (CHT) area in Bangladesh. This phenomenon tends to occur every 40-50 years, lasts 3-5 years, and has a far-reaching and negative impact on the bamboo industry, ecology of the CHT, and lives and livelihoods of communities who depend on bamboo resources. The impacts were particularly dire among the Jhum 6 cultivators in remote areas of the CHT. The Food Assistance Program is implemented by the Ministry of Chittagong Hill Tracts Affairs in three districts (i.e., Bandarban, Khagrachari, and Rangamati) of the CHT area. The program is targeted at ultra-poor women who receive 3.5 kilograms of rice or wheat daily for 30 days for doing public works. Between 2015 and 2018, the number of beneficiaries increased marginally by 3.6% per year, from 744,000 to 828,000, and the total expenditures increased by 6.7% per year, from Tk2.4 billion to Tk2.9 billion during the period. Therefore, the per capita benefit increased by about 2.0% during the period.

Source: ADB. 2022. *Bangladesh: Social Protection Indicator*. Manila.

and contextually appropriate skills training can improve employment opportunities and incomes among marginalized and disadvantaged groups and contribute to reducing poverty, inequality, and exclusion.[40]

---

[40]   OECD. 2018. The Role of Technical and Vocational Education and Training (TVET) in Fostering Inclusive Growth at the Local Level in Southeast Asia. *OECD Local Economic and Employment Development (LEED) Papers.* No. 2018/01. Paris.

III. Trends in the Social Protection Indicator, 2009–2018

- The SPI in Asia increased from 3.3 in 2009 to 4.1 in 2018, driven mainly by the expansion of social insurance.
- The social insurance SPI improved from 2.3 to 3.1; the social assistance SPI increased slightly from 0.8 to 0.9; and the change in the LMP SPI is negligible.
- The social insurance SPI was propelled by the expansion in pension and health insurance coverage.
- There was only modest progress in social protection expenditure in Asia from 2009 to 2018, as the increase in social protection expenditure in Asia was primarily crisis-responsive.

SPI research and data collection present an opportunity to examine trends in the evolution of the indicator in Asia over a considerable timeline. Comparable data are now available for 24 countries in Asia for 2009, 2012, 2015, and 2018, allowing the assessment of close to 1 decade of some key patterns and trends. The analysis in this section includes 24 countries, due to a lack of data for all 4 years for Afghanistan and Kazakhstan. Therefore, the aggregate values for 2018 are different from the analysis based on 26 countries elsewhere in this report.

Progress in the Social Protection Indicator, 2009–2018

Over 2009–2018, social protection expenditure in Asia grew at a moderate pace. The average SPI for Asia increased from 3.3 to 4.1. Within this time period, a substantial increase was observed between 2009 and 2012, after which spending stagnated through 2018. In particular, the average SPI jumped to 4.0 by 2012, rose further to 4.2 by 2015 but then dropped slightly to 4.1 in 2018. This pattern was mainly driven by the rise in the social insurance SPI from 2.3 in 2009 to 2.9 in 2012 and 3.1 in 2015. The social insurance SPI remained steady between 2015 and 2018, but the social assistance SPI declined slightly from 1.0 in 2015 to 0.9 in 2018.

A similar pattern was observed for social protection expenditure in terms of spending as a share of GDP. Expenditure increased from 4.6% of GDP in 2009 to 5.4% in 2018. A major shift in overall spending was recorded between 2009 and 2012, when it increased from 4.6% to 5.5% of GDP. It remained in the range of 5.5% to 5.4% of GDP during 2012, 2015, and 2018.

Figure 9: Trends in the Social Protection Indicator and Social Protection Expenditure by Income Group, 2009-2018

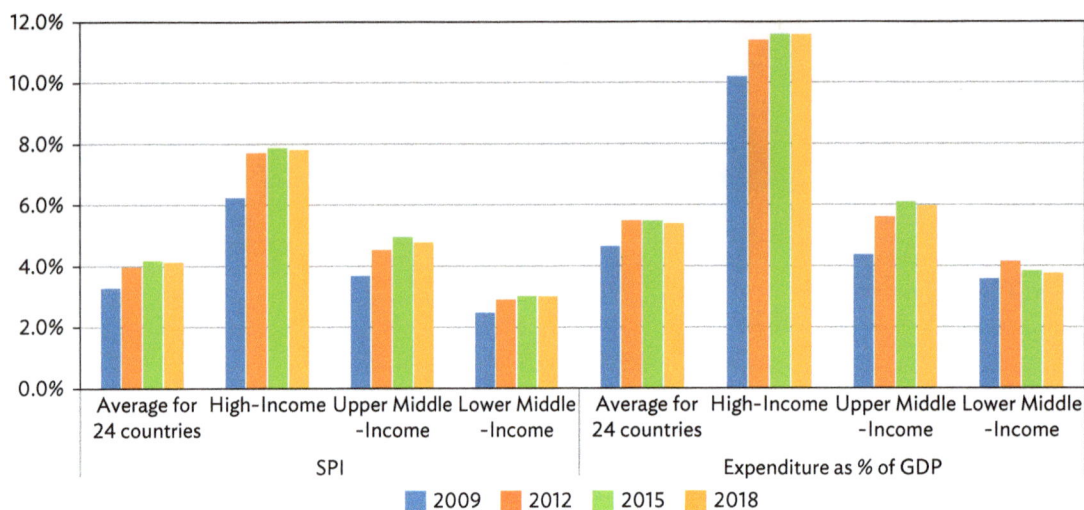

GDP = gross domestic product, SPI = Social Protection Indicator.

Source: ADB estimates.

This picture (Figure 9) suggests overall modest progress in social protection expenditure in Asia from 2009 to 2018. By way of comparison, annual social protection spending in Asia (on average around 5% of GDP) was one-quarter of the Organisation for Economic Co-operation and Development (OECD) average spending of 20% of GDP over this period.[41] Over the past decade, social protection has become an important public policy instrument, and it is used to complement economic and sector policies. Social protection spending in most countries in the region, however, did not outpace growth in GDP and remained lower than what may have been possible given their average income levels.[42]

In fact, social protection in Asia has been primarily responsive to large crises. The 1997 Asian financial crisis was instrumental in stimulating strong demand for social protection among governments, as exemplified by the fivefold increase in the volume of the ADB lending portfolio in 1998-2000 compared with previous years.[43] Similarly, the 2008 global financial crisis and COVID-19 pandemic triggered spikes in social protection spending.[44]

[41]   OECD. OECD Social and Welfare Statistics. https://www.oecd-ilibrary.org/social-issues-migration-health/data/social-expenditure/aggregated-data_data-00166-en (accessed 13 April 2022).

[42]   OECD. 2014. *Society at a Glance: Asia/Pacific 2014*. Paris.

[43]   ADB. 2012. *The Revised Social Protection Index: Methodology and Handbook*. Manila.

[44]   The effects of these events could not be assessed with data collected from the SPI analysis, however.

As part of this study, additional data were collected to capture social protection responses to the COVID-19 pandemic in Asia. Analysis suggests that the pandemic prompted a rise in social protection expenditure across Asia, resulting in new programs as well as in vertical expansion (i.e., increasing benefit size) and horizontal expansion (i.e., extension in coverage) of existing programs. It needs to be established, however, if these measures will remain temporary or form new parts of existing social protection systems.

It is possible to observe annual changes in average social protection expenditure as well.[45] In 2008, the average social protection expenditure for 20 Asia and Pacific countries with available data was 36% higher than with 2007, while in 2009, it increased by 78% compared with 2007. In the following years, social protection expenditure decreased a little but then stabilized at the high levels observed in 2009. This suggests that the 2008 global financial crisis triggered a response that then resulted in a systematic change in social protection. The available 2020 data for 14 countries suggest that once again, the average social protection expenditure increased by 30% compared with 2019.

Progress in the Social Protection Indicator by Income Group, 2009–2018

The SPI increased across all countries' income groups from 2009 to 2018 (Figure 10). The highest increase of 1.6 percentage points was observed in high-income countries. Upper middle-income countries also registered a positive trend, with their SPI rising from 3.7 in 2009 to 4.8 in 2018. Lower middle-income countries showed an increase of 0.5 percentage point. In all income groups, these results were driven by social insurance.

All income groups followed the general regional trend; as the SPI rose substantially between 2009 and 2012, it continued an upward trend into 2015 and dropped slightly by 2018 in high-income and upper middle-income countries, while remaining stable in lower middle-income countries.

Examining individual country-level trends over 2009-2018, the overall SPI increased in 20 of 24 countries for which comparable data are available. Boxes 4 and 5 discuss in greater detail the progress in developing comprehensive social protection systems achieved in the ROK and the PRC. The highest increments are observed in Armenia, Tajikistan, and the PRC, which improved their overall SPIs by more than 2 percentage points. Other countries increased their SPIs within 1-2 percentage points, including Azerbaijan, Japan, the ROK, the Kyrgyz Republic, Nepal, Pakistan, and Singapore.

---

[45] It is important to clarify that the above data on social protection expenditure does not necessarily have the same definition used in the SPI report, in particular in relation to health insurance expenditure, and does not offer the same consistency and comparability. It nevertheless allows discernment of the overall pattern of spending in the region. See ADB. Key Indicators Database. https://kidb.adb.org/.

Figure 10: Social Protection Indicator by Country and Income Group for 2009, 2012, 2015, and 2018

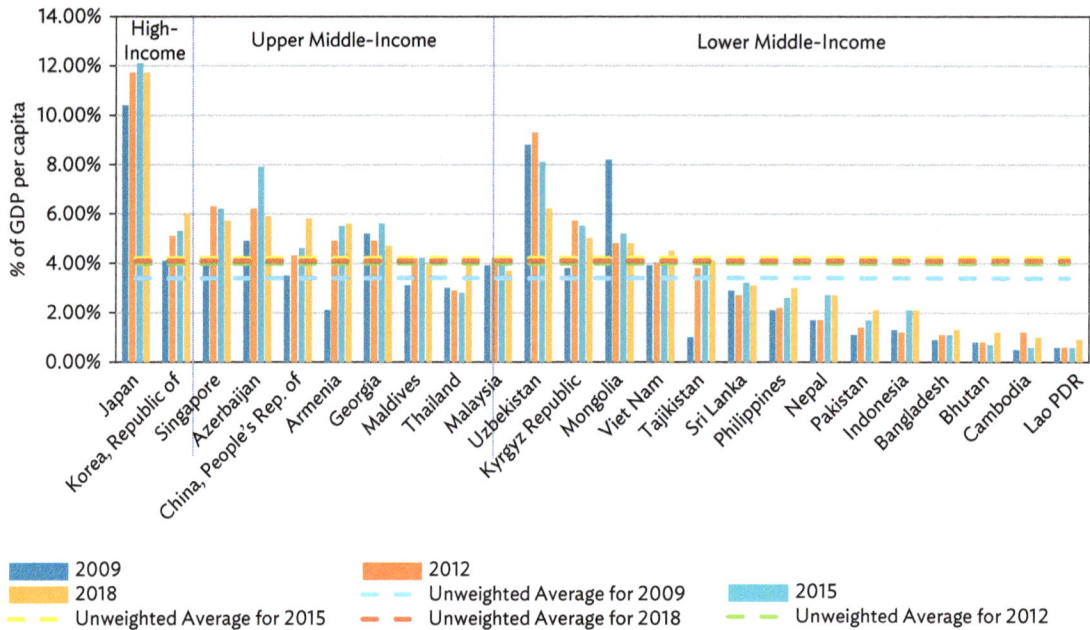

GDP = gross domestic product, Lao PDR = Lao People's Democratic Republic.

Source: ADB estimates based on consultants' reports.

Box 4: Republic of Korea's Comprehensive Social Protection System

The Republic of Korea (ROK) has succeeded in expanding social protection and developing a comprehensive system in the past decade. This was driven by the government's pledge to ensure that "a nation takes responsibility for each individual." The growth rate of social protection expenditure over the past decade was 1.5 times higher than its total spending.

The ROK's total SPI rose steadily from 4.1 in 2009, to 5.1 in 2012, to 5.3 in 2015, and finally to 6.0 in 2018. The social insurance Social Protection Indicator (SPI) increased from 3.2 to 4.6 in this period and accounted for most of the increase in its overall SPI. At the same time, the ROK's social assistance SPI rose from 0.8 to 1.2, and its labor market programs (LMPs) SPI rose from 0.1 in 2009 to 0.2 in 2018.

The expenditure on social protection accounted for 9.6% of the gross domestic product (GDP) in 2018—almost 1.2 percentage points higher than the 8.4% recorded in 2015. This expenditure was predominantly for social insurance, which accounted for 77.9% of the total expenditure and was composed mainly of pensions and health insurance. Social assistance was the second major source of expenditure, accounting for 19.3% of

continued on next page

the total expenditure. LMPs accounted for 2.8%, a threefold increase from the 1.2% recorded in the previous study. The total social expenditure remained still far below the Organisation of Economic Co-operation and Development (OECD) average of 21.0% of GDP. However, the total social protection expenditure–GDP ratio has steadily increased over the years.

The ROK's National Health Insurance was established in 1989 to provide universal compulsory health insurance. It is the country largest social protection program, accounting for 34.0% of social protection expenditure and covering 51.1 million people or 97.0% of the population in 2018. The remaining 1.5 million were included under the Medical Aid System as eligible candidates for the National Basic Livelihood Security System. Health insurance spending doubled from W27.5 trillion in 2008 to W52.6 trillion in 2016.

The ROK's old-age pensions accounted for 26.1% of government social protection expenditure in 2018. It achieved near-universal coverage, and most citizens had pension benefits through one of the four public sector pension schemes, including the largest National Pension Service and the government employees' pension.

The rapid population aging dynamic in the ROK, however, has put pressure on the financing of health care and pensions. The ROK's share of population aged 65 and over steadily expanded, rising from 10.5% in 2009 to 14.3% in 2018. Medical costs from older people accounted for 33.3% of all medical spending in 2009; in 2018, this figure reached 40.8%. According to Statistics Korea, the proportion of older population is expected to reach 44.3% in 2060. Therefore, public expenditures are projected to continue rising as the population keeps aging.

Continued investment in social assistance demonstrates the importance that the government attaches to the need to support vulnerable groups. In fact, social assistance is also used to respond to the challenge of an aging population. Assistance to older people accounted, for example, for 7.0% of all expenditures on social protection in 2018, while health assistance accounted for another 4.3% of the total. Just between 2015 and 2018, expenditure on assistance to older people increased by 25.8%, and that on health assistance rose by 30.6%. Child welfare was another priority area accounting for 4.8% of all expenditures.

In 2018, LMPs constituted the smallest of the three SPI categories, but they still accounted for 2.8% of all social protection expenditures. This was still relatively high for Asian countries. This percentage resulted mainly from a skills development and training program for people with disabilities, which represented two-thirds of all LMP expenditures. The Skills Development Training Program for people without disabilities accounted for the other 1.0 percentage point of total social protection expenditures. In fact, LMP expenditures tripled since 2015, reflecting a change in wage policy, resulting in a 16% increase in the minimum wage in 2018, as well as in the related spending to ease employers' burdens.

Source: ADB. 2022. *Republic of Korea: Social Protection Indicator.* Manila.

Box 5: Developing Comprehensive Social Protection in the People's Republic of China

The People's Republic of China (PRC) has made impressive progress on social protection in recent years. Its overall Social Protection Indicator (SPI) increased from 3.5 in 2009 to 4.6 in 2015 and then rose significantly to 5.8 in 2018. The 2018 achievement is marked by increases across social insurance, social assistance, and labor market programs (LMPs). Between 2015 and 2018, for example, the SPI for social insurance increased from 4.1 to 4.8; the SPI for social assistance increased from 0.4 to 0.6; and the SPI for LMPs increased from 0.1 to 0.4.

Especially noteworthy is the growth in the PRC's social insurance SPI from 3.0 in 2009 to 4.8 in 2018. Social insurance is the dominant form of social protection in the PRC. The Urban Enterprise Employees Pension Scheme (UEEPS) covered 118.0 million participants, and the total pension insurance expenditure was CNY4,464.5 billion in 2018 or nearly 5.0% of gross domestic product (GDP). The Urban and Rural Residents Pension Scheme (URRPS) covered 159.0 million participants, and its total expenditure reached CNY290.5 billion or 0.3% of GDP.

There were two major health insurance schemes. Basic Medical Care Insurance for Urban Employees covered 316.8 million participants in 2018, and its expenditure was CNY1.1 billion or 1.2% of GDP. Basic Medical Care Insurance for Urban and Rural Residents covered 897.4 million people, with an expenditure of CNY628.5 billion. This scheme is currently being consolidated with the former New Rural Cooperative Medical Scheme, which covered 130.4 million and entailed an additional expenditure of CNY81.8 billion in 2018. Together, these two schemes made up 0.8% of GDP.

The PRC's progress in social assistance was less prominent than that in social insurance, as the SPI for social assistance from 2009 to 2018 improved by a low 0.2 percentage point. This, however, partly reflects the success achieved in poverty reduction, especially in rural areas. Dibao is the main social assistance instrument to support the poorest families in both urban and rural areas through cash transfers. In recent years, the number of beneficiaries in both urban and rural areas has substantially decreased. For example, the number of beneficiaries decreased by 14.7% from 53.1 million in 2017 to 45.3 million in 2018. Dibao has been instrumental in establishing a solid institutional base for the entire social assistance system, however. The eligibility for most other social assistance projects is based on Dibao entitlement; that is, Dibao recipients are eligible to apply for benefits of most other social assistance programs.

There is growing recognition that the PRC needs to develop social care services, such as for children, older people, and people with disabilities. This is especially pertinent as the PRC's population has been aging rapidly; 12.6% of the population is now age 65 or older, and this percentage is likely to increase.

The PRC also exhibited an impressive 0.3-percentage point increase in its LMP SPI, from 0.1 in 2009 to 0.4 in 2018, which was the highest level across Asia. Importantly, its LMPs have also been increasingly emphasizing skills development and training, as an integral part of the PRC's new technology-based economic development model. There is clear recognition in the PRC that it needs to expand its support for skills development and training to deal with the rising impact of digitalization and the increasing importance of automation, robotics, and other labor-displacing technologies. For example, the Employment Assistance Program (with a core skills development and training component) benefited about 33.2 million unemployed workers in 2018, at a cost of about CNY84.5 billion.

Another important LMP was the Poverty Alleviation and Development Program, mainly implemented in regions with high levels of poverty. It offered training, marketing services, direct investment, infrastructure services, and small loans for the rural poor. It targeted poor families whose incomes per capita were lower than the local official rural poverty alleviation standard. Total beneficiaries numbered 55.7 million in 2015 and 16.6 million in 2018.

Sources: Government of the PRC, Ministry of Finance. National General Public Budget Expenditures. Beijing (8 years: 2013-2020). http://yss.mof.gov.cn.

Other countries in this income group with substantial improvements in SPI include Armenia, Azerbaijan, Maldives, and Thailand. In Armenia, for example, improvements in SPI were driven by the rise in social insurance spending, mainly for old-age pensions; additionally, the share of both disability pension expenditure and beneficiaries increased in social assistance and social insurance programs.[46] In Maldives, substantial SPI gains were derived from the introduction of the universal health insurance scheme, Aasandha, in 2012. In 2014, this scheme was further developed into Husnuvaa Aasandha with the aim of providing health care for all without a ceiling protection limit. It extended its coverage and removed the annual cap of Rf100,000 per person per year. In Thailand, the rise in SPI was driven by the expansion of coverage by the Universal Health Coverage scheme and Old Age Allowance.

Tajikistan steadily expanded its pension insurance spending, as its social insurance SPI jumped from 0.6 in 2009 to 3.3 in 2012 and kept rising into 2018, resulting in a 3-percentage-point increment over 2009-2018. Thus, from 2015 to 2018, the number of beneficiaries for pensions in Tajikistan increased by 25%, from 511,200 to 687,000 and total expenditure increased by 33%.

Pakistan's progress is also notable, if still modest at times, across all three forms of social protection. Between 2009 and 2018, its social insurance SPI almost doubled from 0.9 to 1.7. Meanwhile, its social assistance SPI moved up from 0.2 to 0.3, and its LMP SPI also increased to 0.1 by 2018 from 0.03 in previous years. Within social insurance, government employee pensions dominated expenditure. In fact, its share to total social protection expenditure grew from 78.0% in 2015 to 82.0% in 2018. Expenditure on social assistance formed just 15.0% of the total social protection expenditures and comprised mainly welfare assistance. The main welfare assistance program is the Benazir Income Support Programme (BISP) flagship conditional and unconditional cash transfer, which achieved success by extending coverage from 1.8 million in 2009 to 5.6 million in 2018 and increasing spending nearly sixfold, from PRs15.8 to PRs102.2 million.[47]

Nepal has had a similar record, starting from an SPI of 1.7 in 2009 but reaching 2.7 by 2018. Nepal's SPI was largely boosted by expenditures on the public sector pension scheme, which rose sharply in 2015 and 2018. Expenditures on pensions increased from NRs26.0 billion in fiscal year 2015 to NRs53.0 billion in fiscal year 2018 due to the rise in the salaries of all public servants by 25.0% in 2017 as well as the expansion of other benefits for public servants. In fiscal year 2018, social insurance accounted for the highest share of total social protection expenditure at 70.1%, with public sector pensions accounting for more than half of total spending.

Along with these improvements, a reduction in SPI between 2009 and 2018 was observed in Uzbekistan by 2.5 percentage points, Mongolia by 0.3 percentage point, and Malaysia by 0.2 percentage point.

[46]   World Bank. 2014. *Republic of Armenia Public Expenditure Review: Expanding the Fiscal Envelope.* Washington, DC. https://documents1.worldbank.org/curated/en/264471468005435366/pdf/885860ESW 0REVI0P13340000PUBLIC000AM.pdf.

[47]   ADB. 2022. *Pakistan: Social Protection Indicator.* Manila.

In Uzbekistan, the decline in SPI was mainly due to low levels of social protection spending relative to the pace of GDP growth. For example, social insurance spending in Uzbekistan rose until 2015, but it then declined from 6.9 to 5.2 in 2018, while social assistance gradually decreased from 2.5 in 2009 to 1.0 2018. The overall social protection expenditure in Uzbekistan increased by 45.8% between 2015 and 2018, while GDP in current prices rose by 93.5%. As a result, the share of social protection expenditures in GDP decreased from 7.9% in 2015 to 6.0% in 2018, with a corresponding decline in the SPI.

The decline in the overall SPI in Mongolia was induced by reductions in social assistance. Mongolia's social assistance increased from 1.6 in 2009 to 2.5 in 2012 but then declined to 1.3 in 2015 and further to 1.1 in 2018. This can be explained by the suspension of universal cash transfers under the Human Development Fund and introduction of targeted benefits, which resulted in budget reductions for social welfare.

Progress in Social Protection Indicator by Category, 2009-2018

Figure 11 provides the disaggregation of the SPI for social insurance, social assistance, and LMPs for 2009-2018. In most Asian countries, increases in the SPI since 2009 were driven mainly by the expansion of social insurance. The social insurance SPI in Asia increased by 0.6 percentage point from 2.3 in 2009 to 3.1 in 2018. The social assistance SPI remained at 0.9 between 2009 and 2018. Spending on LMPs was substantially below the other two categories, and the SPI stayed at 0.1.

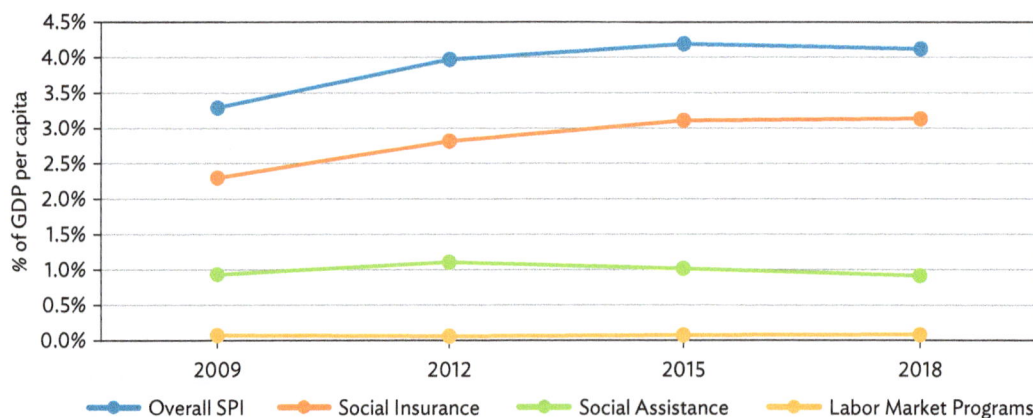

Figure 11: **Progress in Social Protection Indicator by Category, 2009-2018**

GDP = gross domestic product, SPI = Social Protection Indicator.

Source: ADB estimates.

Most countries in Asia showed progress in the social insurance SPI between 2009 and 2018. Most substantial SPI increments were observed in Armenia, the PRC, the Kyrgyz Republic, Maldives, and Tajikistan. It is notable that countries, such as Bangladesh, Bhutan, the Lao PDR, Nepal, and Pakistan—whose social insurance SPI remained modest—doubled their spending over this period, and Indonesia nearly tripled it. Social insurance spending declined in Uzbekistan, as discussed above.

Regarding social assistance, 11 countries improved their SPIs, and another 3 retained their existing spending levels over this period. In most countries, this increase was in small increments. Bangladesh and Sri Lanka doubled—and the Philippines tripled—their spending. These improvements, however, did not result in a discernible change for Asia in aggregate terms, as 10 countries decreased their spending. Among them are Uzbekistan and the Kyrgyz Republic, where social assistance spending declined by more than one-half over this period.

The most substantial progress among all three social protection categories was observed in social insurance in high-income countries, where expenditure increased by 1.2 percentage points (Figure 12). The social insurance SPI increased in the upper middle-income and lower middle-income countries by 0.6 percentage point and 0.5 percentage point, respectively. Social assistance expenditure improved by 0.3 percentage point and 0.5 percentage point in high-income and upper-middle income countries, respectively, but declined in lower middle-income countries. Spending on LMPs remained unchanged in all three income groups.

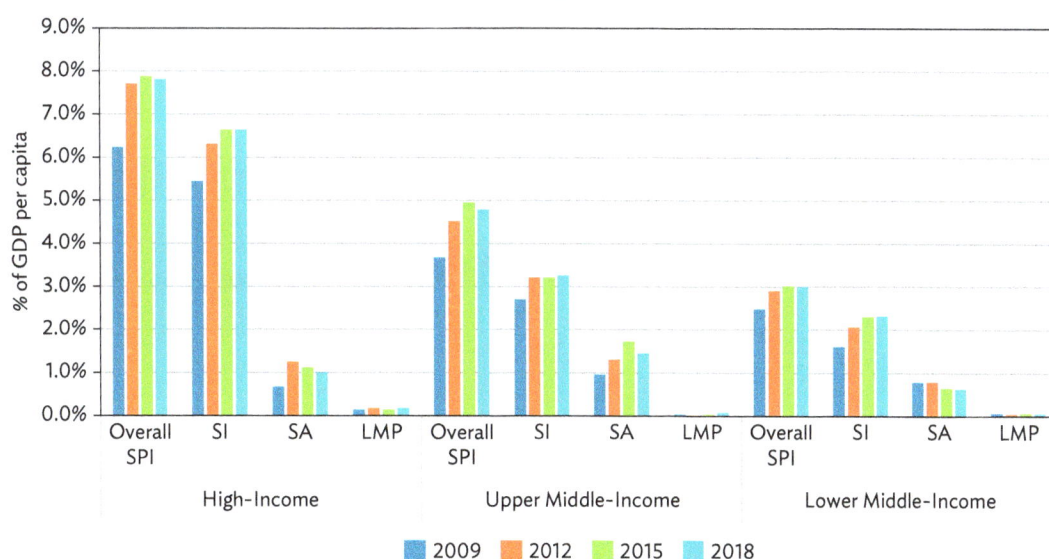

Figure 12: **Trends in Social Protection Indicator by Category and Income Group, 2009-2018**

GDP = gross domestic product, LMP = labor market programs, SA = social assistance, SI = social insurance, SPI = Social Protection Indicator.

Source: ADB estimates.

IV. Depth of Benefits and Breadth of Coverage of Social Protection

This chapter examines the depth of social protection benefits and breadth of coverage of social protection in Asia. The depth indicator represents the average value of the benefits received by each actual beneficiary as a share of GDP per capita. The breadth indicator represents the number of beneficiaries relative to the total target beneficiaries. It thus reflects the number of people receiving benefits in practice. The chapter then examines the trends in depth and breadth from 2009 to 2018.

Depth and Breadth of Social Protection in 2018

- Among 26 countries, the depth of social protection benefits for each actual beneficiary as a share of GDP per capita reached 9.2%, while 65.2% of intended beneficiaries were covered.
- Among the three categories, social insurance had the highest depth of benefits at 36.9% of GDP per capita, social assistance benefits reached 4.6% of GDP per capita, and the depth of LMPs amounted to 5.9% of GDP per capita.
- Social insurance had the widest coverage at 38.5% of intended beneficiaries, social assistance covered 25.1% of all intended beneficiaries, while LMP coverage was very low at 1.6% of intended beneficiaries.
- The majority of Asian countries offered small benefits but achieved high coverage. These countries chose to extend coverage but retained low benefits, with the prospect of raising benefit levels incrementally.
- Only a few countries combined generous benefits with wide coverage; a handful of countries provided generous benefits to a small share of the eligible population; finally, several countries had low benefits and low coverage (i.e., Bhutan, Cambodia, the Lao PDR, Nepal, Sri Lanka, Tajikistan, and Uzbekistan).

The depth indicator allows the assessment of the adequacy of social protection benefits. Given that countries in the region have very different levels of development, it is useful to adopt a relative measure of the value of benefits by expressing the value in terms of percentage of GDP per capita. For example, rather than comparing the absolute value of benefits in Japan with those of Bangladesh, it is more useful to express amounts in relative terms. To convey a more complete picture of benefit adequacy, this report considers the derived monetary value of benefits in addition to assessing the level of expenditure relative to a country's GDP per capita.

The breadth indicator helps identify how far social protection reaches in supporting the beneficiary population. Breadth is a weighted indicator, and its computation for the social protection categories uses the total reference population. As a result, the sum of breadth for each of the social protection categories equals the overall breadth. The unweighted breadth shows the actual coverage of social protection for each category. For example, the social insurance breadth of coverage is estimated at 38.5% of the total target beneficiaries of social protection. However, if examining the unweighted breadth of social insurance, the value is 65.2%. This indicates that social insurance programs covered about 65.0% of the social insurance target beneficiaries, defined as the employed and older people.

The breadth indicator may exceed 100%, as it combines the total number of actual beneficiaries for different programs not adjusted for double counting. In other words, the records for the beneficiaries of social protection programs can count the same person more than once if they are reached by more than one program.

Table 3 shows both the depth and breadth of social protection across the 26 countries in Asia in 2018. The breadth and depth are also included for the three major components of social protection.

Table 3: **Depth of Benefits and Breadth of Coverage by Country, 2018**

Country	Depth of Benefits (% of GDP per capita)				Breadth of Coverage (% of target beneficiaries)			
	Overall Depth	Social Insurance	Social Assistance	Labor Market Programs	Overall Breadth	Social Insurance	Social Assistance	Labor Market Programs
Afghanistan	1.5	258.4	0.9	4.0	17.1	0.0	16.7	0.4
Armenia	11.1	23.0	4.7	9.8	50.1	17.6	32.4	0.1
Azerbaijan	17.1	25.8	9.0	3.4	34.8	17.5	15.2	2.1
Bangladesh	3.7	116.3	2.0	5.7	33.5	0.4	29.3	3.8
Bhutan	11.8	80.6	3.7	16.0	9.8	1.0	8.5	0.3
Cambodia	5.0	53.8	0.6	21.4	19.4	1.5	17.6	0.3
Georgia	5.3	31.5	5.1	5.5	89.1	0.6	88.4	0.1
Indonesia	1.6	2.0	1.3	4.0	129.0	57.0	72.0	0.0
Japan	9.1	9.0	12.3	0.9	128.3	119.1	7.8	1.4
Kazakhstan	13.4	22.7	5.4	7.4	34.6	15.8	17.9	0.9
Kyrgyz Republic	8.8	9.2	7.5	3.4	56.9	42.6	14.1	0.2
Korea, Republic of	5.5	5.3	8.1	2.6	110.3	89.3	14.4	6.6
Lao PDR	1.3	1.2	4.6	0.2	66.2	64.9	0.9	0.4
Malaysia	43.5	58.7	2.9	...	8.5	6.2	2.3	...
Maldives	5.9	4.5	14.6	...	68.1	58.8	9.3	...
Mongolia	4.3	5.3	2.7	0.7	111.9	69.9	39.9	2.1
Nepal	9.4	39.6	3.4	1.0	29.1	4.9	24.2	0.0

continued on next page

Table 3: *continued*

Country	Depth of Benefits (% of GDP per capita)				Breadth of Coverage (% of target beneficiaries)			
	Overall Depth	Social Insurance	Social Assistance	Labor Market Programs	Overall Breadth	Social Insurance	Social Assistance	Labor Market Programs
Pakistan	6.6	81.7	1.1	19.9	32.4	2.1	30.0	0.3
Philippines	2.5	2.1	4.5	4.5	119.1	95.3	23.3	0.5
China, People's Republic of	6.1	6.2	4.0	13.9	95.6	77.5	15.2	2.9
Singapore	5.4	8.4	1.9	3.1	106.2	55.2	41.0	10.0
Sri Lanka	4.8	18.9	1.2	4.3	65.0	13.3	51.5	0.2
Tajikistan	20.9	35.3	5.5	4.6	19.5	10.1	9.2	0.2
Thailand	2.7	3.0	2.4	0.1	135.9	99.7	29.9	6.4
Uzbekistan	26.9	49.9	8.2	6.7	23.3	10.5	11.6	1.2
Viet Nam	4.5	5.8	1.3	11.2	100.2	70.0	29.6	0.6
Unweighted Asia Average	**9.2**	**36.9**	**4.6**	**5.9**	**65.2**	**38.5**	**25.1**	**1.7**

... = no available data, GDP = gross domestic product, Lao PDR = Lao People's Democratic Republic.

Note: 0.0% values are less than 0.1.

Source: ADB estimates.

The average depth of benefits across all Asian countries in 2018 is 9.2%. In other words, relative to GDP per capita, the average expenditures per beneficiary were only 9.2%. The average breadth of coverage is 65.2%. Thus, about two-thirds of all intended beneficiaries received some social protection benefits. This also means that one-third of target beneficiaries were not covered.

The depth of benefits varies by social protection category. The depth for social insurance programs in 2018 is 36.9%, nearly three times higher than the overall social protection regional average. In contrast, the depth for social assistance in 2018 is only 4.6%, and the depth for LMPs is similarly small, about 6.4%.

The depth of benefits is the highest in upper middle-income countries (13.1% of GDP per capita), followed by lower middle-income (8.0%) and high-income countries (6.7%) (Figure 13). Looking at the derived monetary value, the picture is reversed: high-income countries spent $2,995.10; upper middle-income countries, $1,019.00; and lower middle-income countries, $176.40.

Social insurance coverage had the highest level of covered targeted beneficiaries, 38.5%. Social assistance covered 25.1% or one-quarter of all the targeted beneficiaries, while the LMP breadth of coverage was only 1.6%. The breadth of coverage is the highest in high-income countries (114.9% of target beneficiaries), followed by upper middle-income countries (64.6%) and lower middle-income countries (58.2%).

Figure 13: **Depth of Benefits and Breadth of Coverage by Income Group and Category, 2018**

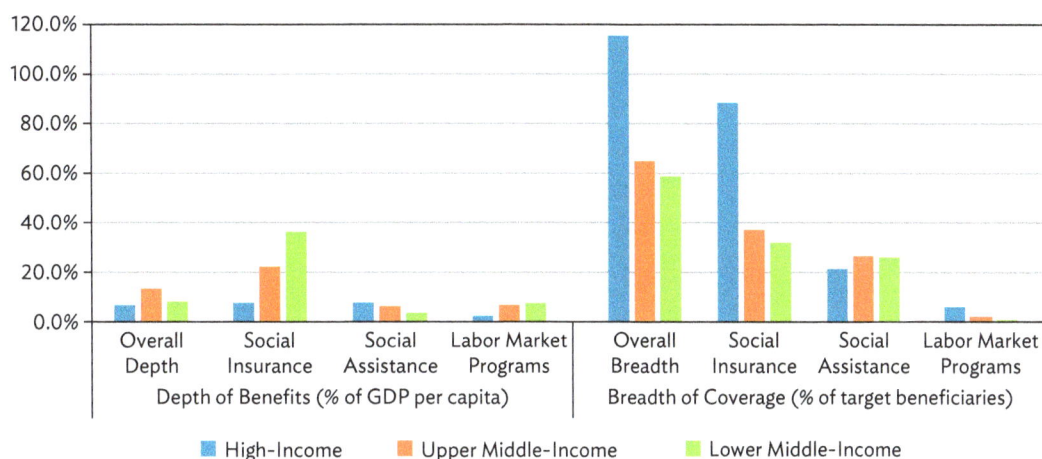

GDP = gross domestic product.

Source: ADB estimates.

To fully assess the significance of the depth of benefits, one needs to evaluate it in conjunction with the breadth of coverage. A high depth could result from high expenditures on a relatively small number of beneficiaries. This effect can sometimes be the case for social insurance, for instance, for pension programs that in some countries are provided mainly for public sector employees.

By examining at the relationship between the aggregate measures of depth and breadth, four broadly defined groups of countries that share general patterns can be distilled:

(i)   **Generous benefits and broad coverage.** These are high-income Japan, the ROK, and Singapore, which have developed relatively generous social insurance systems that reached the majority of their populations.

(ii)   **Small benefits and high coverage.** These countries extended their coverage in small but steady steps by retaining low benefits. The majority of countries in Asia fall into this category. Several countries (i.e., the PRC, Maldives, Mongolia, Thailand, and Viet Nam) established universal coverage for health and/or pension insurance; others (i.e., Indonesia, the Philippines) were moving towards universal health coverage. Similarly, many countries (i.e., Armenia, Bangladesh, Georgia, Indonesia, Mongolia, Pakistan, Sri Lanka, and Viet Nam) substantially extended social assistance coverage.

(iii)   **Generous benefits to a small share of an eligible population.** This category includes Bangladesh, Bhutan, Malaysia, Maldives, and Pakistan.

(iv)   **Low benefits and low coverage.** This includes several countries such as Bhutan, Cambodia, the Lao PDR, Nepal, Sri Lanka, Tajikistan, and Uzbekistan.

Social Insurance

Regarding social insurance, the depth of benefits in eight countries is above the regional average of 28.2% of GDP per capita. The benefit value in some of these countries appears exceptionally high; for example, 116.3% in Bangladesh, 81.7% in Pakistan, 80.6% in Bhutan, and 58.7% in Malaysia. This is because these benefits are high in their value but supported only a small share of workers in the formal economy.

Social insurance benefits were the highest in the lower middle-income countries (i.e., 35.8% of GDP per capita), followed by upper middle-income countries (i.e., 21.9%). However, in terms of their derived monetary values, upper middle-income countries spent $1,640.30, nearly 2.5 times more than lower middle-income countries (i.e., $692.80). High-income countries spent 7.6% on benefits; this amounted to $3,621.00, exceeding benefits in the other two groups.

Looking at the breadth of coverage in social insurance, 12 countries are above the 41.0% average for Asia. The coverage in the remaining countries in the region, however, does not exceed 16.0%, reflecting the fact that social insurance remained underdeveloped and did not reach most of the workers in the informal economy.

Social insurance coverage was the highest in high-income countries (87.9%), due to high coverage in Japan, the ROK, and Singapore, and it was higher than social assistance and LMP coverage across all country income groups in Asia. The coverage in upper middle-income countries was at 36.7%, primarily driven by the PRC, Maldives, and Thailand. Lower middle-income countries covered 31.7% of target beneficiaries, with especially strong performance in Indonesia, Mongolia, the Philippines, and Viet Nam.

The analysis of the relationship between the depth of benefits and breadth of coverage in social insurance allows the categorization of countries into four groups:

(i) **Generous benefits.** In the first group are countries offering generous social insurance benefits across most of the beneficiary population. The depth of benefits was particularly substantial in high-income Japan ($3,538.40), the ROK ($1,769.80), and Singapore ($5,554.90). Social insurance in these countries was the primary social protection instrument, reflecting the central role of the state in financing and regulating social policies.

(ii) **Small benefits but high coverage.** These include Thailand (99.7%), the Philippines (95.3%), the PRC (77.5%), Viet Nam (70.0%), Mongolia (69.9%), the Lao PDR (64.9%), Maldives (58.8%), and Indonesia (57.0%). As mentioned earlier, Thailand, the PRC, Mongolia, and Maldives achieved universal or near-universal pension coverage, while the PRC, Viet Nam, Thailand, and the Lao PDR extended health protection to more than 90.0% of their populations. The Philippines and Indonesia were also moving towards universal health coverage. The depth of social insurance benefits in these countries, however, is below the regional average, with benefits ranging from $606.30 in the PRC to $64.80 in the Philippines and $31.00 in the Lao PDR. These countries chose to extend social protection coverage but retain low benefits, with the prospect of raising benefit levels incrementally.

(iii) **Generous benefits to a small population share.** For example, Malaysia had the highest benefits in the region ($6,494.60) covering 6.2% of the eligible population. Bhutan and Bangladesh offered substantial benefits—$2,751.70 and $1,948.90, respectively—but their coverage did not exceed 1.0% of the population. Similarly, Pakistan combined relatively generous benefits of $1,248.50 with low beneficiary coverage of 2.1%. Relatively generous benefits in these countries reflect the privileged status of public sector workers and the continued government adherence to maintaining a relatively high level of provision for them.

(iv) **Low benefits and low coverage.** Coverage rates in Sri Lanka and Cambodia were 13.3% and 1.5%, respectively, and their benefits were below the regional average; Nepal had coverage of 4.9%, but the actual benefits there were just $395.10. Social insurance schemes were similarly designated to support public sector workers, including former civil servants and their families.

Social insurance in countries with low coverage mainly provides an instrument for supporting workers in salaried employment, leaving out the majority of those engaged in the informal economy. As discussed earlier, extending social insurance to previously uncovered workers is challenging due to various factors, including the limited contributory capacity of low-earning workers and employers and tight fiscal space restricting the extension of coverage through tax financing, especially in lower middle-income countries.[48] At the same time, policy preferences can play a key role in expanding coverage. For example, the impressive progress in the Lao PDR was made possible partly due to the government commitment to promote universal health coverage and its efforts to strengthen the legal, institutional, and financing arrangements for social health protection.[49]

As noted previously, the SPI analysis currently defines the employed population as the intended beneficiary group for health insurance. When health insurance becomes effectively universal, the intended beneficiaries can be expanded to the total population. This factor should be taken into account in assessing progress in a country that is trying to establish universal coverage.

Social Assistance

For social assistance, the depth of benefits in 11 countries is above the regional average of 4.6% of GDP per capita. The benefits were especially high in Maldives (14.6%), Japan (12.3%), and the ROK (8.1%). As for their derived monetary value, benefits only in four countries were above the regional average of $608.80.

[48] ILO. 2021. *Extending Social Security to Workers in the Informal Economy: Lessons from International Experience.* Geneva. https://www.social-protection.org/gimi/RessourcePDF.action?id=55728 .
[49] ILO. 2019. *Lao People's Democratic Republic. Moving towards Universal Social Health Protection.* Volume 6. https://www.social-protection.org/gimi/RessourcePDF.action;jsessionid=70g8jlPI28IsPx7SqNOUQ5Ke7JabxYxPqdmj0vu0p-iQ40e-CD5t!539423187?id=55648.

Social assistance benefits were the highest in the high-income countries (7.4% of GDP per capita or $2,932.30), reflecting the fact that all three exhibited strong results. Benefits reached 6.0% of GDP per capita ($468.10) in upper middle-income countries, and 3.4% of GDP per capita ($71.40) in lower middle-income countries.

Looking at the breadth of coverage in social assistance, 10 countries are above the 25.1% average for Asia. Coverage was especially high in Georgia (88.4%), Indonesia (72.0%), and Sri Lanka (51.5%). Social assistance coverage was the highest in upper middle-income countries (26.3%), mainly driven by Armenia, Georgia, and Thailand. Lower middle-income countries covered 25.8% of target beneficiaries, with especially wide coverage in Bangladesh, Indonesia, Mongolia, Sri Lanka, and Viet Nam. High-income countries covered 21.1% of intended beneficiaries.

The analysis of social assistance benefits and coverage suggests the following three policy configurations.

(i)   **Generous benefits but low coverage.** For example, the derived value of the depth of social assistance benefits in Maldives amounted to $1,517.20, but the breadth of coverage was low at 9.3%. Similarly, high-income countries offered substantial benefits—Japan, $4,835.80; the ROK, $2,704.80; and Singapore, $1,256.50. Unlike social insurance, however, these countries did not combine generous social assistance benefits with high coverage. As discussed earlier, Japan and the ROK have developed comprehensive social protection systems, with social insurance as the main social protection instrument. In Singapore, social protection is offered through the contributory CPF model. Social assistance in these countries systems is deployed to support vulnerable society members who face particular social risks and require more targeted assistance.

(ii) **Low benefits but substantial coverage.** For example, the breadth of coverage was 88.4% in Georgia and 72.0% in Indonesia. Georgia's universal pensions covered the entire population of retirement age (Box 2). Indonesia's conditional cash transfer, PKH, increased its coverage from 1.5 million families in 2012 to 10.0 million families in 2018, or 15.0% of the population. Countries such as Armenia, Bangladesh, Mongolia, Pakistan, Sri Lanka, and Viet Nam, all exceeded the regional breadth of coverage average but offered low benefits.

(iii) **Low benefits combined with limited coverage.** For example, the Lao PDR offered low benefits ($118.90), covering only 0.9% of target beneficiaries. Benefits and coverage in Bhutan, Tajikistan, and Uzbekistan were similarly low.

Labor Market Programs

Regarding LMPs, the depth of benefits in eight countries is above the 6.4% of GDP per capita average for Asia. The benefits were especially high in Cambodia (21.4%), Pakistan (19.9%), Bhutan (16.0%), and the PRC (13.9%). The average derived monetary benefit for this category was $376.70, which is nearly one-quarter of the average social insurance benefit and one-half the size of the social assistance benefit.

Benefits were the highest in the lower middle-income group at 7.4% of GDP per capita, followed by upper middle-income countries at 6.7% of GDP per capita, and higher-income countries at 2.2% of GDP per capita. In terms of monetary equivalent, the amount was highest in high-income countries ($1,090.70), mainly because of the generous benefits in Singapore and the ROK.

In terms of breadth of coverage, seven countries are above the 1.6% average for Asia. Coverage was especially high in Singapore (10.0%), the ROK (6.6%), Thailand (6.4%), and Bangladesh (3.8%). LMP coverage was the highest in high-income countries (6.0%), again driven by Singapore and the ROK. Upper middle-income countries covered 2.1% of target beneficiaries, with high coverage in Thailand and the PRC. Lower middle-income countries covered less than 1% of intended beneficiaries.

Looking at the depth of benefits relative to the breadth of coverage in LMPs, one can identify two broad groups.

(i)   **Small benefits with limited coverage.** For example, half of lower middle-income countries provided less than $100 in benefits, covering less than 2.0% of target beneficiaries. Two countries, Singapore and the ROK, offered relatively high benefits in monetary terms, $2,050.00 and $868.20, covering 10.0% and 6.6% of intended beneficiaries, respectively.

(ii) **Generous benefits with limited coverage.** In particular, the SPI depth of benefits in the PRC constituted 13.9% of GDP per capita and had a relatively high monetary value of $1,359.40 but covered only 2.9% of the target population. The depth of benefits in Bhutan made up 16.0% of GDP per capita ($546.20), covering less than 1.0% of the target population.

Trends in Depth and Breadth, 2009-2018

- Among 24 countries in Asia with complete data for 2009 to 2018, the average depth of social protection benefits remained stable, with only a modest improvement by 0.2 percentage point from 9.1% of GDP per capita in 2009 to 9.3% in 2018.
- The progress in the breadth of social protection coverage over this period was more substantial than that in the depth of benefits, with an increase by 24.1 percentage points, from 42.9% in 2009 to 67.0% in 2018.
- Social insurance coverage increased substantially from 23.1% to 41.0%, as 20 countries improved the breadth of social insurance coverage, propelled by the expansion of pension and health insurance programs.
- Social assistance coverage increased from 17.0% to 25.7%, while LMPs declined from 3.7% to 1.8%.

Figure 14: Progress in Depth and Breadth of Social Protection by Category, 2009-2018

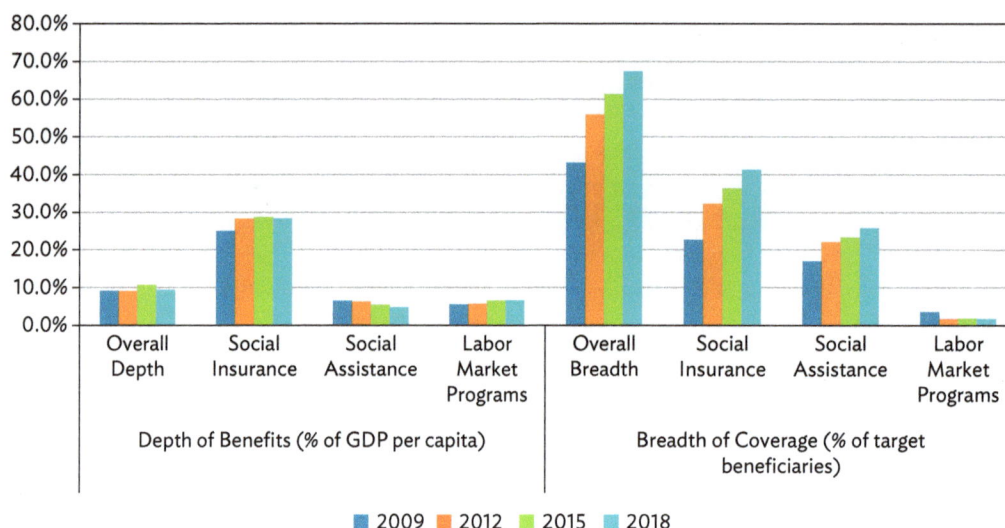

GDP = gross domestic product.

Note: Excludes Afghanistan and Kazakhstan.

Source: ADB estimates.

The depth of social protection benefits in 24 countries in Asia from 2009 to 2018 remained stable, with only a slight improvement by 0.2 percentage point from 9.1% of GDP per capita to 9.3%. The depth of social insurance benefits increased from 24.8% of GDP per capita in 2009 to 28.2% in 2018. The depth of social assistance benefits declined from 6.4% to 4.7%, but LMPs showed some progress, from 5.4% to 6.5% (Figure 14).

The progress in the breadth of social protection coverage over this period was more substantial than that in the depth of benefits. The overall breadth of coverage increased by 24.1 percentage points, from 42.9% in 2009 to 67.0% in 2018. The breadth of social insurance coverage increased from 22.5% to 41.0% during this period, while the breadth of social assistance increased from 16.8% to 25.7%. LMPs saw a 1.7-percentage-point decline in their breadth of coverage from 3.5% to 1.8%.

Between 2009 and 2018, eight countries improved the depth of social insurance benefits. An especially sharp increase, by more than 60 percentage points, was observed in Pakistan, due to an increase in the value of military, government employee, and civil service pensions. The depth of social insurance benefits declined in 16 countries. It dropped substantially in some countries—by 35.4 percentage points in Malaysia, by 25.1 percentage points in Sri Lanka, and by 24.3 percentage points in the Philippines.

In terms of the breadth of coverage, 20 countries experienced improvements in social insurance. Especially strong progress was observed in the Philippines, where social insurance coverage under PhilHealth improved by close to 90 percentage points (Box 6). Japan, Indonesia, and the Lao PDR increased their breadth of coverage by more than 50 percentage points and Viet Nam by 30 percentage points (Box 7).

Box 6: Progress of the Philippines on the Breadth of Social Insurance Coverage

The Philippines made steady progress on social protection since 2009. While in that year, its Social Protection Indicator (SPI) was 2.1, in 2015, its SPI had risen to 2.6, and in 2018, it reached 3.0. Both social insurance and social assistance contributed to this overall increase. The social insurance SPI rose from 1.7 in 2009 to 2.0 in 2018. The social assistance SPI registered just 0.3 in 2009 but rose to 1.0 in 2018, mainly due to the expansion of the Pantawid Pamilyang Pilipino Program. Correspondingly, the overall breadth of coverage increased from about 32% in 2009 to about 119% in 2018. This general increase was driven by social insurance, whose breadth jumped from a mere 6.5% in 2009 to 95.3% in 2018.

Health insurance—mainly provided by the Philippine Health Insurance Corporation and known as PhilHealth—was a major contributor to progress. Funding for this program is based mainly on premiums paid by members plus financial sponsorship by local governments. Membership in the program is designed to be universal, as coverage is mandatory for all, including household help and sea-based overseas Filipino workers. In 2018, health insurance was funded by P124.3 billion and benefited 105 million, almost the entire population.

PhilHealth provides services for both inpatient and outpatient beneficiaries. For inpatients, services cover subsidies for hospital room and board fees, medicines, x-ray and other laboratory examinations, and operating room and professional fees for confinements of over 24 hours. For outpatients, services are provided for day surgeries, dialysis, and cancer treatment procedures such as chemotherapy and radiotherapy. It also provides a maternity care package, outpatient tuberculosis package, outpatient benefits for the poor, health education packages, and emergency and transfer services.

The 2019 Universal Health Care Act provides a legal basis for health insurance. The law aims to expand benefits to include free consultation fees, laboratory tests, and other diagnostic services. It also aims to improve the doctor–patient ratio, upgrade hospital bed capacity and equipment, and establish more health care facilities in remote areas.

An overarching current priority for social protection in the Philippines is to increase its overall breadth of coverage. In 2015, the overall average depth of benefits was only 2.2%, and this increased only to 2.5% in 2018. This implies that the average benefits of social protection that people have received have remained relatively small.

Source: ADB. 2022. *Philippines: Social Protection Indicator.* Manila.

Box 7: Viet Nam's Progress on Social Insurance Programs

Viet Nam made notable progress on social protection between 2009 and 2018. In 2009, its Social Protection Indicator (SPI) was already 3.9, and social insurance was the dominant component, as its SPI was 3.3. It steadily increased from 3.3 in 2012 to 4.0 in 2018. The overall breadth of coverage in Viet Nam rose from 69.3% in 2009 to 100.2% in 2018. This is due mainly to social insurance, whose breadth increased by about 30 percentage points, from 40% in 2009 to 70% in 2018. The driving force behind this increase in breadth was health insurance.

Viet Nam's 2014 Law on Health Insurance seeks to establish universal health insurance coverage with large government subsidies for vulnerable groups on health insurance fees. Indeed, Viet Nam is moving close to achieving the goal of universal health coverage. The total number of health insurance participants increased from 67.9 million in 2015 to 83.5 million in 2018, with an annual growth rate of 71.1%. As a result, health insurance coverage expanded from 74.0% in 2015 to almost 88.2% in 2018.

continued on next page

Box 7: *continued*

The main reason for this success can be attributed to the government policy on health insurance subsidies, which contributes to inclusion of previously uncovered groups. The 2014 Law on Health defines 12 groups eligible to receive subsidies for their health insurance contributions. It envisages full subsidies for eight groups, including those who receive targeted social assistance and ethnic minorities who live in areas with extreme socioeconomic conditions, and partial subsidies for four groups, including the near-poor; students; and households engaged in agriculture, forestry, fishery and salt production. From 2015 to 2018, the number of fully subsidized participants increased at an annual growth rate of 3.70% and partially subsidized participants at 5.77%.

Source: ADB. 2022. *Viet Nam: Social Protection Indicator.* Manila.

For social assistance, eight countries improved the depth of benefits over this period. Despite a modest percentage increase, benefits increased nearly fourfold in the Lao PDR and the Philippines. The depth of social assistance benefits declined in 16 countries.

Conversely, the breadth of social assistance coverage improved in 17 countries and declined in 7 countries. Georgia had the highest increase, by 63.3 percentage points, from 2009 to 2018, mainly due to the introduction of the Universal Healthcare program in 2013, which propelled coverage to exceed 100% by 2015. The subsequent tightening in the eligibility for free health services reduced social assistance coverage to 88.4% in 2018. Indonesia followed with a 57-percentage-point improvement. The breadth of coverage in Bangladesh, Pakistan, and Thailand exceeded 20 percentage points. Substantial reductions, however, were observed in the Kyrgyz Republic by 21.9 percentage points, in the Lao PDR by 17.6 percentage points, and in Uzbekistan by 11.3 percentage points.

As for LMPs in 22 countries for which comparative data were available, the depth of benefits improved in 11 countries, stayed unchanged in Nepal, and declined in 10 countries. The breadth of coverage improved in 7 countries, declined in 13, and stayed unchanged in Viet Nam and Tajikistan. The most notable improvements were observed in Azerbaijan, the ROK, and Singapore.

Examining individual country-level trends in benefits and coverage together, one can identify four distinct patterns in the development of social protection across the region.

First, a small share of countries in the region improved both benefits and coverage of social protection. Among the eight countries that improved the depth of social insurance benefits, the breadth of social insurance coverage increased in five—Armenia, Bhutan, the PRC, the Kyrgyz Republic, and Tajikistan. In social assistance, the depth of benefits similarly increased in eight countries, but only three—the Philippines, Singapore, and Sri Lanka—also improved the breadth of coverage. Regarding LMPs, six countries improved both benefits and coverage, including the PRC, the ROK, and Singapore, while Tajikistan improved the depth of benefits while maintaining its coverage level.

Second, the prevailing trend in the region over this period was to keep the depth of benefits low and to expand the breadth of coverage. The depth of social insurance benefits dropped in 16 countries, but the breadth of social insurance coverage increased in all, except in Uzbekistan, where it declined only slightly. The progress in the breadth of social insurance coverage was driven by the enhancements of pensions and health insurance coverage. The expansion in health insurance was the key driving force in Japan, the ROK, Maldives, the Philippines, Thailand, and Viet Nam, largely due to the progressive universalization of health insurance coverage. The progress in pension coverage is especially notable in Armenia, the PRC, Indonesia, Japan, the ROK, the Kyrgyz Republic, and Tajikistan.

The prioritization of the breadth of coverage over the depth of benefits was also observed for social assistance. Among the 16 countries that decreased the depth of social assistance benefits, 13 improved the breadth of social assistance coverage, including Armenia, the PRC, Georgia, the ROK, Mongolia, Nepal, Pakistan, Thailand, and Viet Nam. The progress in coverage is driven by the expansion of welfare assistance programs in Bangladesh, Indonesia, Pakistan, the Philippines, and Singapore as well as in assistance for older people in Georgia, the ROK, Tajikistan, and Thailand. This trend was less pronounced for LMPs, where 10 countries decreased the depth of benefits, but only Pakistan improved, and Viet Nam maintained the breadth of coverage.

Third, some countries increased the depth of benefits but reduced the breadth of coverage. These include three countries for social insurance (i.e., Cambodia, Georgia, and Pakistan); five for social assistance (i.e., Azerbaijan, Japan, the Kyrgyz Republic, the Lao PDR, and Tajikistan); and four for LMPs (Bhutan, Cambodia, the Lao PDR, and Sri Lanka), while Nepal maintained the LMP depth while decreasing its breadth.

Finally, several countries reduced both benefits and coverage. These include Uzbekistan for social insurance; Cambodia, Maldives, and Uzbekistan for social assistance; and eight countries for LMPs.

Among the country income groups, the depth of benefits in high-income countries declined from 7.5% in 2009 to 6.7% in 2018, caused mainly by the fall in the depth of social insurance across the three countries. In contrast, the depth increased for both social assistance and LMPs. For social assistance, this was driven by both Japan and Singapore; for LMPs, by the ROK and Singapore.

In the three high-income countries, there was a progressive increase in the breadth of coverage between 2009 and 2018—from 81.2% to 114.9%. This trend was driven by the gradual increase in the breadth of social insurance from 57.6% in 2009 to 87.9% in 2018—propelled, to a large degree, by the expansion of health insurance programs.

There was a substantial increase in the breadth of social protection coverage in Japan, from 90.4% in 2009 to 128.3% in 2018. The breadth of coverage in the ROK was similarly remarkable, from 73.1% in 2009 to 110.3% in 2018. Along with social insurance, there was also an overall increase in the breadth of coverage of social assistance in high-income countries. It rose from 16.1% in 2009 to 21.1% in 2018—although there was a dip in breadth during 2012-2015. However, the breadth of coverage for LMPs, which was already narrow, ended up decreasing from 7.5% in 2009 to 6.0% in 2018.

There was an erratic pattern in the depth of benefits for the upper middle-income country group; the depth increased overall between 2009 and 2018, from 11.3% to 13.1%, but oscillated during this period. The depth of social insurance increased progressively between 2009 and 2015—from 21.0% to 25.5%—but then dropped back to 21.8% in 2018. However, the depth of social assistance progressively declined from 9.9% in 2009 to 6.1% in 2018. LMPs increased from a depth of 4.3% in 2009 to 6.5% in 2018, driven by sharp increases in the PRC and Azerbaijan.

The breadth of coverage in upper middle-income countries also increased overall; it rose from 45.2% in 2009 to 68.9% in 2018. The overall increase in the breadth of coverage of social insurance was only modest, from 27.6% in 2009 to 39.7% in 2018. In contrast, the increase in the breadth of coverage of social assistance was more pronounced, from 12.7% in 2009 to 27.5% in 2018. This increase is driven by substantial growth in coverage in Armenia, Georgia, and Thailand. For LMPs, however, a sharp decline in coverage was observed, from 5.0% in 2009 to the very low level of 2.3% in 2018.

In lower middle-income countries, the depth of benefits increased from 8.3% in 2009 to 9.0% in 2015 before declining back to 8.0% in 2018. The depth of social insurance benefits increased by 5.5 percentage points, from 30.0% to 35.5%, but social assistance declined by 2.2 percentage points, from 4.6% to 3.4%.

In lower middle-income countries, an overall sustained increase was noted in the breadth of social protection coverage between 2009 and 2018. This breadth increased progressively from 36.7% in 2009 to 58.2% in 2018 and was driven mainly by the increase in the breadth of social insurance, which rose progressively from 14.3% in 2009 to 31.7% in 2018. The breadth of social assistance for all lower middle-income countries also rose, though modestly, from 20.2% in 2009 to 25.8% in 2018. In contrast, the breadth of LMPs dropped to very low levels, from 2.0% in 2009 to only 0.7% in 2018.

V. Poverty, Gender, and Disability Dimensions

This chapter focuses on the poverty, gender, and disability dimensions of the SPI. It discusses the distribution of social protection expenditure as a share of GDP per capita between poor and nonpoor beneficiaries, between women and men beneficiaries, and on people with disabilities. Disaggregated analysis by poverty, gender, and disability is key to understanding the effectiveness of social protection. It can help design policies that better reach and support the poor and promote gender equality and social inclusion.

Distribution of Expenditure between the Poor and Nonpoor

- The SPI in 26 countries in Asia clearly favored the nonpoor over the poor.
- Intended nonpoor beneficiaries were allocated 3.2% of GDP per capita and intended poor beneficiaries 0.8%.
- Higher spending on the nonpoor was mainly driven by contributory social insurance.
- The SPI gap between the poor and the nonpoor appeared to widen as a country income per capita increases, with social insurance as the primary means of social protection and broad-based coverage in high-income countries.

This section provides the results for the differentials in the SPI for the poor and the nonpoor in 26 countries for 2018 (Figure 15). Such comparisons are based on country-specific poverty lines, and the Asia regional average reflects estimates that are specific to each country's context and are not internationally comparable. They nevertheless provide useful estimates for tracking progress and variation.

Overall social protection spending across Asia favored the nonpoor. As previously discussed, the overall SPI for Asia as a whole in 2018 was 4.0. There was a gap between the SPI for the poor, which was only 0.8%, and the corresponding SPI for the nonpoor, which was 3.2%. Thus, the gap between the two was substantial—2.4 percentage points.

All countries had a higher share of SPI going to the nonpoor than to the poor. Some countries spent proportionally more for the poor, for example, Armenia, Georgia, the Philippines, and Uzbekistan; in Singapore and Japan, almost one-third of the share went to the poor. At the other end of the spectrum, there are countries where less than one-tenth of the share was going to the poor, including Kazakhstan, Thailand, and Viet Nam.

Figure 15: **Poverty Dimension of Social Protection Indicator by Country, 2018**

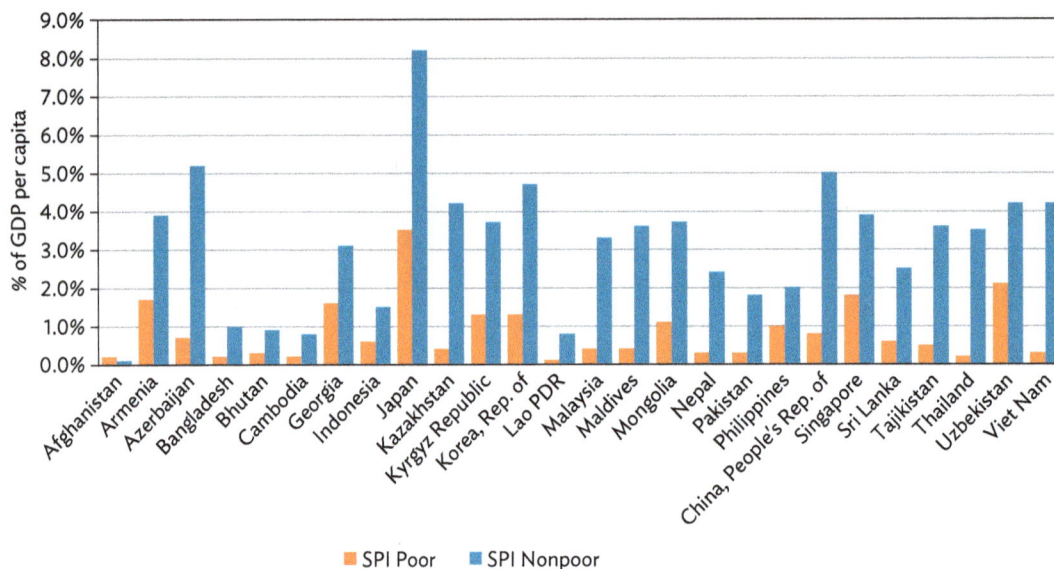

GDP = gross domestic product, Lao PDR = Lao People's Democratic Republic, SPI = Social Protection Indicator.

Source: ADB estimates based on consultants' reports.

This higher spending on the nonpoor was mainly driven by contributory social insurance that made up the largest share of social protection expenditure across all income groups. The main function of social insurance is to provide income support in the face of life-cycle-related risks, such as old age, health, and unemployment. Individuals secure entitlements to income support payments because of their social insurance contributions financed by employees, employers, and the state. Social insurance, therefore, is not specifically targeted at the poor and, in fact, tends to benefit the nonpoor, mainly those in formal sector employment.

The key policy challenge, however, is that the poor were the least represented in social insurance across the region. Some countries have made substantial progress in achieving universal or near-universal pension and health insurance coverage, while many other countries had limited social insurance programs that did not cover the majority of the poor. Most uncovered workers are employed in the informal sector, which represents close to 70% of all workers in the region.[50]

Many social assistance programs provided benefits to all individuals within a specific geographic group or category. These programs did not differentiate according to economic status and supported both the poor and nonpoor. However, most social assistance programs have a clear poverty reduction mandate. These are poverty-targeted

---

50   UNESCAP and ILO. 2020. *The Protection We Want: Social Outlook for Asia and the Pacific.* Bangkok: UNESCAP.

programs that provide basic sustenance to persons considered poor and vulnerable. However, as discussed earlier, the spending on social assistance was limited in most countries, restricting the breadth of coverage and depth of benefits.

Figure 16 provides information on the poor and the nonpoor by income group for 2018. For all income groups, the overall social protection expenditure was higher for the nonpoor. The SPI gap between the poor and nonpoor appeared to widen as a country's income per capita increases. In particular, in the high-income group, there was a significant gap of 3.4 between the poor and nonpoor. The SPI for the nonpoor was 5.6, while the SPI for the poor was only 2.2. There was also a wide gap of 3.2 between the 4.0 SPI for the nonpoor and the 0.8 SPI for the poor in the eight upper middle-income countries. For the lower middle-income countries, the gap between the SPI of the poor and nonpoor was much smaller, only 1.5. The SPI for the poor was only 0.7, while the SPI for the nonpoor, 2.2, was also relatively low.

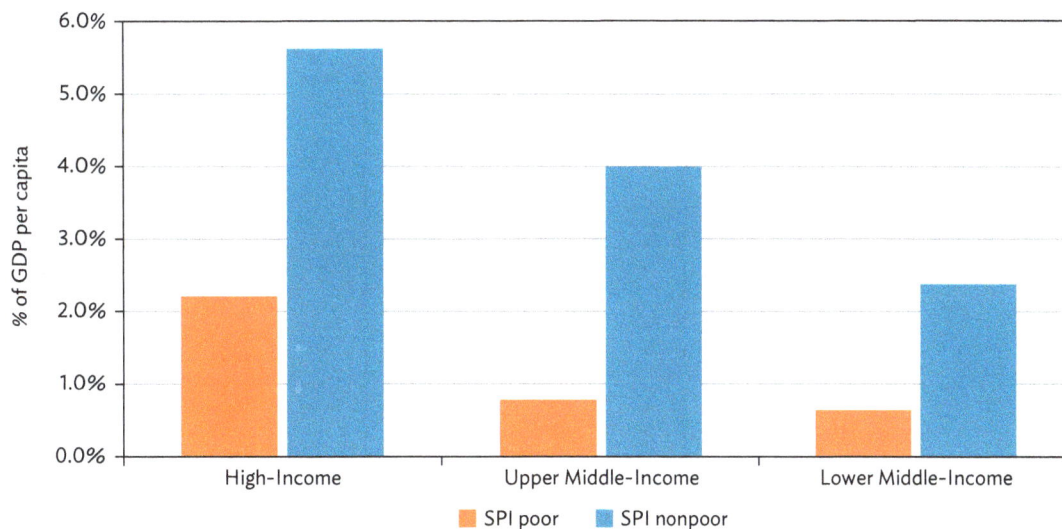

Figure 16: **Social Protection Indicator Poverty Dimension by Income Group, 2018**

GDP = gross domestic product, SPI = Social Protection Indicator.
Source: ADB estimates.

Again, this was because high-income countries used social insurance as the primary means of social protection. They established broad-based social insurance programs that cover the majority of their populations. The domination of social insurance was especially pronounced in countries where universal pensions and health insurance schemes accounted for the bulk of social protection expenditure. These countries thus spent more on both the poor and nonpoor compared with countries in other income groups. In contrast, systems with a narrow reliance on social insurance not only offered limited support to the poor but also tended to focus on a smaller subsection of the nonpoor, i.e., those mainly working in public sector institutions and the civil service.

The key implication from this analysis is that both social insurance and social assistance should be more effective in supporting the poor. These programs need to be developed in a way that they complement each other to address vulnerabilities and to ensure comprehensive protection against risks for the entire population.

Trends in Social Protection Indicator by Poverty, 2009-2018

Figure 17 presents the SPI for the poor and nonpoor from 2009 to 2018. The overall spending on social protection in Asia continued to favor the nonpoor over this time period. In 2009, the SPI for the poor across Asia was only 0.7 while the SPI for the nonpoor was 2.6. In 2018, the SPI for the poor was 0.9, although it rose to 1.0 during 2012-2015. However, the SPI for the nonpoor rose from 2.6 in 2009 to 3.2 in 2018. Therefore, the SPI gap widened between the poor and the nonpoor, from 1.9 in 2009 to 2.3 in 2018.

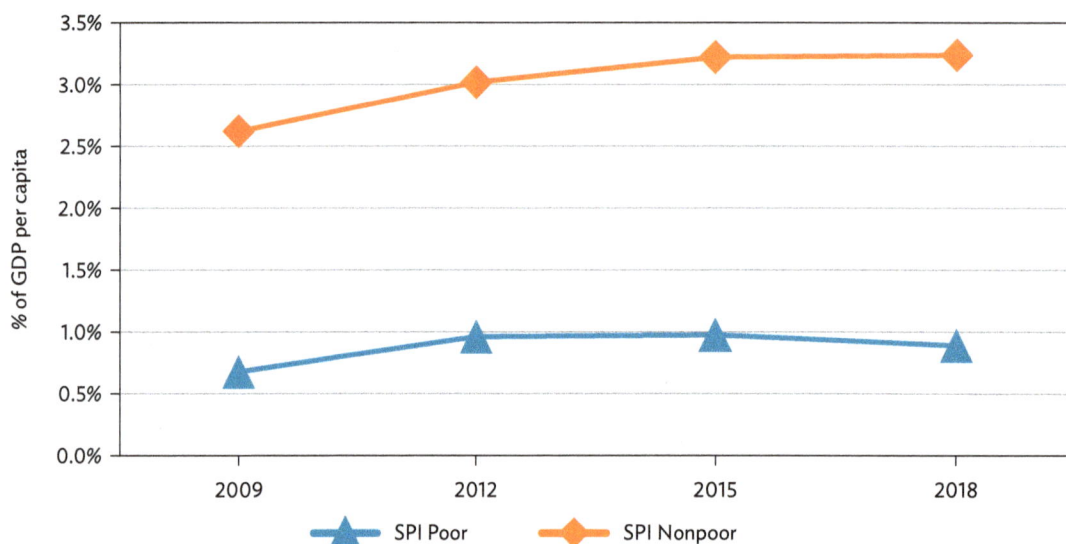

Figure 17: Progress in Poverty Dimension of Social Protection, 2009-2018

GDP = gross domestic product, SPI = Social Protection Indicator.
Source: ADB.

The gap between spending on the nonpoor and poor remained steady across all income groups over this period (Figure 18). The poor were clearly more disadvantaged over time compared with the nonpoor in all income groups. In the high-income group, the SPI of the poor rose from 1.7 in 2009 to 2.2 in 2018, while the SPI of the nonpoor rose significantly more, from 4.5 to 5.6, more than twice as much in absolute terms. In the upper middle-income group, the SPI for the poor rose from 0.7 in 2009 to only 0.8 in 2018, and the SPI for the nonpoor similarly increased by 1.0 percentage point.[51] Finally, in the lower middle-income group, the SPI for the poor increased from 0.4 in 2009 to 0.7 in 2018. The SPI for the nonpoor increased from 1.9 in 2009 to 2.2 in 2018.

Figure 18: Progress in Poverty Dimension by Income Group, 2009-2018

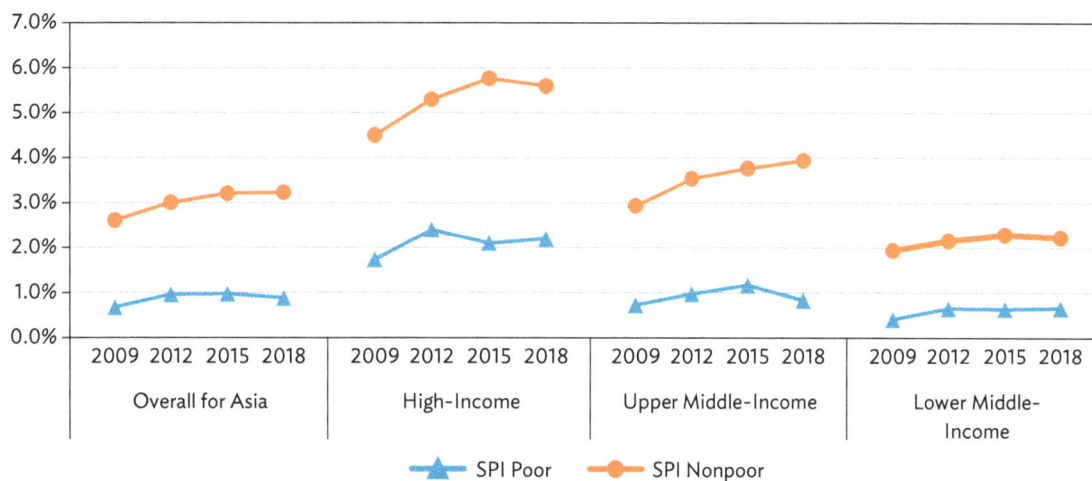

SPI = Social Protection Indicator.

Source: ADB estimates.

While the gap remains, the SPI for the poor increased in all three income groups. The progress was substantial in the high-income countries and more modest in the upper middle-income countries and lower middle-income countries.

There were reassuring improvements at the country level. Out of 24 countries for which complete comparable data were available, spending on the poor increased in 16 countries during this period. In some countries, this improvement was substantial. For example, pro-poor expenditure increased by 1.2 percentage points in Armenia and by over 0.5 percentage point in Indonesia, the Philippines, and Singapore. Spending remained constant in Bangladesh, Cambodia, the Lao PDR, and Malaysia. Some reduction was also observed in Azerbaijan, Thailand, and Viet Nam.

---

[51]   The SPI for the nonpoor in upper middle-income countries for 2018 was 3.9, different from that in Figure 17 for 2018 (4.0). This is because it is used to present progress over time and is based on the series average that includes countries for which comparable data were available.

Gender Gaps in Access to Social Protection in Asia

> - The 2018 SPI in 26 countries in Asia was equally split between men and women, with the SPI for each sex accounting for 2.0% of GDP per capita.
> - The SPI appeared to be more favorable for women in countries with broad-based social insurance programs, and it was more favorable for men in countries with limited social insurance.
> - The gender gap in access to social protection decreased between 2009 and 2018, as the SPI for women increased from 1.4 to 2.1, while it hovered around 2.0 for men.

This section discusses how social protection expenditures were distributed between men and women. In 2018, the SPIs for women and men in 26 countries were roughly the same, 2.0. This denotes overall gender equality in terms of access to social protection in Asia as whole. Spending favored women in nine countries, mainly in post-Soviet Union transition countries, and was equal for both sexes in Cambodia and the Philippines (Figure 19 and Table 4). However, spending on men was higher in 15 countries.

Gender inequities were primarily a consequence of the differential access to social insurance programs that accounted for the bulk of social protection expenditure in the region. Countries with broad-based social insurance programs that reached the majority of their populations tended to have a more equal distribution of expenditure by sex. Conversely, countries where social insurance programs had a narrow reach tended to be more favorable to men.

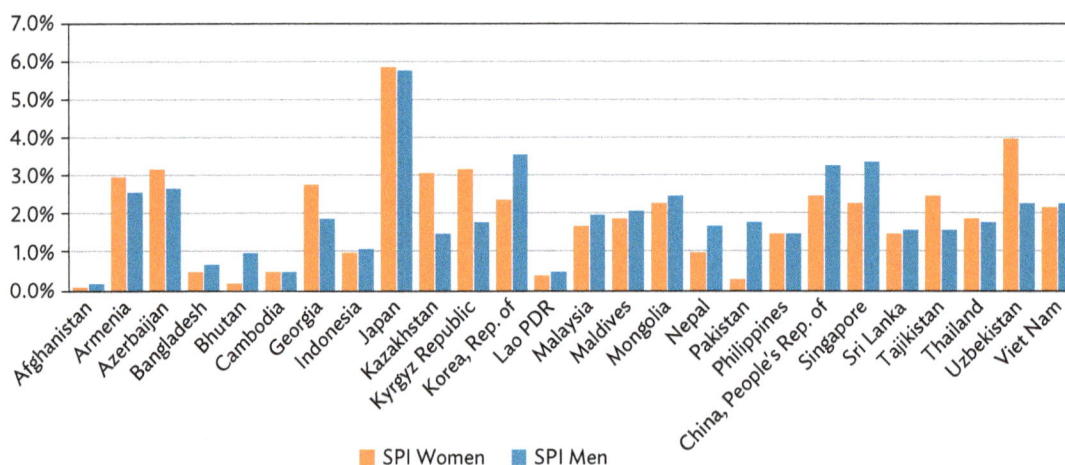

Figure 19: **Gender Dimension by Country, 2018**

Lao PDR = Lao People's Democratic Republic, SPI = Social Protection Indicator.

Source: ADB estimates based on consultants' reports.

Table 4: Gender Dimensions of Social Protection by Country, 2018 (% of GDP per capita)

	Overall SPI	SPI Women	SPI Men
Afghanistan	0.3	0.1	0.2
Armenia	5.6	3.0	2.6
Azerbaijan	5.9	3.2	2.7
Bangladesh	1.3	0.5	0.8
Bhutan	1.2	0.2	1.0
Cambodia	1.0	0.5	0.5
China, People's Republic of	5.8	2.5	3.3
Georgia	4.7	2.8	1.9
Indonesia	2.1	1.0	1.1
Japan	11.7	5.9	5.8
Kazakhstan	4.6	3.1	1.5
Kyrgyz Republic	5.0	3.2	1.8
Korea, Republic of	6.0	2.4	3.6
Lao PDR	0.9	0.4	0.5
Malaysia	3.7	1.7	2.0
Maldives	4.0	1.9	2.1
Mongolia	4.8	2.3	2.5
Nepal	2.7	1.0	1.7
Pakistan	2.1	0.3	1.8
Philippines	3.0	1.5	1.5
Singapore	5.7	2.3	3.4
Sri Lanka	3.1	1.5	1.6
Tajikistan	4.1	2.5	1.6
Thailand	3.7	1.9	1.8
Uzbekistan	6.2	3.9	2.3
Viet Nam	4.5	2.2	2.3
Unweighted Asia Average	**4.0**	**2.0**	**2.0**

GDP = gross domestic product, Lao PDR = Lao People's Democratic Republic, SPI = Social Protection Indicator.

Source: ADB estimates based on consultants' reports.

These were countries with limited social insurance programs that benefitted mainly a small share of workers in the formal economy, often public sector employees. These programs did not extend to the majority of workers in the informal economy, and a high proportion of them were women. Due to sex discrimination in the labor market in these countries, fewer women have salaried employment, and they are mainly engaged in informal, low-wage, and irregular economic activities.[52] For example, 64.1% of women (70.5% of men) in employment are likely to be engaged

---

R. Holmes and L. Scott. 2016. Extending Social Insurance to Informal Workers—A Gender Analysis. *ODI Working Papers*. No. 438. London: ODI.

in informal employment in Asia and the Pacific, but in South Asia, more women (90.7%) than men (86.8%) are in informal employment.[53] Limited contributory capacity restricts women from qualifying for social insurance, resulting in coverage gaps, especially where there is limited provision to extend coverage by financing individual contributions from government revenues.

Social assistance generally disproportionally reaches women, as women are more likely to belong to poor and vulnerable groups. Its contribution to gender equality is especially substantial in countries that have invested in broad-based programs.

Among all countries in this study, social protection expenditure appeared to be more favorable for women in post-Soviet Union transition countries. In fact, the results for these countries appeared to be a major factor driving the overall results of greater gender equality in 2018. Figure 19 shows that women actually had greater access to social protection than men in Armenia, Azerbaijan, Georgia, Kazakhstan, the Kyrgyz Republic, Tajikistan, and Uzbekistan. For example, in both Uzbekistan and the Kyrgyz Republic, the SPI for women was 1.6 percentage points higher than that for men.

This was primarily because of higher coverage of women by social insurance in these countries. More specifically, most post-Soviet Union transition countries had broad-based contributory pensions that equally covered men and women, reflecting the relatively equitable participation in the labor market by men and women who currently claim pension benefits. Contributory programs in all of these countries were accompanied with basic or social pensions that cover those without contributory history.

In addition to social insurance, social assistance in post-Soviet Union transition countries tended to be more equally distributed between men and women. Georgia was the only post-Soviet Union transition country that entirely relied on social assistance, i.e., social pensions, to cover most of the older population. This achieved near-universal coverage, with women making up about 70% of all beneficiaries. Georgia spent 3.6% of GDP on its pensions, and the SPI for women was 2.8, while that for men was 1.9. In the welfare assistance subcategory of social assistance, Armenia, Azerbaijan, and Georgia spent 0.9%, the highest share of expenditure to GDP in Asia. This expenditure mainly supported cash transfers that had relatively equal reach. The Kyrgyz Republic spent more than other Asian countries on child welfare programs at 1.2% of GDP. It included maternity grants and a one-time allowance at childbirth. The largest share of social assistance in Uzbekistan went to programs targeted at women, including child-care allowance, family allowance, and old-age allowance.

Spending on women and men was equal in the Philippines and Cambodia, and several other countries came very close to achieving gender equity in access to social protection. Specifically, spending in Indonesia, the Lao PDR, Sri Lanka, and Viet Nam

---

53   ILO. 2018. *Women and Men in the Informal Economy: A Statistical Picture*. Geneva. https://www.ilo.org/wcmsp5/groups/public/---dgreports/---dcomm/documents/publication/wcms_626831.pdf.

favored men only by 0.1 percentage point. Some of these results were driven by spending in social assistance. Countries such as Cambodia, Indonesia, and the Philippines had strong social assistance programs that prioritized women as their main beneficiaries. Many others were targeted at children, with mothers designated as the main benefit recipients on their behalf, such as the 4Ps in the Philippines and PKH in Indonesia. In the Lao PDR and Viet Nam, results were instead due to high social insurance coverage. Viet Nam extended pensions and health insurance to more than 90% of its population, and the Lao PDR achieved near-universal coverage in health insurance.

Where pensions had wide coverage, they tended to cover a high share of women partly due to their longer life expectancy. Data show that women tend to outnumber men in a significant number of countries in Asia.[54] In 13 countries in the study, women's life expectancy exceeds that of men by an average of 4 years. This includes in most post-Soviet Union transition countries as well as in Japan, Mongolia, the Philippines, Sri Lanka, Thailand, and Viet Nam. There is a gap of 8-10 years between the life expectancy of men and women in Georgia, the Kyrgyz Republic, Mongolia, the Philippines, Uzbekistan, and Viet Nam. Thus, there appears to be a strong correlation between a higher life expectancy for women and a higher, or at least comparable, SPI for women relative to men.

It was also apparent in many countries in Asia that women who did qualify for pensions on the basis of their work experience were able to retire earlier than men. In many pension programs in Asia, women can retire, in fact, 5 years sooner than men. This is another part of the explanation for the prevalence of women as beneficiaries of pensions.

In other countries in Asia, men still had somewhat greater access to social protection than women. Social insurance programs in these countries remained rigid and offered limited opportunities for greater engagement of workers in the informal economy. Such programs did not address gendered inequalities in the labor market and thus excluded women engaged in low-wage, casual, and irregular work. The following are some examples of countries with gender inequalities in social protection:

(i)   **Pakistan.** The 2018 SPI for men (1.8) was substantially higher than that for women (0.3). Overall, women received fewer social insurance benefits than men. The existing social insurance programs largely benefitted men, mainly public sector employees. This was despite the government's introduction of a 10% quota for women in public sector employment, with Punjab Province raising this to 15%. Women benefitted the most from social assistance programs. More specifically, the BISP offered cash transfers to women as its primary recipients with their families designated as the beneficiaries. The skills development programs in Sindh and Punjab provinces also supported training for women. However, the expenditure on these initiatives was smaller than that on social insurance to influence gender equity in a substantial manner.

---

54   UNDESA. World Population Prospects. https://population.un.org/wpp/ (accessed 4 April 2022).

(ii) **Nepal.** Social protection spending favored men (1.7) over women (1.0). This was due to the higher number of men employed in the public sector. Only 30% of women were receiving pensions from public sector employment. Similarly, the gender gap in Bangladesh was significant with an SPI for men at 0.8 and women at 0.5. The disparity between men and women was especially pronounced in social insurance, mainly due to the large share of men in the formal economy covered by social insurance. Spending in both social assistance and LMPs favored men.

(iii) **People's Republic of China.** The PRC made major advances in social protection, but it did not achieve gender equality. In 2018, its overall SPI was 5.8; the SPI for women was only 2.5, while that for men was 3.3. The variation in expenditure on benefits is a significant factor that contributed to the gendered gap.

Basic Medical Care Insurance for Urban Employees had the highest level of benefits and financing of the existing three health insurance schemes. This scheme, however, mainly benefitted urban workers in the formal economy, and men made up the higher share. This insurance is an employment-based scheme and ties eligibility to one's work unit, which restricted women working in the informal sector from accessing the scheme. The 1998 social insurance reform excluded other family members from its coverage. Empirical analysis suggests that the gender gap in accessing the scheme was especially prevalent among older women.[55] Thus, women over age 50 had significantly lower coverage than men. These women, especially those with low education, were more likely to be laid off and have difficulty being reemployed. These women could be covered by Basic Medical Care Insurance for Urban and Rural Residents; however, the benefits received under this scheme would be substantially lower.

Similar inequities existed in the PRC's old-age pensions. The basic social pension benefits offered by the existing three major pension schemes varied in size, resulting in equalities among the subgroups that they covered.[56] These inequalities worsened when taking into account the effect of commercial and occupational (or employee-provided) pensions. Sex and age are the key variables that exacerbated inequalities in pensions. Women were particularly disadvantaged. For example, their average pension in 2013 was 30% lower than that of men.

Among the high-income countries, the SPI for men in 2018 was 4.3, significantly higher than that for women, at 3.5 (Figure 20). Among the three high-income countries, two countries did not achieve gender equality in access to social protection (Box 8).

55   M. Zhou, S. Zhao, and Z. Zhao. 2021. Gender Differences in Health Insurance Coverage in China. *International Journal for Equity in Health*. 20 (52).

56   H. Zhu and A. Walker. 2018. Pension System Reform in China: Who Gets What Pensions? *Social Policy and Administration*. 52 (7). pp. 1410–1424.

Figure 20: Gender Dimension by Income Group, 2018

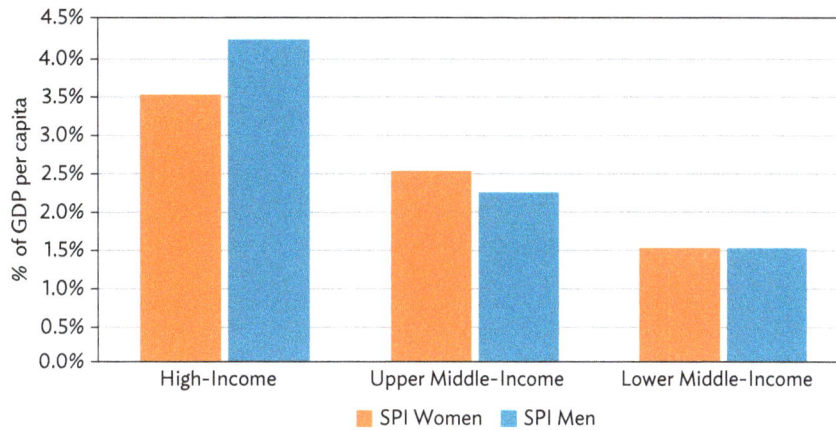

GDP = gross domestic product, SPI = Social Protection Indicator.

Source: ADB estimates based on consultants' reports.

Box 8: Gender Disparities in Social Protection in Singapore and the Republic of Korea

When disaggregated by the sex of social protection program beneficiaries, the Social Protection Indicator (SPI) for women in Singapore in 2018 was only 2.3, while the SPI for men was 3.4. This suggests that women were somewhat disadvantaged compared with men in terms of social protection expenditure.

The overall male bias of social protection expenditure was driven by a large share of expenditure that was allocated to social insurance, which was dominated by formal sector employment. This reflects the fact that the labor force participation rate among women was 60.2%, compared with 75.6% among men. In this rapidly aging society with a lower level of past education, a much higher share of women remains outside of the labor force. There were also very few social protection programs that targeted women, and some did not qualify as social protection programs in this study context, further contributing to a low SPI value for women.

Overall, the SPI for women in Singapore progressed, from 1.8 in 2009 to 2.3 in 2018. As older people in recent years are encouraged to continue working even during their advanced age, and due to greater women involvement in the formal labor market, the labor force participation rate of women will continue to improve, which will more likely favor the SPI value for women in the future.

In the Republic of Korea (ROK), the overall 2018 SPI for women was 2.4% of the per capita GDP and that for men was 3.6%. There has been little improvement in the SPI of women since 2012. The gender disparity in the ROK is primarily the result of inequalities in social insurance. The social insurance SPI for men was nearly 1.5 times as large as that for women. The employment ratio between men and women in the ROK was 59–41 and, proportionately, the SPI for men and women was 63–37. This gender employment rate gap has been gradually improving, falling from 24.7% in 2003 to 20.4% in 2017. However, more time is needed for these changes to increase the social insurance beneficiary numbers and expenditure. The spending in social assistance was roughly equal for men and women in social assistance, mainly because allowances are paid without differentiating by sex in child-care programs.

Sources: ADB. 2022. *Singapore: Social Protection Indicator*. Manila; and ADB. 2022. *Republic of Korea: Social Protection Indicator*. Manila.

Among the upper middle-income countries, on the contrary, the overall SPI for women in 2018 was 2.5, which was higher than the SPI of 2.2 for men. These results were driven mainly by three post-Soviet Union transition countries: Armenia, Azerbaijan, and Georgia. For the lower middle-income countries, the overall SPI in 2018 for women was 1.5, the same as that for men. In other words, there was roughly gender equity in access to social protection across the income group. This group includes another three post-Soviet Union transition countries— the Kyrgyz Republic, Tajikistan, and Uzbekistan—that had gender equitable programs as well as several other countries, such as Cambodia, Mongolia, the Philippines, and Sri Lanka, which had equal spending or only modest disparities in their spending.

Trends in Social Protection Indicator by Gender, 2009-2018

Figure 21 presents the SPI progress in the gender dimension from 2009 to 2018 across 24 countries, for which data series are complete. Overall, there was significant progress in the access of women to social protection between 2009 to 2018. In 2009, the SPI for women was only 1.4 while that for men was 1.9. By 2018, the gender gap in access to social protection improved as spending on women increased by 0.7 percentage point, while spending on men increased only by 0.2 percentage point.

Figure 21: **Progress in the Social Protection Indicator Gender Dimension, 2009 to 2018**

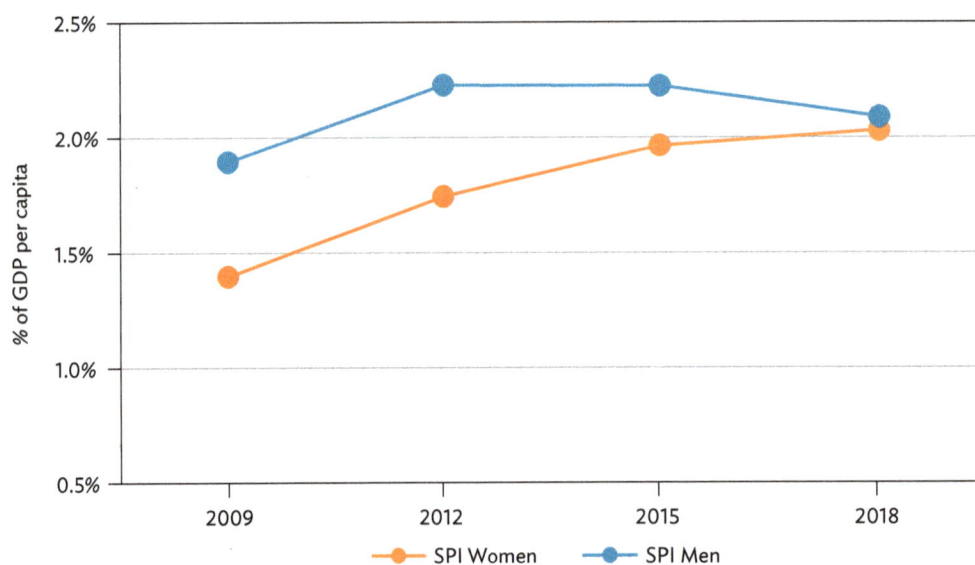

GDP = gross domestic product, SPI = Social Protection Indicator.

Source: ADB estimates.

Spending on women increased in all income groups from 2009 to 2018 (Figure 22). The most significant was the increase of 0.9 percentage point in upper middle-income countries, followed by 0.7 in high-income countries and 0.5 in lower middle-income countries. Spending on men increased by 0.8 percentage point in high-income countries and by 0.2 percentage point in upper middle-income countries and 0.1 percentage point in the lower middle-income group.

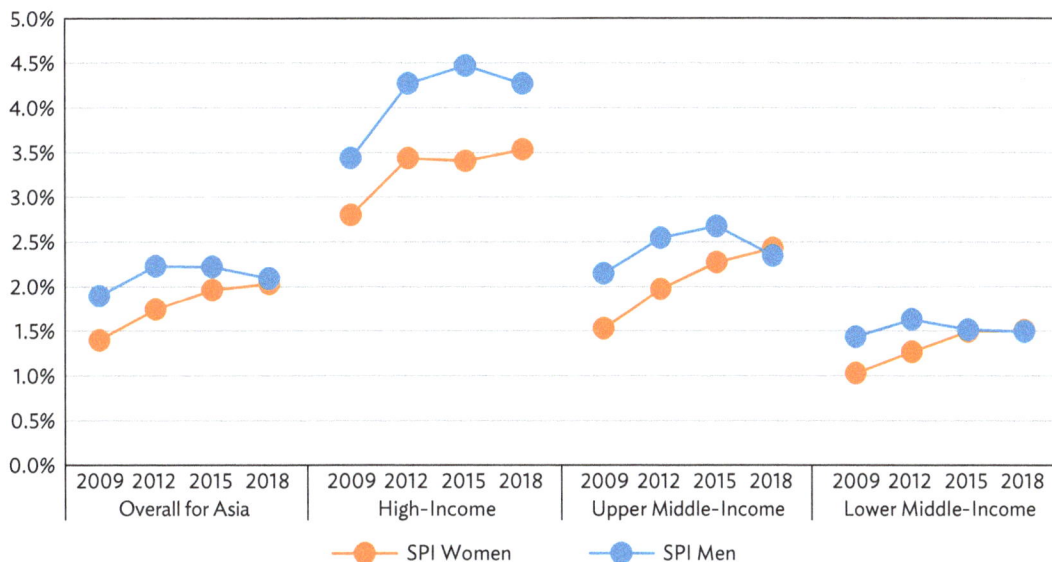

Figure 22: **Progress in the Gender Dimension by Income Group, 2009-2018**

GDP = gross domestic product, SPI = Social Protection Indicator.

Source: ADB estimates..

Most countries increased their expenditure on women in 2018, except Bhutan and Uzbekistan. This was an important achievement, especially given that all 24 countries spent more on men than women in 2009. The most significant was the increase by 2.1 in both Armenia and Tajikistan, followed by 1.8 in the Kyrgyz Republic. The increase in spending in several other countries, such as Cambodia, the Lao PDR, and Nepal, was more modest in terms of the SPI value but doubled over this period.

The expansion of social insurance coverage, including pensions and health insurance, is likely to contribute to greater inclusion of women relative to men in terms of their overall access to social protection. This pertains to both government-led contributory schemes and noncontributory financing arrangements to cover those with limited contributory capacity. Additionally, expansion in social assistance programs targeted at women and children will help reduce gender disparities in coverage.

Social Protection Expenditure for People with Disabilities

- For the 26 countries, the SPI for people with disabilities was 0.5% of GDP per capita of the 4.0% overall SPI in 2018.
- Most countries had a national disability-targeted program and/or reached people with disabilities through general social protection programs.
- The average spending for people with disabilities in Asia increased from 0.15% of GDP in 2009 to 0.23% of GDP in 2018.

This section presents the disaggregated SPI for people with disabilities. This indicator shows the social protection expenditure and coverage of people with disabilities as a share of the SPI. These data are gathered for the first time and help introduce an additional dimension to the SPI analysis.

Table 5 and Figure 23 present the data on the proportion of the overall SPI that reached people with disabilities. The data that generate the SPI for people with disabilities are not yet fully developed. Therefore, the report identifies disability target rates for each general social protection program. For programs that specifically target people with disabilities, a 100% rate was used. However, for general programs, where there were no disaggregated data on the number of people with disabilities as program beneficiaries, the nationally defined disability prevalence rates from national surveys were used. Disability prevalence rates show the total number of people with disabilities in a country.

Table 5: Expenditure for People with Disabilities as a Share of the Overall Social Protection Indicator, 2018

	Overall SPI	People with Disabilities	People without Disabilities
Afghanistan	0.3	0.1	0.2
Armenia	5.6	1.2	4.4
Azerbaijan	5.9	1.8	4.1
Bangladesh	1.2	0.1	1.1
Bhutan	1.2	0.0	1.2
Cambodia	1.0	0.1	0.9
China, People's Republic of	5.8	0.2	5.6
Georgia	4.7	0.5	4.2
Indonesia	2.1	0.1	2.0
Japan	11.7	1.7	10.0
Kazakhstan	4.6	0.8	3.8
Kyrgyz Republic	5.0	0.6	4.4

continued on next page

Table 5: *continued*

	Overall SPI	People with Disabilities	People without Disabilities
Korea, Republic of	6.0	0.4	5.6
Lao PDR	0.9	0.1	0.8
Malaysia	3.7	0.8	2.9
Maldives	4.0	0.4	3.6
Mongolia	4.8	0.7	4.1
Nepal	2.7	0.0	2.7
Pakistan	2.1	0.2	1.9
Philippines	3.0	0.1	2.9
Singapore	5.7	0.7	5.0
Sri Lanka	3.1	0.2	2.9
Tajikistan	4.1	0.8	3.3
Thailand	3.7	0.2	3.5
Uzbekistan	6.3	1.2	5.1
Viet Nam	4.5	0.2	4.3
Unweighted Asia Average	**4.0**	**0.5**	**3.5**

Lao PDR = Lao People's Democratic Republic, SPI = Social Protection Indicator.

Source: ADB estimates based on consultants' reports.

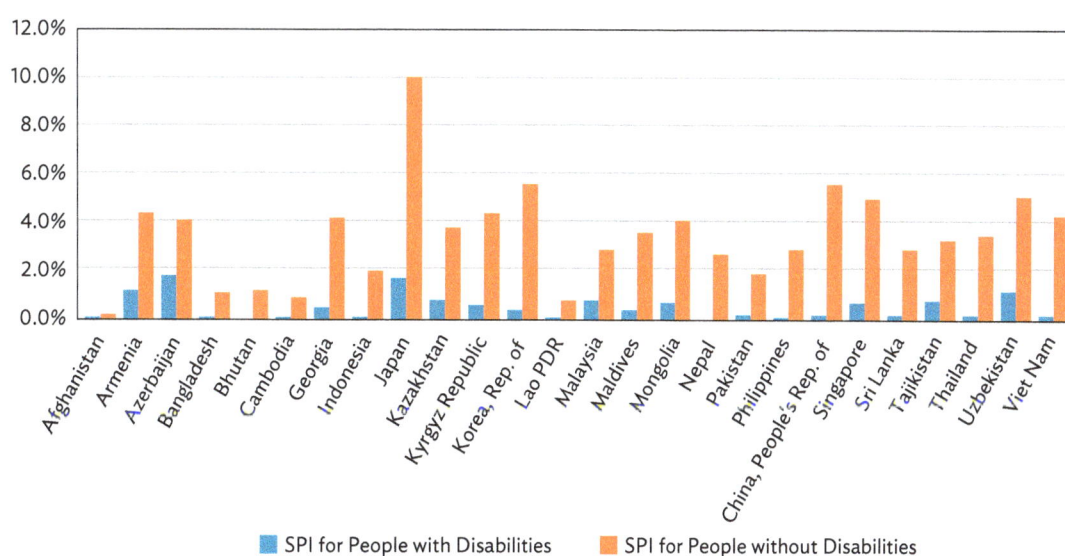

Figure 23: **Expenditure for People with Disabilities as a Share of the Overall Social Protection Indicator, 2018**

Lao PDR = Lao People's Democratic Republic.

Source: ADB estimates based on consultants' reports.

The use of prevalence rates to assume that people are benefiting from general social protection programs can be considered only illustrative given the challenges that people with disabilities experience in accessing social protection programs; given that people with disabilities are generally underrepresented in the workforce and therefore unlikely to benefit from social insurance programs and measures; and given that people with disabilities can experience difficulties in accessing mainstream health and education programs and services.

Nevertheless, the SPI on disability can demonstrate the weight of disability within an overall social protection system.

On average across the 26 countries, the SPI for people with disabilities was 0.5% of GDP per capita of the 4.0% overall SPI in 2018. The SPI for disability was generally a small part of the overall SPI for all Asian countries in this study. This is to be expected, as the population of people with disabilities is a small proportion of the overall population. The SPI in 10 countries was above the regional average of 0.5% (and equaling 0.5% in Georgia). In some countries—Armenia, Azerbaijan, Malaysia, and Tajikistan—the weight of expenditure for disability in the SPI was considerably more than in others.

These data confirm that most countries in Asia spent a portion of social protection expenditure to support people with disabilities. Most countries had at least one disability-targeted program—and many had more than one—under both social insurance and social assistance, where all expenditures (or at least 90% to allow for inclusion errors) can be assumed to have been spent on people with disabilities. Programs targeted only to people with disabilities were not identified in Indonesia, the Lao PDR, the Philippines, and Singapore. Pakistan had a program in one province but no national disability-targeted program. However, people with disabilities in these countries may still have been benefiting from other social protection programs.

The following are examples of social protection programs supporting people with disabilities in Uzbekistan, Mongolia, and Japan. Expenditure on people with disabilities was driven by spending on both social insurance and social assistance and social support services, including social care services.

(i)   **Uzbekistan.** The main programs that benefitted people with disabilities were social insurance-based disability pensions and two social assistance programs, allowances for people with disabilities from childhood and allowances for children with disabilities aged 0-16. Together, these three programs covered 622,000 beneficiaries in 2018. A high level of disability-related expenditure in Uzbekistan reflected a range of other allowances and services provided by the government, including disability allowances for persons without work experience; medical, social, and vocational rehabilitation of people with disabilities; home care services; provision of prosthetic and orthopedic products; and free basic food and hygiene products for older people and people with disabilities. However, the number of registered people with disabilities was likely to be underestimated as not all people with disabilities were registered as such, reflecting the challenges in motivating people to register and targeting people with disabilities.[57]

---

57   ADB. 2022. *Uzbekistan: Social Protection Indicator*. Manila.

(ii)   **Mongolia.** People with disabilities were entitled to a disability pension and other insurance programs such as employment injury and occupational disease and benefits insurance. The disability pension covered 80,300 persons in 2018, while social pensions covered 41,000 people with disabilities who were unable to pay insurance contributions for a minimum of 20 years. The government subsidized health insurance contributions for people with disabilities. The caregiver allowance was also provided for caregivers of people with disabilities and persons in need of permanent care, including children with disabilities. It is estimated that about 66% of people with disabilities received benefits from at least one social assistance program, and this rose to 87% when only children with disabilities under age 16 were considered.[58]

(iii)   **Japan.** Three programs offered support: the disability pension, welfare for people with disabilities, and LMPs for people with disabilities. Together, these programs covered roughly 87% of the adult population (i.e., working age plus those over age 60), assuming little overlap in their benefits. In 2019, the government introduced the Comprehensive Support for Daily and Social Lives of People with Disabilities, which is focused on promotion of self-sufficiency and social participation of people with disabilities.[59]

Trends in Social Protection Expenditure by Disability, 2009-2018

The Convention on the Rights of People with Disabilities (CRPD) introduced in 2006 recognizes in Article 28 the right of people with disabilities to an adequate standard of living and social protection.[60] This recognition includes access to appropriate and affordable services, devices, and other assistance for disability-related needs and expenses as well as access to programs focused on social protection, poverty alleviation, public housing, and retirement schemes. The Incheon Strategy to "Make the Right Real" for People with Disabilities in Asia and the Pacific is an action plan on disability-inclusive development agreed by nearly all governments in the region to accelerate the implementation of the convention.[61] Goal 4 of the Incheon Strategy underscores the centrality of ensuring that people with disabilities have access to social protection on an equal basis with others, including having access to affordable disability-specific services to enable independent living (footnote 61).

To examine trends over time in social protection expenditures targeted to people with disabilities, this report examines expenditures recorded in previous SPI studies as a share of GDP (Table 6). In 2009, the average expenditure for people with disabilities was 0.1% of GDP; in 2018, it was 0.2% of GDP, an increase of almost 50%.[62] Spending increased in small increments since 2015 in 10 countries.

---

[58]   ADB. 2022. *Mongolia: Social Protection Indicator.* Manila.
[59]   This program was not included in the 2018 SPI calculation.
[60]   United Nations. 2007. *Convention on the Rights of Persons with Disabilities.* New York.
[61]   UNESCAP. 2017. *Incheon Strategy to "Make the Right Real" for Persons with Disabilities in Asia and the Pacific.* Bangkok.
[62]   The analysis on trends over time for disability is presented here in "share to GDP" values, as data were not available in the early rounds.

This could reflect commitments under the CRPD and Incheon Strategy having an impact on social protection expenditure. Ratification of the CRPD and the Incheon Strategy placed disability inclusion on the social protection map in the region, as evidenced by several disability-focused social protection strategies, policies, and mechanisms for coordination since the last SPI report (2015 data) (Box 9). This effort has also led to harmonization of legislation and legal definitions of disability with the CRPD even in countries, such as Bhutan, which have not yet ratified the CRPD.

In some countries, disability expenditures increased significantly between 2009 and 2018, notably in Japan (even when adjusted for social insurance expenditures). In some others, however, they decreased, particularly in Uzbekistan and Georgia. The increases may indeed reflect increased expenditures. In Japan, there is a rapidly growing older population with disabilities, and disability social assistance expenditures more than doubled as a percentage of GDP compared with 2009. The decreases in expenditure as a percentage of GDP per capita in some countries seem to be linked more to a significant increase in the GDP per capita than to a decrease in expenditure on programs intended for people with disabilities (Table 6).

Box 9: Key Disability Documents Introduced in Selected Countries since 2015

Bhutan. Bhutan introduced the National Policy for People with Disabilities in 2019. The policy strengthens and extends community-based rehabilitation and provision of assistive technology and devices to people with disabilities as well as improves reasonable adjustments in access to health services. The Gross National Happiness Commission Secretariat is responsible for making sure the rights of people with disabilities are upheld until a separate responsible entity is established.

Kazakhstan. Kazakhstan began to strengthen online services for people with disabilities in 2020 to help them identify social and rehabilitation services and push for a barrier-free environment. People with disabilities welcomed the online portal as it removes the intermediary of state procurement, which affected the quality of services and assistive devices and technology. An interactive accessibility map allows users of the portal, with or without disabilities, to enter information about accessibility of buildings, transport hubs, or other infrastructure. Users with limited mobility can go online before visiting a building or making a journey to assess accessibility and the degree and quality of adaptations that have been introduced.

Uzbekistan. In 2019, the government established a new information system, Single Registry of Social Protection, which is an interagency e-government data transfer network. It aims to introduce efficiencies in administering disability benefits and provide information on disability status from the Ministry of Health's medical and social expertise committees, among other aspects of social protection programs.

Republic of Korea. The Republic of Korea has begun to expand access to social services that can support independent living and increase participation of people with disabilities in education and economic activities. In 2019, the government extended eligibility for activity assistant services to all people with disabilities. The budget for these services was drastically increased by 45.3%, from W609.7 billion in 2018 to W1.0 trillion in 2019. The budget for support projects for the people with developmental disabilities rose fourfold from W8.5 billion in 2018 to W42.7 billion in 2019.

Sources: ADB. 2022. *Bhutan: Social Protection Indicator.* Manila; ADB. 2022. *Kazakhstan: Social Protection Indicator.* Manila; ADB. 2022. *Uzbekistan: Social Protection Indicator.* Manila; and ADB. 2022. *Republic of Korea: Social Protection Indicator.* Manila.

Table 6: Share of Disability Expenditures to Gross Domestic Product, 2009-2018
(%)

	2009	2012	2015	2018
Afghanistan	0.000	0.000	0.000	0.000
Armenia	0.030	0.120	0.160	0.110
Azerbaijan	0.020	0.110	0.150	0.150
Bangladesh	0.010	0.010	0.020	0.040
Bhutan	0.000	0.000	0.000	0.000
Cambodia	0.000	0.000	0.000	0.020
China, People's Republic of	0.020	0.050	0.050	0.060
Georgia	0.640	0.580	0.530	0.420
Indonesia	0.002	0.001	0.001	0.000
Japan	0.250	0.450	0.420	0.880
Kazakhstan				0.500
Korea, Republic of	0.040	0.050	0.070	0.100
Kyrgyz Republic	0.270	1.140	1.120	1.030
Lao PDR	0.000	0.000	0.000	0.000
Malaysia	0.100	0.110	0.120	0.150
Maldives	0.020	0.340	0.260	0.220
Mongolia	0.940	0.840	0.850	0.760
Nepal	0.020	0.020	0.020	0.040
Pakistan	0.000	0.000	0.020	0.005
Philippines	0.040	0.000	0.000	0.000
Singapore	0.010	0.000	0.010	0.000
Sri Lanka	0.003	0.010	0.010	0.010
Tajikistan	0.050	0.030	0.040	0.050
Thailand	0.002	0.060	0.100	0.110
Uzbekistan	1.910	1.420	1.160	1.000
Viet Nam	0.040	0.100	0.100	0.110
Unweighted Asia Average	**0.150**	**0.190**	**0.180**	**0.230**

Lao PDR = Lao People's Democratic Republic, SPI = Social Protection Indicator.

Note: Mongolia does not include the disability pension under social insurance, as data were not available for 2009 and 2012.

Source: ADB estimates.

In addition to allowances and pensions, several countries introduced innovative employment services to support people with disabilities to access employment and assistive devices and technology, not only in keeping with the provision of the CRPD, but also in a drive toward increasing employment of people with disabilities and reducing reliance on social assistance (Box 10). Employment quotas and support for reasonable accommodations in the workplace were reported by several countries in Asia; however, it is not clear

the extent to which these measures impacted the desired results.
Other innovations include inclusive employment services and social services,
such as providing personal assistants who can support independent living and
inclusion of people with disabilities in the open labor market.

Box 10: Innovative Labor Market Programs and Employment Services Supporting People with Disabilities

Mongolia. Mongolia is developing inclusive employment services using coaching and case management methods to try to increase the number of people with disabilities in salaried employment in the open labor market and to move away from reliance on self-employment and sheltered employment for people with disabilities in the intermediate labor market. At the same time, through an intersector approach to social protection, the government is developing community-based services, including personal assistant services that can further support people with disabilities in employment and independent living.

Japan. Japan introduced legislation in 2019 that aims to increase support for independent living and employment for people with disabilities. Employment quotas have been in force since 1976, but a new levy and grant system has been introduced to incentivize employment of people with disabilities. The levies pay subsidies to employers for each person with disabilities employed above the minimum quota and take levies from employers who do not meet the quota. The grants support the additional costs of employing people with disabilities, including workplace attendants, and support the commutes of people with severe disabilities, provision of workplace facilities, and skills development of people with disabilities. In addition, services to support people with disabilities into employment have been introduced, including job coaches, vocational ability development centers, and services to support employers to prepare for people with disabilities in the workplace. Job coaches help improve the support system in the workplace and assist the person with disabilities in adjusting to the workplace.

Kazakhstan. Kazakhstan has increased its focus in actively supporting employment of people with disabilities based on the following legislative innovations: (i) a norm limiting participation in public procurement for large and medium-sized enterprises that do not fulfill the quota for the employment of people with disabilities; and (ii) a mechanism whereby the company, instead of fulfilling the quota for the employment of people with disabilities, can pay compensation. The collected funds accumulate into a specially created fund to help people with disabilities find employment (e.g., for training, paid internships, and special jobs). These measures have been introduced in part to mitigate the concerns of employers that the job quota system and support for reasonable accommodations introduced in 2018 were not realistic. The real costs of adjusting workplaces were often much higher than the subsidies provided to employers by the government.

Republic of Korea. The Republic of Korea launched the Employment Project for People with Disabilities in the early 2000s as a national initiative to expand the social participation and income security of people with disabilities by providing them with job opportunities tailored to their disability. Until now, it has focused on quantitative growth. The number of participants tripled in 11 years, from 4,900 individuals working in two kinds of jobs in 2007, to 17,400 people working in seven types of jobs in 2018; the project budget has increased by 766%. However, its scale is still largely insufficient compared with the participation rate in economic activities and the unemployment rate of people with disabilities. At around the same time, a program was launched to provide 80% of the purchase cost of information technology devices and technical aids, such as screen readers and print-to-voice converters, to people with disabilities to support digital life and to bridge the information gap. The program prioritizes people with severe levels of disabilities and aims to target jobseekers and students.

Sources: ADB. 2022. *Mongolia: Social Protection Indicator*. Manila; ADB. 2022. *Japan: Social Protection Indicator*. Manila; ADB. 2022. *Kazakhstan: Social Protection Indicator*. Manila; and ADB. 2022. *Republic of Korea: Social Protection Indicator*. Manila.

VI. Social Protection and COVID-19 in Asia

This chapter takes stock of the immediate social protection response to the COVID-19 pandemic in 26 Asian countries. It presents COVID-19-related social protection expenditures as well as innovative approaches, programs, and developments in the social protection ecosystem in Asia. The chapter distills policy lessons emerging from the pandemic period as well as the new reality for social protection systems in Asia, as countries gradually come out of the crisis and embark on recovery. This chapter draws on the data collected by ADB as part of the SPI study as well as on other publicly available information.

The COVID-19 Crisis in Asia

Since 2020, the COVID-19 pandemic has exerted immense social and economic strain on countries around the world. As of May 2022, the World Health Organization (WHO) reported over 524 million confirmed cases of COVID-19 globally, including over 6 million deaths.[63]

In addition to the unprecedented health crisis, preventive measures taken in response to the pandemic have severely affected the global economy, with global growth estimated to have dropped from 2.9% in 2019 to –3.1% in 2020.[64] In addition, new global stressors—such as the crisis triggered by the Russian invasion of Ukraine, which has spurred a significant spike in inflation and increased food and energy prices—are anticipated to further complicate recovery. Global growth, which recovered to 6.1% in 2021, is projected to drop to 3.6% in 2022 and 2023, with significant variations across income groups and regions (footnote 64).

For developing Asia, ADB estimations indicate that growth in this region dropped from 5.0% in 2019 to –0.8% in 2020 in the wake of the pandemic. In 2021, growth is estimated to have recovered to 6.9% in developing Asia, but new global stressors and the scattered, yet continuing, COVID-19 pandemic, are lowering growth estimates to 5.2% and 5.3% in 2022 and 2023, respectively.[65]

63   WHO. WHO Coronavirus (COVID-19) Dashboard. https://covid19.who.int (accessed 19 May 2022).
64   IMF. 2022. *World Economic Outlook April 2022: War Sets Back the Global Recovery*. Washington, DC. https://www.imf.org/en/Publications/WEO/Issues/2022/04/19/world-economic-outlook-april-2022.
65   ADB. 2022. *Asian Development Outlook (ADO) 2022: Mobilizing Taxes for Development*. Manila. https://www.adb.org/sites/default/files/publication/784041/ado2022.pdf.

The adverse implications of COVID-19 and measures imposed to contain its spread are anticipated to impact particularly vulnerable groups, including low-income households and the poor. This effect could strike a severe blow to the progress already made across the world on various key development indicators, such as the reduction of extreme poverty since the 1990s.[66]

The COVID-19 pandemic triggered a social protection response of a previously unseen magnitude. Several organizations, including the World Bank and the International Labour Organization (ILO), have been actively tracking the global social protection response to the pandemic. By the end of 2020, more than 200 countries around the world, including those in Asia, announced or implemented over 1,414 social protection measures in response to the pandemic, with most measures falling under the category of social assistance. Cash assistance is estimated to have accounted for more than 50% of such measures, offered for an average duration of 3.3 months, by the end of 2020.[67] However, the long nature of the crisis forced many governments to extend emergency social protection support well past 2020, with the available estimates indicating over 3,856 measures introduced globally by January 2022.[68]

In addition to the already large number of vulnerable individuals residing in Asia, the pandemic also created large numbers of newly vulnerable people, many of whom previously fell outside of the often-limited scope of social protection systems in many low- and middle-income countries. ADB simulations indicate that in 2020 alone, the pandemic is estimated to have pushed an additional 75 million to 80 million people into extreme poverty in developing Asia.[69]

As discussed previously, social protection coverage in Asian countries was at 65.2% of intended beneficiaries. While this is an improvement in comparison to the coverage recorded in earlier rounds of SPI research, it still implies that significantly large sections of the intended population were not covered by social protection at the onset of the COVID-19 pandemic. Countries often had to quickly adapt by scrambling to direct available resources to protect their populations against the health, social, and economic fallout from the pandemic, with their social protection systems often functioning at unsustainable levels throughout the critical period of the initial outbreak.

[66] IMF. 2020. *World Economic Outlook Update, June 2020*. Washington, DC. https://www.imf.org/en/Publications/WEO/Issues/2020/06/24/WEOUpdateJune2020.

[67] U. Gentilini, M. Almenfi, I. Orton, and P. Dale. 2020. *Social Protection and Jobs Responses to COVID-19: A Real-Time Review of Country Measures*. Washington, DC: World Bank. https://openknowledge.worldbank.org/handle/10986/33635.

[68] U. Gentilini et al. 2022. *Social Protection and Jobs Responses to COVID-19: A Real-Time Review of Country Measures*. Washington, DC: World Bank. https://documents.worldbank.org/en/publication/documents-reports/documentlist?colti=COVID-19%20Living%20Paper.

[69] ADB. 2021. *Key Indicators for Asia and the Pacific 2021*. Manila. https://www.adb.org/sites/default/files/publication/720461/ki2021.pdf.

The Social Protection Response to COVID-19

The next sections review social protection measures and the estimated expenditures incurred in the 26 Asian countries in their immediate responses to COVID-19. This analysis draws on the data collected by ADB for the SPI study. More specifically, along with the SPI, data were collected on national responses to COVID-19. Consultations were conducted with in-country sources to verify some information. These data were then used to identify key social protection measures and expenditures in the region presented here. However, the data collection was undertaken at a time when available data on COVID-19-related social protection measures were still largely estimations of national commitments, based on announced or proposed responses rather than administrative or program data from implementing agencies—and hence should be treated as such.

The analysis of these data is complemented by information from other sources, including government websites, publications and announcements, media reports, and global repositories of COVID-19 measures maintained by World Bank, ILO, and International Monetary Fund (IMF).[70] This information has helped further identify innovative approaches and programs to address the effects of the pandemic.

Like most countries around the world, those in Asia deployed social protection as a critical component of their pandemic responses. Measures introduced in Asia range across social assistance, social insurance, and LMPs. Most countries introduced a range of new programs, primarily composed of ad-hoc or temporary measures, including various forms of welfare transfers for vulnerable groups, wage subsidies to retain employees, and other targeted subsidies invoked to cushion the socioeconomic burden on vulnerable groups. Many countries also utilized vertical expansion (i.e., increasing benefit size) and horizontal expansion (i.e., extension of coverage) of existing social protection programs for vulnerable individuals and households that were previously not recipients of social protection benefits.

Sixty-three percent of the measures introduced constitute new programs, and the remaining 37% are almost equally split between coverage or benefit expansions of existing programs (Figure 24).

---

[70]   See U. Gentilini et al. 2022. *Social Protection and Jobs Responses to COVID-19 : A Real-Time Review of Country Measures.* Washington, DC. https://documents.worldbank.org/en/publication/documents-reports/documentlist?colti=COVID-19%20Living%20Paper; ILO. 2021. Social Protection Responses to COVID-19 Crisis around the World. https://www.social-protection.org/gimi/ShowWiki.action?id=3417; and IMF. 2021. Policy Responses to COVID-19. https://www.imf.org/en/Topics/imf-and-covid19/Policy-Responses-to-COVID-19.

Figure 24: New Social Protection Programs, Coverage Expansions, and Benefit Expansions during the COVID-19 Crisis

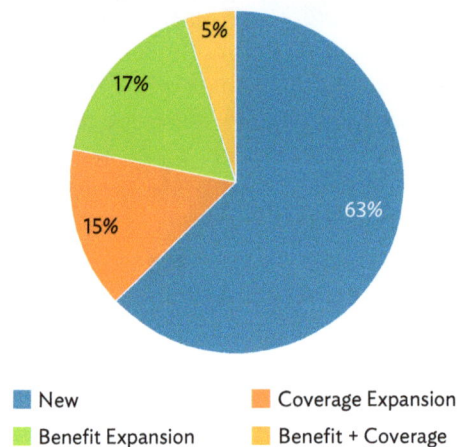

- New
- Coverage Expansion
- Benefit Expansion
- Benefit + Coverage

Source: ADB estimates.

Overall, the social protection response to the pandemic is dominated by social assistance, which accounted for about 67% of all the measures introduced. Social insurance and LMPs made up comparatively smaller shares of the response across Asia, accounting for about 16% each (Figure 25).

Figure 25: Social Protection Response to COVID-19 by Category and Subregion

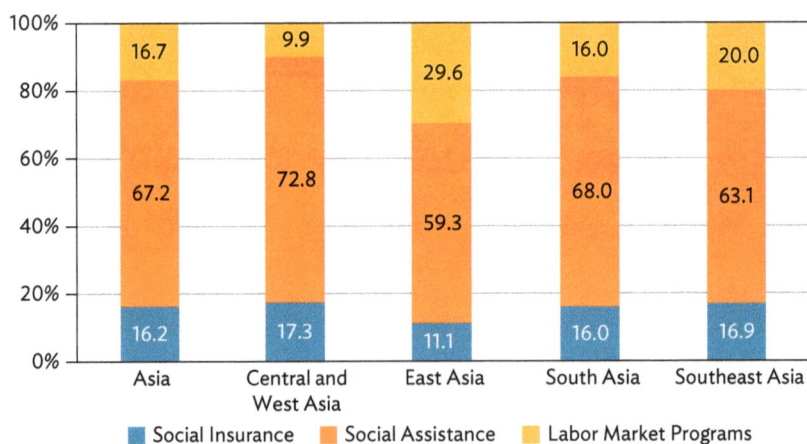

- Social Insurance
- Social Assistance
- Labor Market Programs

Source: ADB estimates.

The social assistance response in Asian countries constituted different forms of welfare transfers, both cash and food, and other targeted subsidies for vulnerable groups. Cash transfers dominated the social assistance measures introduced.

Social insurance measures have ranged across adjustments to pension programs (e.g., Georgia, Kazakhstan, and the Kyrgyz Republic), health insurance measures (e.g., the PRC and Indonesia), unemployment benefits (e.g., Azerbaijan, the PRC, and Japan), sickness benefits (e.g., Uzbekistan), and contribution rates for social security payments (e.g., Cambodia and Viet Nam).

LMPs introduced include wage subsidies, skills training, and short-duration public works and employment programs. Several countries (e.g., Armenia, Azerbaijan, Bangladesh, Japan, Sri Lanka, and Thailand) introduced wage subsidies, often to retain employment in the hardest-hit industrial sectors. Only a few countries introduced skills training (e.g., Bhutan, Cambodia, and Indonesia) and public works or employment programs (e.g., Indonesia, Nepal, and Pakistan). Restrictive measures invoked to contain the spread of the pandemic made employment and training programs challenging to implement during the critical months of the outbreak.

Social assistance has been the dominant form of response across all subregions[71] and country income groups in Asia. The largest share is recorded among the Central and West Asian countries, accounting for nearly 73% of all measures. In lower middle-income countries, these accounted for close to 69% of the measures introduced.

Social insurance measures have been prominent among Central and West Asian countries and Southeast Asian countries, where they accounted for about 17.0% of the measures introduced, but were least prominent among East Asian countries, where they accounted for about 11.0%. In terms of country income groups, social insurance measures are prominent across upper middle-income countries, where they have represented 22.0% of the overall response, and were least prominent among high-income countries, representing only 3.3%.

LMPs seem prominent in East Asian countries, but least prominent among Central and West Asian countries. Correspondingly, they have been most prominent—close to 37% of the overall response—among high-income countries that include the East Asian countries of Japan and the ROK. These results were driven by the sizable wage subsidies and other employment stabilization and retention programs offered in the high-income countries (Figure 26).

Global evidence on COVID-19-related cash transfers indicates that some of the largest programs, in terms of the number of people reached, are in Asian countries. Countries, such as India (reaching over 200 million people), Japan and Pakistan (reaching over 100 million people each), the PRC (reaching over 80 million people), and the Philippines (reaching close to 70 million people) are examples. High-income countries in the region, such as Japan, the ROK, and Singapore, are also among the top countries globally in terms of the percentage of population reached, due to the intensifying impact of largely universal programs.[72]

---

[71] ADB classifies economies in Asia into the following four subregions: Central and West Asia, East Asia, South Asia, and Southeast Asia.
[72] U. Gentilini et al. 2022. *Social Protection and Jobs Responses to COVID-19: A Real-Time Review of Country Measures.* Washington, DC. https://documents.worldbank.org/en/publication/documents-reports/documentlist?colti=COVID-19%20Living%20Paper.

Figure 26: **Social Protection Response to COVID-19 Shares by Category and Income Group**

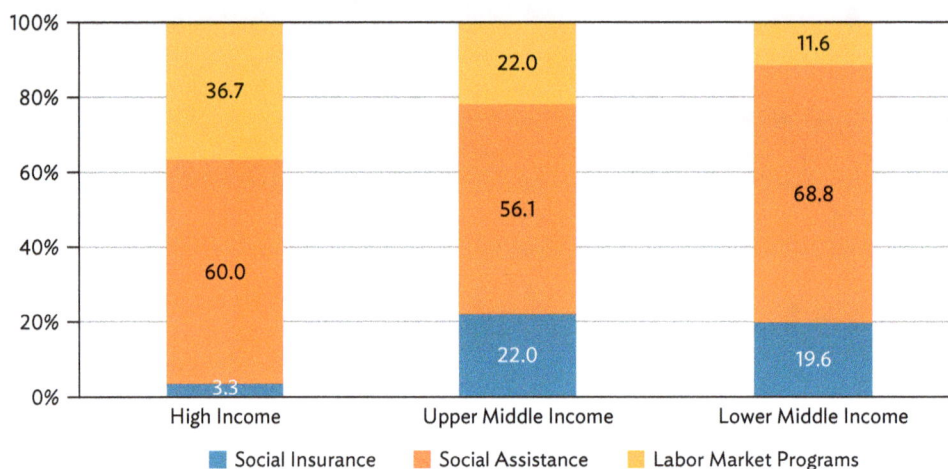

Source: ADB estimates.

Estimates of COVID-19-Related Social Protection Expenditures

With the pandemic still unfolding across Asia, verifiable administrative data on COVID-19-related social protection expenditures are atypical. COVID-19-related emergency expenditures in 2020 may be in addition to already-budgeted social protection expenditures in countries for that year—data that will only be available in forthcoming rounds of the SPI. Most countries in Asia have committed further resources to tackle the ongoing crisis, as new variants of the virus and new outbreaks emerge. The expenditures discussed here thus represent significant underestimations based on available data on emergency social protection commitments through the critical months of the initial outbreak in 2020. However, tentative estimations can be calculated based on the size and nature of the proposed measures in various countries.

On average, COVID-19-related emergency social protection spending across the 26 Asian countries is estimated at 2.0% of GDP for 2020 (Figure 27).

However, the weight of this average among Asian countries may be biased by high spending estimates among the three high-income countries included in this report, which was almost 8.2% of GDP for 2020. If the high-income countries are excluded from this estimation, the average spending drops by almost 40.0%, to 1.2% of GDP for 2020.

Figure 27: Estimates of COVID-19-Related Social Protection Expenditure by Region and Subregion, 2020

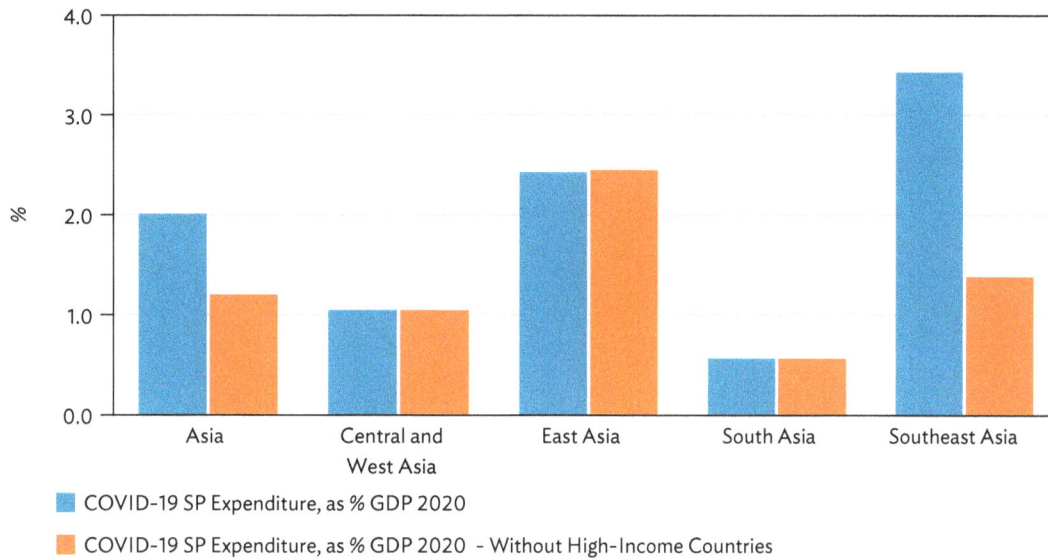

GDP = gross domestic product, SP = social protection.

Source: ADB estimates.

Across subregions, Southeast Asian countries are estimated to have the largest average COVID-19-related spending, at about 3.4% of GDP for 2020. However, this estimate is again biased by the rather high estimates for Singapore (at over 15.0% of GDP for 2020). Excluding high-income countries, East Asia emerges as the subregion with the highest average spending, at 2.4% of GDP for 2020. This percentage is determined by the large emergency packages announced in Mongolia—close to 5.0% of GDP for 2020—which delivered, among other benefits, substantial top-ups to existing universal social protection programs. South Asian countries are estimated to have the lowest COVID-19-related spending, averaging only about 0.6% of GDP for 2020.

Across income groups, estimated spending drops from 8.2% of GDP among high-income countries, to 1.8% of GDP among upper middle-income countries and to 1.0% among lower middle-income countries (Figure 28).

The upper middle-income group average is driven by relatively high estimations in countries such as Malaysia (over 5.0% of GDP for 2020) and Georgia (almost 2.5% of GDP for 2020). The spending estimates for lower middle-income countries are quite diverse, ranging from close to 0.2% of GDP in Cambodia and Sri Lanka, to almost 5.0% in Mongolia.

In general, it appears that high-income countries that have consistently reported a relatively high SPI value from 2009 to 2018—and have more developed social protection systems—were able to commit the largest comparative share of GDP in emergency expenditures in 2020. In addition, countries such as Mongolia, where

Figure 28: **Estimates of COVID-19-Related Social Protection Expenditure by Income Group, 2020 (% of GDP)**

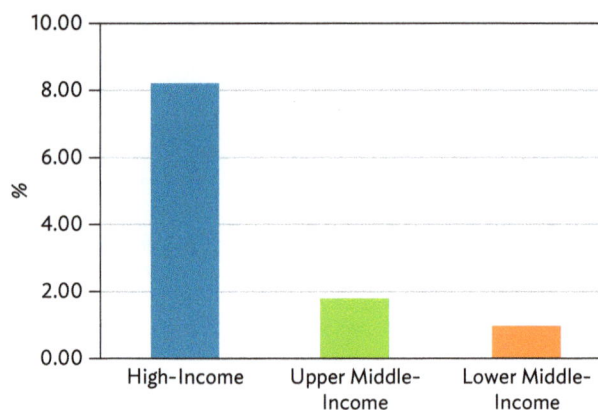

GDP = gross domestic product.

Source: ADB estimates.

existing universal or near-universal programs could be expanded with immediate effect, demonstrated considerably higher potential in channeling emergency support and reaching larger shares of the vulnerable population quickly. Such trends provide important evidence toward the benefits of investing in comprehensive social protection systems in times of no crisis to effectively capitalize on such systems and to provide critical support to people through periods of crisis.

Innovations Supporting Social Protection Expansion

Social protection programs and systems, which form an important pillar of the overall policy response in countries, have been subjected to overwhelming pressure during the pandemic. It also brought to the surface the fragility of the level of sustenance of large sections of the population in Asia. As well as compounding existing vulnerabilities in the region, it added large numbers of newly vulnerable individuals—now increasingly referred to as the "missing middle"—who, in most countries, normally fall outside of the purview and limited scope of existing social protection systems.

In response to this turmoil, countries have adopted a range of innovative means to quickly extend social protection support to those bearing the brunt of the pandemic's negative consequences. This group includes poor households, marginalized groups, women and children, people with disabilities, older people, those in vulnerable and informal employment, and migrant workers.

The pandemic has triggered leapfrogging in the deployment of social protection strategies, programs, and systems across Asia to respond to the overwhelming demand for additional protection. Some countries have capitalized and piggybacked on pre-pandemic reforms and investments, while others have adopted new approaches and interventions in a rushed manner as the pandemic unfolds. Such innovations hold great potential to contribute to the shock responsiveness and strengthening of social protection systems in the future. The section below takes stock of a few such innovative approaches and programs observed in Asia.

The scale and impact of the pandemic made it essential to facilitate horizontal expansion. Considering the limited pre-pandemic social protection coverage levels in Asia—and the fact that the pandemic created many newly vulnerable individuals—rapid coverage expansion proved to be challenging. Countries, such as Cambodia and Pakistan, relied on timely investments made in developing digital capabilities prior to the pandemic, to rapidly expand coverage through the crisis (Boxes 11 and 12).

Box 11: Digital Infrastructure Supporting the Ehsaas Emergency Cash Programme in Pakistan

To deliver the substantial pandemic response deployed in 2020, Pakistan drew on timely investments made in 2019, prior to the pandemic, which included a new biometric payment system, a new wealth profiling mechanism, and a demand-driven registration system to facilitate rapid enrollment in various social protection programs.

The new payment system combines a limited mandate account with a savings wallet and is delivered in collaboration with two commercial banks, through their branchless banking platforms (in retail settings and especially established payment sites) and biometrically enabled ATMs. A total of over 11,500 cash-out points were made available in over 2,270 sites across the country.

Pakistan's existing National Socio-Economic Registry is currently being updated, and the 2017 census data lack relevant information for targeting emergency transfers. Hence, a hybrid targeting approach was adopted, combining the known vulnerable population with demand-driven support for the new poor. The demand-driven desk and SMS-based registration system developed in 2019 were also leveraged. The system enabled eligibility verification across a range of databases, supported by a wealth-profiling data analytics mechanism developed in collaboration with Pakistan's National Database Registration Authority (NADRA). The wealth-profiling mechanism uses a range of wealth proxies validated by household income and expenditure data to minimize the risk of exclusion, especially for those in the poorest two quantiles.

These mechanisms were further supported by the massive reform undertaken at the national implementation agency, the Benazir Income Support Programme (BISP) in 2019. This effort includes substantial changes to information technology safeguards, digital monitoring, and payment systems.

Thus, the one-time Ehsaas Emergency Cash Programme delivered benefits to 14.8 million families by its close in September 2020. Overall, this effort was estimated to impact over 100.0 million individuals, including minorities. It was made possible through a whole-of-government approach, including public–private partnerships, real-time evaluations to address challenges on-the-go, and significant deployment of technology solutions. It was also backed by timely investments in developing the capabilities of information technology systems and digital pathways supporting social protection in the country, including a biometric payment system, and a demand-side SMS-based request-seeking platform.

Sources: S. Nishtar. 2020. *Ehsaas Emergency Cash: A Digital Solution to Protect the Vulnerable in Pakistan during the COVID-19 Crisis.* Islamabad: Government of Pakistan. https://www.pass.gov.pk/Document/Downloads/Ehsaas%20 Emergency%20Cash%20Report%20Oct%202020_Dec15_2020.pdf; and Government of Pakistan. 2021. *Ehsaas Emergency Cash (All Categories).* https://pass.gov.pk/ecs/uct_all.html.

Box 12: Cambodia's IDPoor Program and Rapid Coverage Expansion during COVID-19

IDPoor was established in 2006 as part of the Government of Cambodia's ongoing efforts to support poverty alleviation and socioeconomic development in the country. It provides regularly updated information on poor households for targeted pro-poor measures to several agencies, both government and nongovernment. Specifically, IDPoor aims to reduce duplication of efforts, improve the targeting accuracy of programs, and streamline the approval of beneficiaries for the different agencies involved.

Overview of Cambodia's IDPoor Program

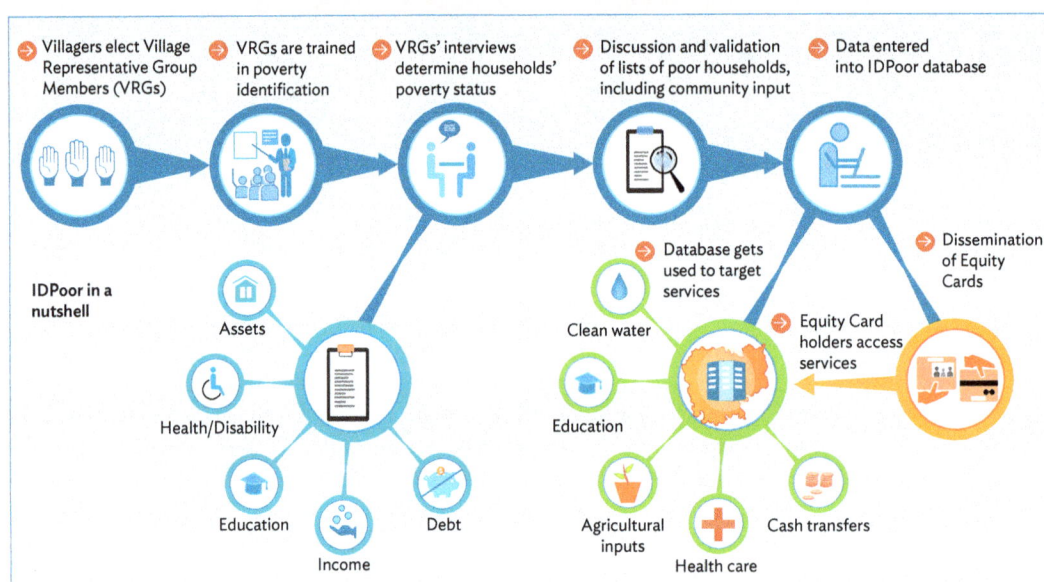

IDPoor is a community-driven proxy means test implemented by residents of each village, and further validated by the community. The process is coordinated by the Ministry of Planning and its provincial departments nationwide. Households on the final list of the poor are issued an equity card, which poor households use to avail themselves of services and assistance, making it easier for service providers to also quickly validate their eligibility.

In implementing the Cash Transfer for Poor and Vulnerable Households during COVID-19, coverage was expanded through the acceleration of an on-demand IDPoor process. Since the start of implementation, the number of beneficiaries has continuously increased from 2.1 million in June 2020 to 2.7 million in February 2021, along with the total amount of cash transferred, from $23.6 million to $30.7 million, respectively. A slight increase is also observed in the average amount per beneficiary, from $11.00 in June 2020 to $11.20 in February 2021.

Sources: Government of Cambodia. IDPoor Process. https://www.idpoor.gov.kh/about/process; and ADB. 2022. *Cambodia: Social Protection Indicator*. Manila.

While rapid horizontal expansion through coverage extension has been key in most countries in the region, countries like Mongolia with large universal social protection programs have relied on increasing impact through substantial vertical expansion, in addition to other measures. Benefit levels of Mongolia's universal Child Money Programme and pension scheme have been rapidly increased to safeguard large shares of vulnerable groups. In fact, the vertical expansion introduced by Mongolia for its Child Money Programme in 2020 is among the largest benefit increases recorded globally in response to COVID-19. It registered almost a fourfold increase in comparison to pre-COVID-19 benefit levels (footnote 72).

Although many of the notable social protection responses to COVID-19 have been in the form of social assistance, social insurance and LMPs also have played important roles in the response. Contributory insurance measures offer a range of protective functions, but benefits are often extended only to those in formal employment. In the initial stages of the pandemic, some innovative approaches were adopted for growing claims of workplace insurance benefits. Modified paid sick-leave provisions emerged as an informative and innovative case study in this respect.

In Japan, for example, the government introduced an income compensation subsidy for all regular and nonregular employees, covering a maximum of ¥8,330 for leave used between 27 February and 31 March 2020. The scheme used a combination of contributory insurance payments (for those enrolled in unemployment insurance) and payments from general government accounts (for those not enrolled in unemployment insurance) to cater to a wider range of workers than originally eligible for social insurance benefits.[73]

The LMPs introduced in response to the pandemic also provide some promising examples of innovative approaches. While containment and social-distancing measures made regular work/training-based LMPs difficult to implement, some countries responded by diverting public employment to meet basic social service and health care requirements.

In the Philippines, for example, the Tulong Panghanapbuhay Sa Ating Displaced/Disadvantaged Workers Program implemented by the Department of Labor and Employment offered temporary wage employment to displaced, underemployed, and self-employed individuals for 10 days in the early stages of the outbreak. The work offered included disinfecting and sanitation of houses and immediate vicinities, with beneficiaries also offered a basic orientation on health and safety measures.[74] The initiative addressed the dual objectives of community health and job creation, pressing issues throughout the pandemic period.

In the ROK, in addition to the emergency social protection measures undertaken to safeguard lives and livelihoods, the government announced the "Korean New Deal." The Korean New Deal is among the first forward-looking strategic initiatives in the region addressing the medium- and long-term changes to the labor market and social protection system induced by COVID-19. It consists of two main components, the Digital New Deal and Green New Deal, underpinned by an overarching policy to strengthen employment and social safety nets.

---

[73]   *The Mainichi.* 2020. Japan Gov't to Subsidize Paid Leave to Care for Children amid School Closures. 3 March. https://mainichi.jp/english/articles/20200303/p2a/00m/0na/008000c.

[74]   Government of the Philippines, DOLE. 2020. Department Order No. 210—Guidelines for the Implementation of the Tulong Panghanapbuhay Sa Ating Displaced/Disadvantaged Workers Program (Tupad) #Barangay Ko, Bahay Ko (TUPAD #BKBK) Disinfecting/Sanitation Project. https://www.dole.gov.ph/news/department-order-no-210-guidelines-for-the-implementation-of-the-tulong-panghanapbuhay-sa-ating-displaced-disadvantaged-workers-program-tupad-barangay-ko-bahay-ko-tupad-bkbk-disinfecting/.

These policy areas are intended to increase the resilience of economic agents against the uncertainty that results from changing economic structures.[75] The program includes a strong focus on job creation, training, and human resources development, with a particular focus on digital jobs and digital skills building, thereby keeping up with the evolving nature of the labor market and mapping of a new normal in labor conditions.

This new deal will also shift the focus of large-scale public works programs from physical infrastructure to digital infrastructure and services, such as data analysis, artificial intelligence, cybersecurity, and promotion of the green economy sector for climate change response. It aims to cover a scope of "untact" (i.e., contactless) services, and the digitalization of social overhead capital (i.e., capital goods available for all), which is usually provided by the government.[76]

Emerging Evidence of the Impact of Social Protection Measures

The evidence base on social protection's role during crisis scenarios had been on the rise even before the COVID-19 crisis. Previous crisis scenarios, such as the 1997 Asian financial crisis, had already demonstrated the need for social protection as a critical tool in protecting people and facilitating their recuperation from such shocks.[77]

The response to the COVID-19 pandemic forms the latest—and one of the most important lessons—on this front. Unlike in previous crisis scenarios, COVID-19 is not just a localized regional stressor. It has unraveled globally as a covariate shock, pushing millions of people into poverty and exacerbating vulnerabilities for countless others. The investment case for inclusive, adaptive, and shock-responsive social protection is one that is indelibly etching itself on the aftermath of the pandemic and through the devastation it continues to cause, together with new risks and stressors in the region.

Verifiable evidence on the impact of emergency social protection measures in achieving their objectives throughout the COVID-19 period is only just emerging. However, given that the pandemic is still unfolding at varying rates

75   Government of the Republic of Korea, Ministry of Economy and Finance. 2020. *National Strategy for a Great Transformation: Korean New Deal*. Seoul. https://english.moef.go.kr/pc/selectTbPressCenterDtl. do?boardCd=N0001&seq=4948.

76   K. Dongwoo. 2020. South Korea's "New Deal:" An Example for Post-COVID Economic Recovery. Toronto: Asia Pacific Foundation of Canada. https://www.asiapacific.ca/publication/south-koreas-new-deal-example-post-covid-economic-recovery.

77   M. Ramesh. 2009. Economic Crisis and Its Social Impacts Lessons from the 1997 Asian Economic Crisis. *Global Social Policy*. 9. pp. 79-99.

across the region, only in the coming years will a robust and comprehensive assessment of its impact and the effectiveness of policy responses be possible. At the same time, a number of studies help shed light on the possible repercussions of the pandemic.

ADB simulations indicate that the pandemic pushed an additional 75 million to 80 million people into extreme poverty in 2020 alone.[78] The compounding and multidimensional nature of poverty imply that the pandemic will further set the region back across a range of development indicators, including educational attainment, maternal and child mortality, and unemployment.

Many other studies have attempted to undertake ex-ante evaluations of the impact of COVID-19-related social protection measures on a range of factors, including poverty, inequality, and consumption expenditures. In one study, three scenarios were compared for Mongolia: (i) a baseline scenario pre-pandemic, (ii) the effect of the pandemic (i.e., what could have happened), and (iii) the mitigation effect of adopted social protection measures (i.e., what is likely to have happened as a result).[79]

This exercise was underpinned by several assumptions, including the length and depth of the shock and ideal implementation of planned social protection measures.[80] The study used microsimulations to access the impact of COVID-19-related social protection measures on national poverty rates and inequality on different socioeconomic groups. Findings from the simulations estimated that in the absence of the Government of Mongolia's mitigating policies, the pandemic would have reduced household income by almost 10% in comparison to a baseline pre-pandemic scenario.[81]

The cumulative distribution (Figure 29) plots the expected shift in monthly consumption per capita throughout the different scenarios above and indicates the estimated positive effect of the government's social protection policies throughout the COVID-19 period. Similarly, Figure 30 plots the impact of the government's social protection response on poverty.

[78] ADB. 2021. *Key Indicators for Asia and the Pacific 2021*. Manila. https://www.adb.org/sites/default/files/publication/720461/ki2021.pdf.

[79] ADB. 2020. Mongolia: Building Capacity for an Effective Social Welfare System: Assessment of the Social Protection Response to COVID-19 in Mongolia. Consultant's report. Manila (TA 9893-MON). https://www.adb.org/sites/default/files/project-documents/51387/51387-001-tacr-en.pdf.

[80] Social protection measures considered in the study also include some measures that do not fall under ADB's SPI definitions, such as general income tax waivers and nontargeted subsidies for the general public.

[81] ADB. 2020. Mongolia: Building Capacity for an Effective Social Welfare System: Assessment of the Social Protection Response to COVID-19 in Mongolia. Consultant's report. Manila (TA 9893-MON). https://www.adb.org/sites/default/files/project-documents/51387/51387-001-tacr-en.pdf.

Figure 29: Simulated Effect on Mongolia's Monthly Consumption per Capita

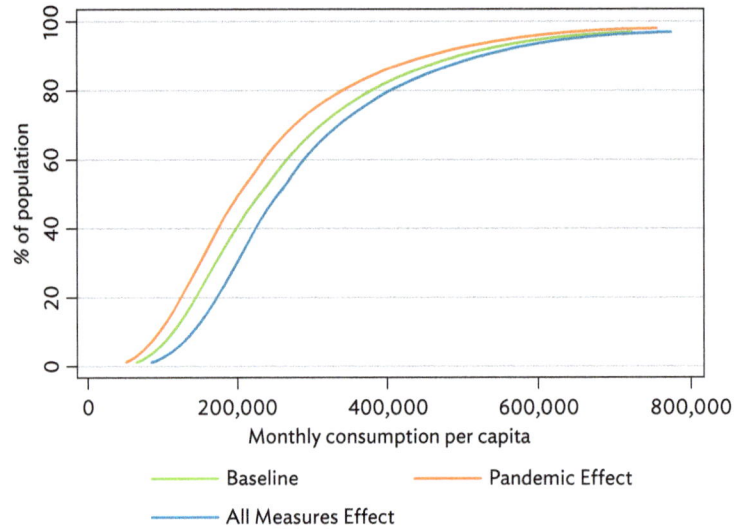

Source: ADB. 2020. Mongolia: Building Capacity for an Effective Social Welfare System: Assessment of the Social Protection Response to COVID-19 in Mongolia. Consultant's report. Manila (TA 9893-MON). https://www.adb.org/sites/default/files/project-documents/51387/51387-001-tacr-en.pdf.

Figure 30: Mongolia's Poor under Different Scenarios of Simulation, April–September 2020 (MNT)

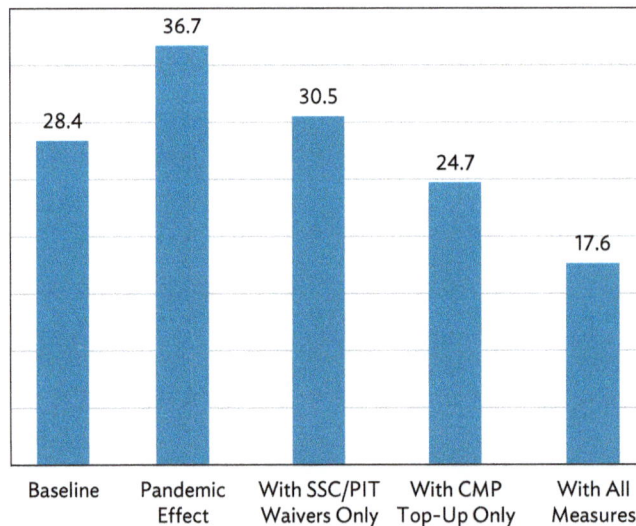

CMP = Child Monitoring Program, MNT = togrog, PIT = personal income tax, SSC = social security contributions.

Source: ADB. 2020. Mongolia: Building Capacity for an Effective Social Welfare System: Assessment of the Social Protection Response to COVID-19 in Mongolia. Consultant's report. Manila (TA 9893-MON). https://www.adb.org/sites/default/files/project-documents/51387/51387-001-tacr-en.pdf.

To build up an evidence base, the United Nations Children's Fund (UNICEF) has made available a sizeable repository of rapid impact assessments for several countries, including those in Asia, which evaluate the pandemic's impact on child poverty.[82] Several of these assessments also provide insights on the role and effectiveness of social protection measures introduced in countries to mitigate the pandemic's negative consequences.

In Indonesia, for example, it is estimated that without the government's emergency response and temporary expansion of the social protection system, COVID-19 would have increased child poverty by almost 14% (Figure 31), poverty among the working-age population by almost 17%, and among older people by 8% in 2020 in comparison to a baseline no-COVID-19 scenario.[83]

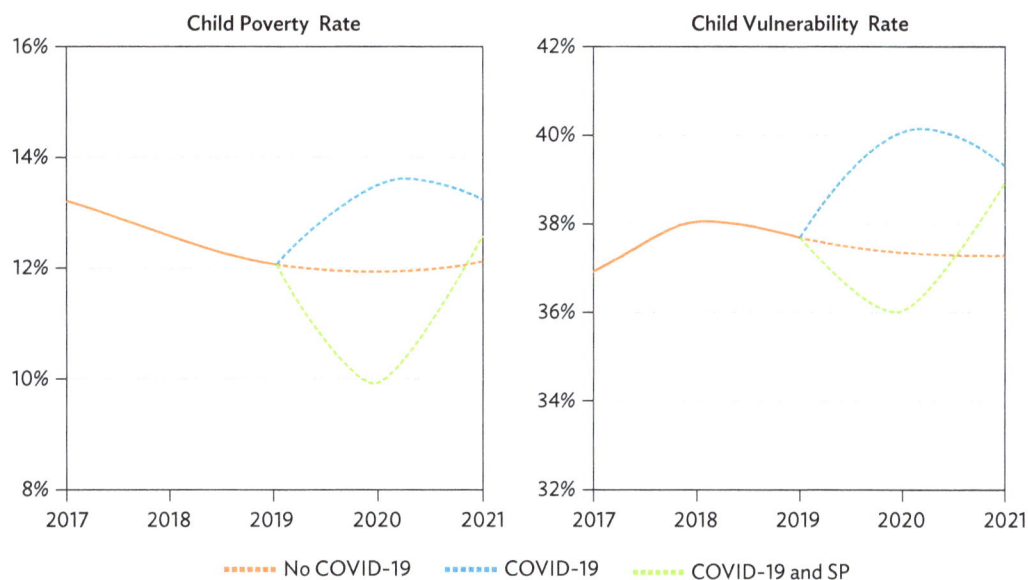

Figure 31: **Children Living below the National Poverty and Vulnerability Lines by Scenario in Indonesia (%)**

SP = social protection.

Source: Government of Indonesia, Ministry of Finance, Fiscal Policy Agency and UNICEF Indonesia. 2021. *The Impact of COVID-19 on Child Poverty and Mobility in Indonesia.* Jakarta: UNICEF Indonesia. https://www.unicef.org/indonesia/media/8456/file/The%20impact%20of%20COVID-19%20on%20child%20poverty%20and%20mobility%20in%20Indonesia.pdf.

---

[82] UNICEF. COVID-19 Impacts on Child Poverty. https://www.unicef.org/social-policy/child-poverty/covid-19-socioeconomic-impacts.

[83] Government of Indonesia, Ministry of Finance, Fiscal Policy Agency and UNICEF Indonesia. 2021. *The Impact of COVID-19 on Child Poverty and Mobility in Indonesia.* Jakarta: UNICEF Indonesia. https://www.unicef.org/indonesia/media/8456/file/The%20impact%20of%20COVID-19%20on%20child%20poverty%20and%20mobility%20in%20Indonesia.pdf.

Granted, such estimations are optimistic, assuming perfect implementation. Nevertheless, they do imply the potential that social protection measures and systems can be effective tools throughout periods of shock. They also highlight the need to improve the implementation efficiency of social protection systems in countries to benefit most from social protection's protective, preventive, and transformative functions.

While the degree of effectiveness of policies often depends on historical contexts, demographic compositions, vulnerability profiles, and capability of implementing mechanisms, the scale of its deployment through the current crisis is already testament to the role of social protection as a critical tool for governments to safeguard people against vulnerabilities and crises.

New Realities for Social Protection Systems

The pandemic has slowly but steadily altered perceptions of normality—the nature of work, structure of labor markets, even day-to-day activities. Most importantly, it has obliged nations to reevaluate the people's vulnerabilities and, consequently, the strategic approaches to social protection.

While some countries capitalized on existing social protection infrastructure to deliver an immediate pandemic response, others have continued to struggle to keep up with the devastation of the pandemic. Social protection systems in many were already facing substantial challenges before the onset of COVID-19, including low coverage, inadequacy of benefits, and limited administrative capacities. In addition to starkly reminding us of such realities, the pandemic also puts existing social protection systems to the test in terms of both shock responsiveness and effectiveness of delivery systems. With significant shares of vulnerable groups falling outside of the purview of existing social protection provisions, rapid expansion of social protection programs and more effective delivery of their services continue to be key challenges.

Most countries are and continue to be overwhelmed by the extended duration of the shock as well as economic and social repercussions that it triggered. This condition has been exacerbated by the financial strains of delivering expensive emergency support to the millions of existing and newly vulnerable populations. The unsustainability of emergency relief has also been a prime factor, leading many countries to cap their emergency support for a limited duration of time. Moreover, as countries slowly edge toward recovery and sustained development pathways, social protection systems must also evolve to support the corresponding stages of progressive development.

The pandemic has also created the idea of a new normal for the world and Asia, and new realities for social protection systems in the region. With new vulnerabilities emerging—and existing vulnerabilities and structural inequalities reinforced—the new normal may result in a much more urgent need for collective progress toward the Sustainable Development Goals (SDGs), including those on social protection and universal health coverage.

While reliable evidence on the setbacks and persistent changes induced by the pandemic may only emerge in upcoming periods, certain indications of a changing socioeconomic landscape may already be evident. As previously discussed, the pandemic has significantly accelerated progress on digital transformation in Asia. Many essential functions, like education, financial inclusion, work, social protection, and social services, are now increasingly reliant on digital delivery mechanisms. While this may help accelerate, for example, social protection delivery, it also imposes the risk of exclusion for those with limited access to digital technology and low digital literacy. Such challenges may often be particularly consequential for the most vulnerable groups in society.

The pandemic has also drastically reshaped labor markets around the world. It has altered working conditions for many, with countless businesses forced to close, while many others have been forced into remote operations. This impact on the labor market has accelerated trends in unemployment and loss of income and given rise to new workplace-related challenges.

ADB estimates indicate that unemployment rates soared by almost 10% in 2020 in many Asian countries, relative to the previous year, while in several others, it was close to 20%.[84] Countries reported staggering increases in unemployment insurance claims throughout the pandemic period,[85] while data on the informal sector impact continue to be speculative and patchy.

Furthermore, as restrictive measures were lifted and individuals returned to work, they were increasingly faced with risks of a skills shortage and competency mismatch in a post-COVID-19 labor market, particularly in low-skilled jobs. Such discrepancies will limit the equitable distribution of gains from any projected post-COVID-19 economic and social recovery, imposing additional levels of inequality for already marginalized groups, such as low-income households, women, youth, the older people and people with disabilities. Such realities also translate into added strains on social protection systems in a recovering Asia.

---

[84] ADB. 2021. *Key Indicators for Asia and the Pacific 2021*. Manila. https://www.adb.org/sites/default/files/publication/720461/ki2021.pdf.

[85] G. Petropoulos. 2021. Automation, COVID-19, and Labor Markets. *ADBI Working Papers*. No. 1229. Tokyo: ADBI.

Vaccinations have been a key factor aiding recovery around the world. Among developing states in Asia, however, progress on vaccinations remains uneven, with vaccination rates falling way behind those of more advanced economies. Countries that were able to roll out vaccinations quickly were able to limit new outbreaks, avoiding further restrictive measures. This allowed such countries to capitalize on the growing global economic demand while protecting health and jobs.[86] However, countries that were unable to procure sufficient vaccinations stand at high risk of further outbreaks and consequently prolonged durations of lockdowns and other restrictive measures. Scaling up the rollout of vaccinations is essential to ensure that the modest growth path observed in the initial half of 2021 is sustained and improved in the coming period. It will also enable individuals to safely return to work.[87]

The pandemic has also highlighted how risks cascade, for example, with respect to the growing incidence of adverse climate events in Asia against the backdrop of the pandemic. Climate change has long been identified as a high risk, capable of slowing developmental gains in countries throughout the region. Coupled with the onset of biological hazards and global pandemics, the evolving risk parameters give rise to a set of regional hotspots where the impact of systemic and cascading risks converge and become unusually severe.[88] Similarly, the Russian invasion of Ukraine and its implications on Asian countries are anticipated to impact the poor particularly, against the backdrop of an already slow recovery from COVID-19—another important example of cascading risk factors.[89]

Existing social protection systems may not be equipped to address the renewed risk profiles afflicted by COVID-19 and the array of other evolving factors in the region. Hence, unless strategic interventions are developed to help address such shortcomings, a tremendous risk exists of the pandemic's immediate effects becoming long-term structural barriers for large sections of the population in Asia, including the newly vulnerable. This trend can include reinforced intergenerational poverty and significant declines in education, health, and other development indicators.

In the wake of such realities, social protection systems must evolve to ensure an equitable and inclusive development trajectory for countries in Asia. The following section discusses a few policy lessons that can already be derived from the ongoing COVID-19 period in Asia and help develop a build back better agenda, and with it stronger, effective social protection systems.

---

[86] ADB. 2021. *Asian Development Outlook 2021 Update: Transforming Agriculture in Asia*. Manila.
[87] ADB. 2021. Surge in COVID-19 Cases Highlights Need to Ramp up Vaccinations in Asia and the Pacific. 9 August. https://www.adb.org/news/features/surge-covid-19-cases-highlights-need-ramp-vaccinations-asia-and-pacific.
[88] A. S. Alisjahbana. 2021. Resilience in a Riskier World. 21 August. UNESCAP. https://www.unescap.org/op-ed/resilience-riskier-world.
[89] ADB. 2022. *Asian Development Outlook (ADO) 2022: Mobilizing Taxes for Development*. Manila. https://www.adb.org/sites/default/files/publication/784041/ado2022.pdf.

Policy Lessons

The COVID-19 crisis serves as an important reminder of the need for inclusive, adaptive, and shock-responsive social protection. It continues to demonstrate that everyone—irrespective of vulnerability classification—is susceptible to the sudden onset of risks. It also provides an invaluable opportunity to reflect on the efficacy of social protection measures and learn associated policy lessons.

Preliminary evidence suggests that countries with comprehensive social protection systems were quickly able to leverage these existing systems to accelerate their beneficial impact for large population groups at the onset of the crisis. In contrast, countries with limited social protection provisions and systems struggled to identify and to reach newly vulnerable populations when the pandemic hit.

Similarly, as is observable from the COVID-19 emergency social protection spending patterns, the capacity to leverage and to disburse emergency financing differs significantly across the region. In comparison to high-income countries with developed social protection capabilities, the vast majority of Asia's developing countries contain a disproportionately higher share of at-risk populations. Thus, the populations most susceptible to vulnerabilities in Asia are also the least protected. This inequitable scenario may damage inclusive and sustainable development in the region, especially if prolonged shocks—such as the COVID-19 pandemic—continue and reinforce vulnerabilities in Asia.

As countries move toward transition and recovery from the pandemic, the vision for resilient and adaptive social protection needs to be strongly embedded in development plans and strategies. While for many countries in Asia this may not become an immediate reality, an increased strategic emphasis should be part of the build back better agenda.

Observations from the COVID-19 crisis period, associated emergency response, and new normal offer some important policy lessons for the way ahead in Asia. A few such lessons are discussed below.

Coverage Expansion to the "Missing Middle" and Other Vulnerable Groups

One of the realizations of the COVID-19 period is the plight of the "missing middle"—individuals who are not entitled to contributory social insurance and do not qualify for government-funded social assistance and LMPs. Developing inclusive policies to extend coverage to them is essential, considering that they constitute large shares of the informal sector workforce, youth, migrant workers, older people, women and children, and other vulnerable groups. The pandemic response in many countries in Asia have seen efforts to extend social protection support to the missing middle, albeit temporarily through the critical phases of the initial pandemic stages. Efforts to continue extending support to this population group must be sustained in the future, however, through more institutionalized measures and as part of regular social protection programming.

Sensitivity to Evolving Risks in Asia

Factors contributing to vulnerabilities in Asian countries are fast evolving, including the increased incidence of adverse climate events, biological disasters, and conflicts. As countries rebuild and repair their social protection systems, they should incorporate sensitivities to such factors. Social protection planning and strategic developments in countries should consider these varying and intersecting risk factors when planning for the way forward.

Capacity Development of Social Protection Systems

The limitations encountered by social protection systems in Asia through the critical periods of the outbreak in 2020 provide a unique opportunity to gauge leakages in respective country systems. Such limitations are often manifested in the form of limited capacity in countries to undertake emergency planning; constraints in the delivery of services, including in identification, registration, and payment processes; and restraints in data systems and human resources. The pandemic has accelerated the demand for social protection for large sections of the population in Asia. With increased demand comes the increasing pressure to deliver. Given the already strained state of social protection systems in many countries in the region and the foreseeable strains of achieving recovery, developing system capacity quickly and efficiently is a key priority. This task includes strengthening the capacity of planning mechanisms, delivery systems (e.g., identification, registration, and payment), data systems, monitoring and evaluation mechanisms, and human resources.

Developing Shock Responsiveness of National Systems

The majority of new ad-hoc measures introduced in the COVID-19 responses imply that existing programs and systems in countries lack adequate shock responsiveness and the adaptability to rapidly expand vertically and horizontally during shocks. Strengthening the shock responsiveness of systems is critical, considering the compounding patterns of social, economic, and climate risks emerging across the world and in Asia. The immediate crisis response in Asia also witnessed several innovative on-demand mechanisms to aid the expansion of social protection provisions in many countries. Asia is rich with examples of such innovations, including the deployment of technology solutions and key partnerships with other stakeholders such as nongovernment organizations (NGOs) and the private sector. Such innovative mechanisms should be considered for integration with regular social protection programming in identifying the way forward to improve the shock responsiveness of national systems.

Diversification of Social Protection Instruments

Social assistance measures formed the most prominent form of response throughout the COVID-19 period. However, social insurance and LMPs also have great potential in helping share the overall risk burden in countries in the event of future shocks. Several countries invoked innovative methods to expand social insurance coverage, such as subsidized contributions for vulnerable groups and innovative expansions of sickness and health insurance programs for informal workers and those in nonstandard employment. Such measures could be adopted as part of regular social protection programming and could provide innovative solutions for risk pooling and financing.

Similarly, the evolving state of labor market demands calls for equally evolved and compatible LMPs to facilitate employment as well as employability, especially for vulnerable groups such as youth, women, and older people. For example, the fast-paced digital transformation and evolving working conditions for many occupations induce substantial risks of skills and competency mismatches for individuals returning to the labor market. This problem may prove particularly prominent for low-skilled jobs and workers with less transferable skill sets. Measures such as skills training and retraining, job search support, and increased provisions for public works could offer much-needed support for such vulnerable workers by aiding their effective reintegration and reactivation. Such measures can also serve as important tools in rekindling the economy through the transition and recovery. An effective combination of active and passive labor market interventions should be developed to facilitate the transition to recovery, reactivation, and in anticipation of future shocks.

Capitalizing on Digital Transformation

The COVID-19 response saw some stellar examples in the use of digital systems. Digital payment systems, such as mobile money and digital wallets, on-demand registration mechanisms, national/unique identification systems, robust social registries, and interoperable databases, were all leveraged, often in haste, to facilitate the rapid expansion of social protection provisions. Moreover, countries such as Pakistan and Cambodia effectively demonstrated the advantages of investing in strong digital systems in noncrisis periods to reap benefits at times of crisis. Strengthening the digital backbone for social protection needs to be a priority area of development in countries across the region. However, there should also be a focus on ensuring that the digital transformation is equitable and inclusive.

Supplementing Social Protection with Social Services

Social services, especially care services, nutrition, education, and prevention of violence against women and children, played a critical role in many countries in delivering last-mile support for some of the most vulnerable groups, who are often difficult to reach for regular social protection provisions. Throughout the pandemic, many governments leveraged care services by fostering partnerships with key stakeholders such as NGOs, community groups, and the private sector. In the wake of evolving demand, governments need to consider leveraging this approach further in times of no crisis to establish robust support mechanisms underpinning regular social protection provision. Such initiatives can also serve as an effective pathway to raise community service-based public works in many countries, as in Indonesia.

Sustainable Financing Options

Finally, all of the above actions need to be backed by adequate and sustainable financing options to ensure effectiveness. The economic downturn caused by COVID-19 and the immediate crisis response imposed severe financial strains on governments around the world and in Asia. In addition, the transition and recovery stages of the pandemic are likely to induce new expenditures in light of the added demand for social protection and the reanimation of labor markets and supply chains. Finding sustainable financing options to ensure that social protection continues to be a priority area is essential through the transition and recovery and should be sustained for the longer development path. This effort will require governments to undertake effective fiscal space assessments, explore options for domestic resource mobilization, and facilitate, early on, adequate and effective planning, such as for shock-responsive financing options.

VII. Social Protection Data and Statistics in Asia and the Pacific

This chapter focuses on the importance of social protection data and statistics for the overall development of social protection in Asia and the Pacific. It presents the main challenges that countries and regional stakeholders face when collecting and analyzing data in the region. It considers the barriers that constrain the creation and collation of quality social protection statistics both at the regional and national levels. This chapter argues that a more coordinated effort from international organizations can facilitate the synergies required to push for more significant advances in this field.

Based on these conclusions and on the aggregator potential of the SDGs and their respective monitoring framework, this chapter proposes practical steps toward a coordinated framework for the collection of social protection data in Asia and the Pacific. As a corollary, it suggests the development of a regional flagship program for statistics in Asia and the Pacific to aggregate development partners' support to countries to develop their own data and statistics and to enhance the creation of more consistent regional statistics.

Importance of Data in Monitoring Progress in Social Protection

Despite positive recent developments and the growing consensus of the importance of social protection in Asia and the Pacific, social protection policies and programs lag, with more than half of the population without access to any form of social protection.[90] Several factors help explain this situation, including low public expenditure on social protection, the structure of the labor market and inadequacy of existing social protection systems, and the informality of economic units. To develop evidence-based solutions to address these challenges, national and regional stakeholders must be equipped with more accurate data and in-depth diagnostic tools. In this regard, upgraded monitoring and evaluation systems can play an essential role; therefore, strong national statistical systems for social protection are necessary.

The COVID-19 crisis exposed the importance of social protection and the urgent need to close gaps in existing systems. At the same time, it also emphasized the need to improve the capacity to better track and to understand the reality of social protection in each country. Indeed, the crisis bared the deficiencies of the national social protection

---

90   ILO. 2021. *ILO World Social Protection Report 2020-22: Social Protection at the Crossroads—In Pursuit of a Better Future.* Geneva.

statistical systems for policy makers, who—faced with difficult policy decisions—were not always equipped with the level and depth of information required to make the best-informed decisions. This acknowledgment comes in addition to the fact that the Agenda 2030 for Sustainable Development and the associated SDG framework created a favorable context—but also additional pressure—for countries to intensify their efforts to improve national social protection monitoring and evaluation systems, including strengthening their statistical systems.[91]

In comparison with its predecessors, such as the Millennium Development Goals, the SDG framework presents a more explicit connection to social protection, with SDG Target 1.3 aiming to "implement nationally appropriate social protection systems and measures for all, including floors, and by 2030, achieve substantial coverage of the poor and the vulnerable." In this regard, SDG Indicator 1.3.1 seeks to measure the "proportion of population covered by social protection floors/systems, by sex, distinguishing children, unemployed persons, older people, people with disabilities, pregnant women, new-borns, work-injury victims and the poor and the vulnerable."[92] Thus, the indicator measures the proportion of persons who are effectively covered by a social protection system. According to this definition, the monitoring must address the multiple dimensions of social protection systems and effective coverage; therefore, it includes the number of those who are either actively contributing to a social insurance scheme or receiving benefits from contributory or noncontributory schemes (footnote 92).

Independent of the SDG framework, monitoring and evaluation systems are key to the development of national social protection systems. They enable informed and evidence-based decision-making by those responsible for designing and implementing social protection policies and programs. According to ILO:

> Members should monitor progress in implementing social protection floors and achieving other objectives of national social security extension strategies through appropriate nationally defined mechanisms, including tripartite participation … they should regularly collect, compile, analyse and publish an appropriate range of social security data, statistics and indicators.[93]

Thus, the production of timely reliable, accurate, and comparable data through nationally defined and comprehensive mechanisms is crucial for social protection systems to achieve their goals. Well-established statistics and monitoring mechanisms help to

(i)   understand and assess the current situation by mapping the social protection system; discovering the needs and vulnerabilities that are insufficiently covered; and highlighting the gaps in social protection systems, including the efficiency and effectiveness of existing schemes and need to develop new schemes;

---

[91]   United Nations. 2015. *Transforming Our World: The 2030 Agenda for Sustainable Development.* New York. A/RES/70/1.

[92]   UNDESA. SDG Indicators Metadata Repository https://unstats.un.org/sdgs/metadata/.

[93]   ILO. 2012. *Social Protection Floors Recommendation, 2012 (No. 202).* Geneva. para. 19 and 21.

(ii)   inform policies about relevant options to fill gaps (e.g., extending coverage, increasing benefit levels, reducing system limitations, and promoting further integration);

(iii)   simulate effects and impacts, and estimate the cost of reforms of existing schemes or development of new schemes; and

(iv)   monitor regularly the extension of coverage and effects of social protection, such as poverty and inequality reduction and income maintenance in line with objectives of programs.

Robust statistical systems are also essential for planning purposes. A good example is the area of actuarial projections, which is necessary to assess social security schemes' financial situations, project their mid- and long-term developments, and provide the required evidence for effective decision-making and planning. The robustness of estimations produced by actuarial models is fully dependent on the quality of the data inputs; thus, comprehensive management and information systems are required.

Another important added value of stronger social protection statistical systems and respective data accessibility is their contribution to building up public trust in these systems. The capacity of social protection institutions to disclose and to make statistics regularly available (e.g., to demonstrate who benefits from the public resources allocated to the programs, how exactly they benefit, and how public resources are spent) is essential to promote a broader understanding and buy-in within a society and to strengthen the social contract. Inversely, the lack of robust statistical systems—including the scarcity of data on coverage gaps to determine which groups are being left behind, as well as on the financing needs associated with such coverage gaps—can put at risk the realization of the policy objectives under the 2030 Agenda for the SDGs.[94]

Overview of Data Availability

Indicators of Effective Coverage by Social Protection Program

Despite progress in recent years in monitoring effective coverage as part of the 2030 Agenda for the SDGs, significant challenges remain. The current SDG data set for the region contains estimates for overall coverage by social protection (at least one contingency) for 40 countries, older people for 39 countries, people with severe disabilities for 31 countries, mothers with newborns for 34 countries, children for 30 countries, the unemployed for 42 countries, vulnerable populations for 39 countries, and employment injuries for 33 countries. Additionally, data on affiliation with a social health protection program, as an indicator of effective coverage outside of the SDG framework, were available for 21 countries. This information shows notable progress and efforts made by many countries in data compilation and analysis.

---

[94]   United Nations. 2015. *Transforming Our World: The 2030 Agenda for Sustainable Development.* New York. A/RES/70/1.

The first category of Figure 32 focuses on the availability of data to estimate SDG Indicator 1.3.1, showing that 42% of the countries (i.e., 19 countries) have enough information available to cover most of the SDG Indicator 1.3.1 components, while the rest have medium and low data availability.

However, regarding disaggregation and monitoring over time, gaps in statistical information become more substantial. For example, less than 45% of countries (i.e., 20 countries) have recent information available for 2018-2020, while the remaining countries have outdated statistics, including 12 countries in which available indicators date from before 2015. This situation poses difficulties for effective monitoring of SDG Indicator 1.3.1 for these countries, as the SDG agenda was developed after 2015.

Figure 32: **Data Availability and Accessibility for Sustainable Development Goal Indicator 1.3.1 and Its Components**

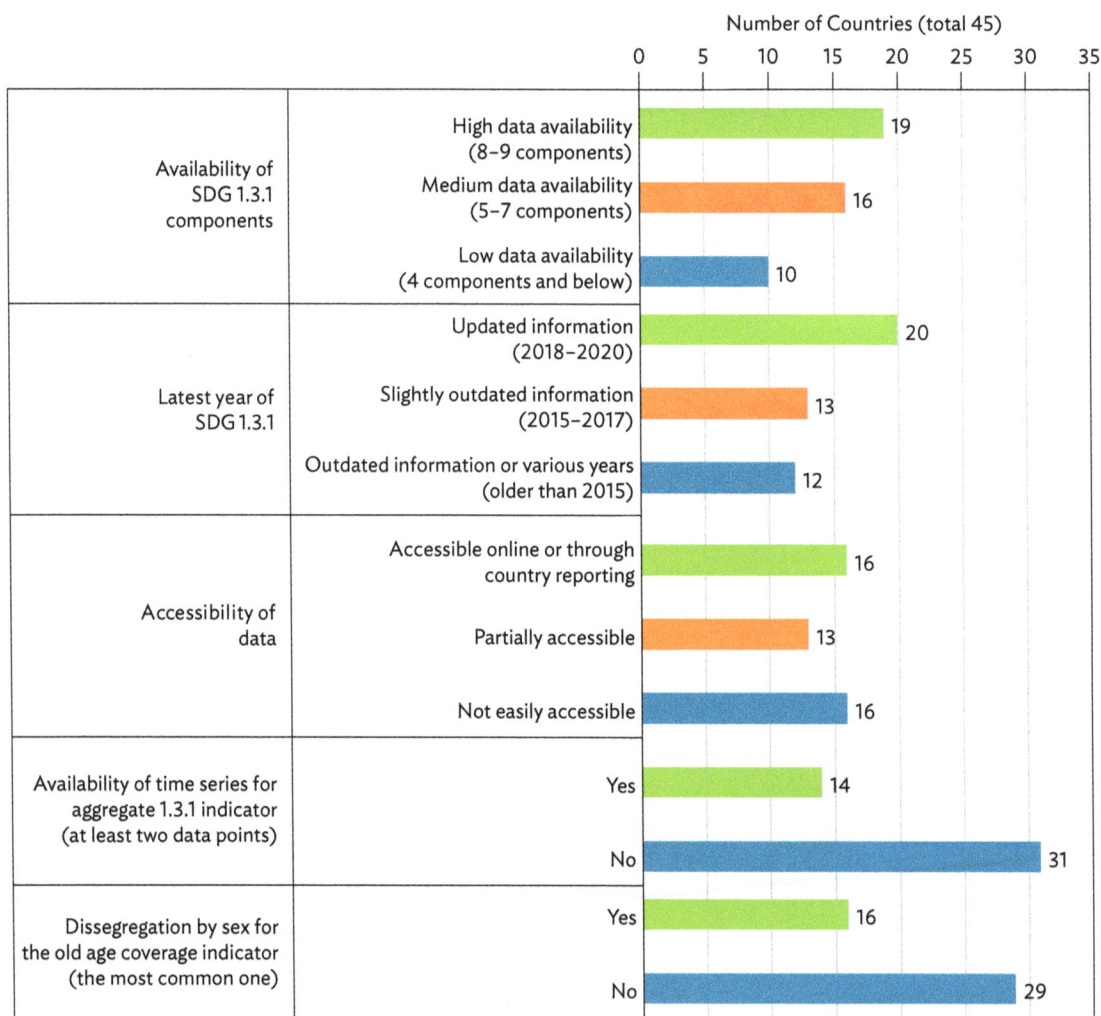

SDG = Sustainable Development Goal.

Source: ILO estimates based on data availability for the Asia and Pacific countries in ILO. World Social Protection Data Dashboards. https://www.social-protection.org/gimi/WSPDB.action?id=32 (accessed 15 January 2020).

Thirty-six percent of countries (i.e., 16 countries) share data on social protection either by reporting directly to ILO or through regular online publications. Several countries have well-organized systems of social protection statistics (e.g., the PRC and Mongolia) where all information is centralized within one organization responsible for national statistics, which ensures consistency of information in the country and easy access to available data. However, it takes significant effort to compile information from other countries.

Regarding disaggregation of data by sex, national or nonnational (e.g., provincial) status, and other classifications, information is very limited. For example, for the indicator with the highest data coverage rate—coverage by old-age benefits—disaggregation by sex is available for 16 countries only. The situation is even less adequate for other indicators and classifications.

To be able to measure progress toward SDG Target 1.3, it is crucial to analyze the situation over time; however, time series for the aggregate SDG Indicator 1.3.1 are available for less than one-third of the countries (i.e., 14 countries). The picture is more promising when looking at the indicators with a long history of data compilation, such as coverage of the unemployed by cash benefits and coverage of older people by old-age pensions, for which time series are available for 37 and 39 countries, respectively.

Tracking some of the more traditional coverage indicators (e.g., old-age benefits coverage, coverage by unemployment benefits, and children covered by cash benefits) seems straightforward, and data for these are usually available from the administrating institutions and reports. However, it is still important to consider how these data were collected and organized and to clarify their basic characteristics (e.g., definitions, concepts, methods of collection, geographic and age coverage, and reference periods) before interpreting the results.

For example, special attention should be given to the age brackets for the indicators on old-age and child benefits coverage. Definitions of a "child" or "retirement age" varies across countries in Asia and the Pacific, using different age groups depending on law. Statutory retirement age sometimes differs even between sexes in countries where women and men become eligible for a pension at different ages (i.e., in six countries). Also, within the same country, unemployment rates can be estimated by labor force surveys, or they can be assessed based on those registered in public employment services, leading to different numbers. Thus, various sources, concepts, and methodologies may lead to different outcomes in terms of indicators and data analysis.

For the purposes of SDG Indicator 1.3.1, in practice, where possible, coverage of the population of older people is estimated separately for men and women; a statistical definition of a "child" is used; and unemployment numbers from labor force surveys are taken into account.

For the coverage indicators related to health care protection, difficulty in measurements occurs when entitlements are implicit (i.e., implicit benefit packages), and there are overlapping benefits provided by different schemes (e.g., primary care financed by one institution and secondary and tertiary care by social insurance, including other supplementary arrangements). Therefore, one needs to thoroughly assess relevant legislation to identify groups covered and to avoid double counting. These issues are pertinent for estimates of both legal and effective coverage.

Furthermore, estimates of the number of persons affiliated with social health protection schemes bring about other difficulties associated with various national concepts across countries and a variation in decentralized registration procedures. An ILO report reflects this complexity, as it includes information on coverage from 30 countries and territories as well as data on effective coverage from 18 countries and territories, representing 90% of the population of the region.[95]

Furthermore, the SDG framework highlights the importance of measuring new indicators, as it created an internationally recognized methodology only in 2016. Hence, it is crucial to continue building national capacities on the indicators of the coverage of people with disabilities, vulnerable populations covered by social assistance, and population groups covered by at least one social protection cash benefit.

Special attention should also be given to the denominators comprising the number of people with disabilities and various vulnerable populations. As national legal definitions of people with disabilities vary significantly across the region, the prevalence estimates of disability rates for groups of countries published by WHO are used to ensure cross-country comparability.[96]

In 2016, ILO conducted a study on definitions of vulnerable groups, using legal instruments of various organizations; however, it concluded that there is no single definition of "vulnerability" at the international level, let alone at national levels.[97] As a result, while establishing the SDG indicators framework and methodology, the Inter-agency and Expert Group on SDG Indicators came up with a statistical definition of a vulnerable population, comprising all children, adults, and older people not covered by benefits from contributory programs.[98]

The aggregate SDG Indicator 1.3.1—measuring the number of people who are effectively covered by at least one contributory and noncontributory benefit—does not pose difficulties under this definition but, in practice, requires attention at the calculation stage. There is always a possibility for one person to be covered by and/or benefit from several social protection programs at the same time. Therefore, a clear distinction should be made between basic and supplementary benefits, population

---

95   ILO. 2021. *Extending Social Health Protection: Accelerating Progress towards Universal Health Coverage in Asia and the Pacific.* Bangkok. https://www.ilo.org/wcmsp5/groups/public/---asia/---ro-bangkok/documents/publication/wcms_831137.pdf.

96   WHO and World Bank. 2011. *World Report on Disability.* Geneva.

97   ILO. 2016 Internal Study to Propose a Definition to the Washington Group on Sustainable Development Goal Indicator 1.3.1. Unpublished.

98   United Nations. 2022. *SDG Indicator Metadata.* https://unstats.un.org/sdgs/metadata/files/Metadata-01-03-01a.pdf.

groups covered by each scheme, eligibility to receive benefits from each scheme, and other metadata required along with quantitative information. To achieve this, a thorough and detailed mapping of the national social protection system in each country is required. Several countries in the region, such as Cambodia, Pakistan, Thailand, and Viet Nam, have conducted such mapping exercises through national dialogues with the participation of relevant institutions involved in social protection.

Indicators of Expenditure on Social Protection and Level of Benefits

Data on social protection expenditures are collected and classified according to different standards in the region. Hence, there are difficulties in compiling this information by social protection scheme and benefit level. Ideally, the information on expenditure for each social protection scheme should be disaggregated by economic type (i.e., expenditure on benefits, administrative costs, and transfers to other schemes) and function (i.e., health care, disability, old-age, survivor, family/children, unemployment, and maternity) to follow indicators of effective coverage and to establish the correlation between the two, and then by type of benefit (e.g., cash/benefit in-kind, periodic, or lump sum).

To date, 41 countries have disseminated data on public social protection expenditure excluding health care, but only 14 of them have data available for 2018-2019, while the rest have older information (Figure 33). Additionally, only 25 countries have disaggregated social protection expenditure by each of the internationally accepted basic income security guarantees (i.e., expenditure on income security for children, working-age adults, and older people), and even fewer countries have more detailed information by function. The most underdeveloped information pertains to social protection expenditure on children.

Figure 33: Availability of Social Protection Expenditure by Guarantee

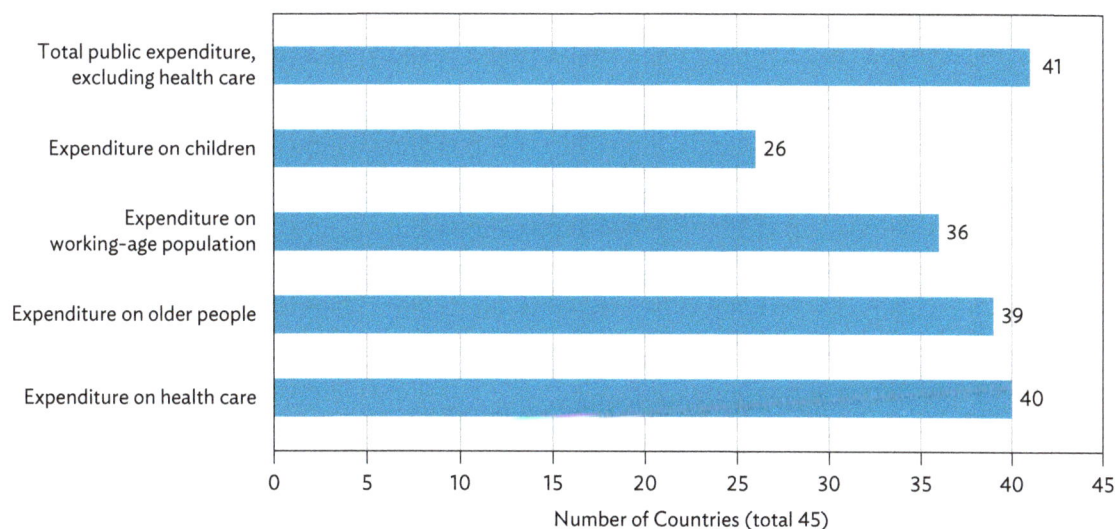

Source: ILO estimates based on data availability for the Asia and Pacific countries in ILO. World Social Protection Data Dashboards. https://www.social-protection.org/gimi/WSPDB.action?id=32 (accessed 15 January 2022).

The main national sources of data on expenditure in the region are ministries of finance, central banks, national statistical offices, and other relevant line ministries. Major international sources include ADB, ILO, IMF, World Bank, and United Nations Economic and Social Commission for Asia and the Pacific (UNESCAP). However, it should be kept in mind that data taken from various sources may differ due to definitions, coverage, and methodology. [99] In addition, general government health expenditure figures are available through the WHO database for 40 countries.[100] For the rest of the countries, it is possible to compile fragmented expenditure information on income security guarantees from various sources and years, which does not give a complete picture and does not allow progress assessment.[101]

As for indicators on benefit levels, which are essential for the assessment of benefit adequacy, a significant amount of work is done at the national level in the process of costing exercises and fiscal space analyses within evidence produced under reviews of national systems to inform national policy dialogue processes. However, despite a growing concern about the adequacy of benefits provided through the various components of different systems and their capacity to keep people out of poverty, global and regional efforts to produce estimates of the benefit adequacy are limited. There are several reasons for this, including the complexity of the subject and limited availability of required data, as many dimensions need to be taken into consideration, including benefit levels, duration of benefit payment, coherency with other benefits available, effective administration, timeliness, and sustainability.

Nevertheless, ILO regularly conducts analyses on the adequacy of noncontributory benefits in comparison with minimum wages, national poverty lines, subsistence levels, and other thresholds available at the national level as well as the assessment of the duration of these benefits and the sustainability of the programs. The assessment of contributory benefit adequacy is part of continuous work at the individual country level, as the interpretation of replacement rates, as set out in national legislation, requires careful attention with the objective of securing adequacy of benefits in the future. However, it is challenging to design a methodology to measure the adequacy of benefits that can be applicable globally.

---

[99]   For more details on the expenditure data sources, see ILO. 2019. *Fiscal Space for Social Protection: A Handbook for Assessing Financing Options*. Geneva. https://www.social-protection.org/gimi/RessourcePDF.action?id=55694.

[100] WHO. Global Health Expenditure Database. https://apps.who.int/nha/database (accessed 15 January 2022).

[101] To a certain extent, comparable data are available through the IMF Government Finance Statistics Database and through the WHO Global Health Expenditure Database on health care guarantees. Figures on social protection expenditure are usually presented both including and excluding general government expenditure on health, with a view to disaggregating cash and care benefits. However, issues regarding the inconsistencies in categorizing national data using international classification persist, along with the incomplete and fragmented information often with only a few data points, breaks in series, and limited historical figures. See IMF. Government Finance Statistics. https://data.imf.org/?sk=a0867067-d23c-4ebc-ad23-d3b015045405 (accessed 15 January 2022); and WHO. Global Health Expenditure Database. https://apps.who.int/nha/database (accessed 15 January 2022).

In terms of cash benefits, the minimum benefit levels in the ILO Social Protection Floor Recommendation can be considered adequate if and when they provide a beneficiary with the means to a life with dignity.[102] Long-term benefits can be considered adequate when they are provided in a manner that also protects against the erosion of the beneficiary's purchasing power. The ILO Social Security Minimum Convention set out minimum standards for the level of social security benefits and conditions under which they are granted.[103]

Challenges in Data Production and Compilation in the Region

Information on social protection coverage in Asia and the Pacific is mainly obtained from the administrative records of institutions managing social protection schemes. Administrative data are the primary or "traditional" source of data. Information on beneficiaries, benefits, and persons covered is indispensable for the administration, monitoring, and evaluation of programs, and it should be regularly collected and published by the institutions administering the programs.

Although there is little or no additional cost to produce data from administrative records, these data are often unexploited, as the initial use is not meant for analytical or research purposes. The use of administrative data requires thorough work before producing estimates, including mapping of the social protection schemes in the country, multiple metadata compilations (e.g., eligibility criteria, groups of population covered, and information on the design of the scheme), and identification of the possible overlaps in beneficiaries among the schemes to avoid double counting. In many countries in the region, the administrative data are of poor quality, have little or no disaggregation available, and are fragmented as they originate from different sources.

Data from household surveys are complementary to administrative data and can be used to identify existing gaps in coverage, gain information about potential beneficiaries, analyze the causes and effects of the absence of coverage, and gauge the impact of social protection in household income distribution.

Despite improvements in the past few years, very few countries include a sufficient number of appropriate questions on social protection in regular survey instruments, and even fewer countries systematically analyze and use this information if it is available. The cost of a representative household survey at the national level is high, and sample sizes are often not sufficient to enable useful data. ILO has been working with several countries in the region (e.g., Cook Islands, India, Pakistan, and Viet Nam) on the inclusion of a social protection module in regular labor force survey data collection.

The ongoing advances in databases, instruments, and processes of data collection have led to significant improvements in available data on social protection in terms of

---

[102] ILO. 2012. *Social Protection Floors Recommendation, 2012 (No. 202)*. Geneva.
[103] ILO. 1952. Minimum Requirements in ILO Social Security Standards. https://www.social-protection.org/gimi/RessourcePDF.action?id=55516.

the number of countries covered, data content, data quality, and degree of updating the information collected. Nevertheless, substantial challenges remain, including the different definitions of social protection and classifications of functions, such as adequate linkages with the overarching public financial management frameworks; fragmentation of data sources and lack of instruments to promote consolidation; lack of coordination in national monitoring and evaluation processes; partial or nonexistent disaggregation of data; and limited public availability of data.

Today, different agencies in social protection collect qualitative and quantitative information and develop indicators that are not easily comparable. While much needed, there is no consistent or systematic methodology shared by the community of practice regarding the collection of data on the provision, coverage, cost, or impact of social protection. The lack of consistent and systematic data-gathering methodology has concrete and damaging consequences both at the individual country and global levels.

At the country level, social protection schemes are administered by multiple actors and institutions responsible for its planning, financing, implementation, and governance. Coordination among institutions is often limited, without a clear ownership of processes, which creates obstacles to harmonization and integration of data. Often, this reflects the lack of comprehensive policy and legal frameworks, absence of a clear institutional setup, established coordination functions, and lack of well-defined mandates for data collection and compilation. In some cases, this problem reflects the lack of an agreed definition of what social protection entails.

Not surprisingly, data are fragmented, and the availability and quality of such data vary across countries, as well as across schemes and programs within countries. In the absence of coordination mechanisms, many countries encounter difficulties in assessing existing social protection gaps and needs, and changes over time. Coordination requires a shared methodology and agreed principles regarding data to be collected.

As mentioned earlier, without access to a minimum set of social protection data over a sustained period, countries are not able to take stock of and to identify gaps to define adequate policy options for social protection. They are even less able to monitor changes, progress, and efficiency of social protection provisions over time as well as the capacity of social protection systems to meet national policy objectives and population needs.

Thus, the need for the progressive harmonization of social protection data is evident. The process of harmonization involves developing common standards to help determine which data to collect, how to classify data, and how to categorize programs and benefits. This will ensure comparability of data and allow use for multiple purposes.

The issues at the national level are echoed at the international level. When data are not collected and aggregated at the individual country level with a clear and consistent methodology, the process of gathering internationally comparable data is difficult and often impossible.

In addition to the existing challenges at the individual country level, there have not always been agreements on the conceptual definitions and methodologies that different international and regional organizations use to collect, classify, and analyze social protection data. This means that not only are there inconsistencies in the figures presented by the different organizations, but that the efforts and resources invested to support the improvement of the social protection statistical landscape at the national level are not always consistent and therefore not as effective as they could be.

Moreover, within different social protection areas, it is especially challenging to produce comparable statistics on the coverage of people with disabilities. This is largely conditioned by the challenges facing countries in accurately defining people with disabilities, which affects the establishment of the reference population for social protection programs that are targeting people with disabilities. Due to various sociocultural, institutional, and administrative barriers, people often have little motivation to register their disability status. Disability prevalence estimates based on registered people with disabilities, therefore, can result in undercounting of the number of people with disabilities within a population. Furthermore, the diversity of methods used to capture disability status as well as the variation in people's subjective understanding of what constitutes a disability constrain international standardization of a definition.

The Way Forward: Improving Data Production and Compilation in the Region

As mentioned earlier, the consensus around SDG Target 1.3 creates an opportunity for new joint efforts by international organizations to support the development of social protection data and statistical systems in Asia and the Pacific. This section details some ideas that could guide this collaboration.

Better Coordination and Collaboration at the Country Level

Effective formal coordinating mechanisms among different actors and institutions allow countries to have a complete picture of their social protection systems, across various schemes and programs; to assess gaps and efficiency; and to track progress over time. This knowledge is crucial for adjusting the design of programs based on identified inefficiencies and for identifying new solutions and future planning.

Coordination implies the harmonization of concepts, methods, standards, and principles to guarantee data comparability and quality so that data can be used for different purposes. This is the basis for the compilation of data from multiple sources, which then allows for comprehensive analysis of social protection systems.

An important step followed by some countries was the establishment of national bodies in charge of supervising the design and implementation of social protection. In some countries, such bodies—which can assume different forms such as councils, committees, and working groups—have a clear mandate to collect data on social protection. A clear legal definition of this mandate is also a strong enabler of this function. Additionally, some countries have developed social protection monitoring and evaluation frameworks to help guide activities of different social protection stakeholders.

Technological developments can also be an enabling factor to help achieve these goals. In the past, sharing information was often—from an operational perspective—a heavy exercise. In the current technological context, however, this should no longer be a barrier. In fact, the ability to share data online without great technical complexity has the potential to facilitate harmonization and to enable definition and coordination of respective mandates and responsibilities.

Standardization of Conceptual Definitions and Methodologies

International standards are crucial to ensure the validity, consistency, accuracy, reliability, timeliness, and comparability of social protection statistics produced around the world. Conventions, recommendations, and resolutions guide countries in building statistical systems and monitoring and evaluation frameworks in an efficient, consistent manner.

An internationally adopted resolution encouraged the development of a system of social security statistics in 1952, covering the nine contingencies identified in the Social Security (Minimum Standards) Convention. It provides guidelines and definitions on the main types of data to be collected—participants (i.e., persons protected, contributors, and persons covered); beneficiaries; benefits; and expenditure and income—as well as some examples and basic principles regarding measurement issues.[104] More recently, the methodology agreed for the classification, collection, and computation of SDG Indicator 1.3.1 is based on the social protection functions specified under ILO Convention No. 102 and a resolution concerning the development of social security statistics from 1957.[105]

Closely linked with this issue, it is imperative that the definition of core data collected ensures comparability and allows for the use of the data by various organizations as well as the creation of bridges between different classifications. The scope and level of disaggregation of these data, however, currently vary widely from one organization to another, resulting in data sets that are incomplete in terms of periodicity of collection and geographic coverage.

---

[104]   ILO. 1952. Minimum Requirements in ILO Social Security Standards. https://www.social-protection.org/gimi/RessourcePDF.action?id=55516.

[105]   ILO. 2012. Social Protection Floors Recommendation, 2012 (No. 202). Geneva; and ILO. 1957. Resolution Concerning the Development of Social Security Statistics. https://www.ilo.org/global/statistics-and-databases/standards-and-guidelines/resolutions-adopted-by-international-conferences-of-labour-statisticians/WCMS_087550/lang--en/index.htm.

A set of core data should thus be defined, also allowing each organization to calculate its respective indicators according to its mandate and needs. This will be the first step toward coordination and harmonization among organizations on social protection statistics. For countries that have not yet progressed on this matter, SDG Indicator 1.3.1 reporting requirements offer a sound and objective set of indicators for initial discussion.

Reference Tools and Methodology to Collect Information

The ILO Social Security Inquiry (ILO/SSI) is the main comprehensive questionnaire used by countries to collect data on social protection as well as the main global source of administrative data on social protection.[106] The data collected—including the main characteristics of schemes and benefits, coverage, benefit levels, and revenue and expenditure—allow the tracking of social protection-related SDG targets, costing and fiscal space analyses, and other studies.

The ILO/SSI was revised to better reflect the agreed metadata for SDG Indicator 1.3.1 and is now recognized as the main methodological reference for the SDG Indicator 1.3.1 metadata. As a further development, the ILO/SSI is available online with a user-friendly interface and integrated survey and user management, enabling simultaneous collaborative work through secured access. The new version allows automatic survey management, centralized user and status management, simultaneous multiusers, and secure access to information.

The general objective of the ILO/SSI is to collect quantitative data on social security to calculate a set of indicators, which are comparable across countries, over time, and available on a regular basis. Information collected through the ILO/SSI should also assist in building national monitoring and evaluation frameworks on social protection; contribute to the establishment of a national system to track, process, and analyze social protection data; promote evidence-based policy culture in decision-making; constitute a basis for analysis within the framework of studies and research work in a country; give a comprehensive overview, and contribute to measuring progress with respect to national social protection coverage, detection of gaps, and specific vulnerable groups of the population; and contribute to monitoring social protection data and coordination of data collection, including developing national methodology on social protection data compilation and monitoring or action planning among stakeholders.

Enhanced Collaboration at the Regional Level

Despite the growing consensus around the importance of social protection data and the wide acknowledgment of existing gaps at the national level, the methods used by international and regional organizations are not always harmonized or consistent. This impedes standardization and sets an additional barrier to the enhancement of consistent and comparable social protection statistics at the regional level.

---

[106] ILO. ILO/SSI. https://qpss.ilo.org/SSI/.

Considering that most of, if not all, development partners working in the area of social protection are bound by the SDGs, the goal of supporting countries to adequately report on SDG Indicators 1.3 and 3.8 could bring development partners together to support the enhancement of regional, and consequently national, statistics on social protection. In this regard, a regional interagency group could be established to agree on a core set of data, which should consider each organization's data needs in calculating its respective indicators and reflect their respective mandates. This could be the first important step toward coordination and harmonization among organizations on social protection statistics.

This group could engage in a discussion on data collection tools. The fact that countries receive different requests to fill in different surveys and questionnaires constitutes an additional burden for countries, particularly for those with limited technical resources. The agreement on a set of appropriate data collection tools could be a step toward streamlining the process and avoiding the duplication of national-level activities and efforts to collect data. A collective road map could be agreed, defining joint targets and key timing for data collection.

This agreement could result in closer collaboration at the individual country level and to a clearer division of labor among agencies depending on their respective areas of strength. It would also introduce certain standards in the area of social protection statistics to be applied by organizations and in countries. Some principles would be defined progressively, as the minimum core set of social protection data grows. Qualitative and contextual information (including wider issues such as demographic and labor market structures that help interpret results and indicators) will be collected and published along with the quantitative information.

An example of a potential collaboration is the current parallel exercise conducted by ILO to collect data for its World Social Protection Database and the ADB data collection process to produce the SPI. Despite a dialogue and joint effort between the two organizations, these two exercises are still being conducted separately. A preliminary exchange of data has allowed the identification of some differences in relation to each organization's approach, and it did not show significant methodological differences between the two studies.

Improvement of Knowledge Sharing and Capacity Building

The inconsistency between the work of organizations at the regional level and their respective tools do not favor the process of collecting and compiling data. It is also important to acknowledge that the problem with regional data does not start with the process of data collection and compilation by international organizations. As mentioned earlier, the root causes of the problem lie at the core of the national statistical production. Despite good intentions, a harmonization effort at the regional level is hardly sufficient to address the challenges in the production of regional social protection data that remain at the national level.

Therefore, any effort made at the regional level should also be accompanied by support provided at the individual country level. In this regard, a set of definitions and instruments agreed by different organizations at the regional level could offer a strong foundation to jointly support countries in the development of their own statistical definitions and data collection instruments, if possible, in alignment with regional (and global) instruments.

Considering the challenge faced, bringing the resources of various partners under one joint effort could be relevant to increase the effectiveness of each resource and initiative, whether in terms of technical assistance or through the provision of training services. For instance, the development of a single joint training package, which could be implemented by different organizations to support countries to build their national statistical capacities, could also be instrumental in raising regional capacity toward social protection statistics.

One option is to create a regional flagship program to improve social protection statistics in Asia and the Pacific, aiming to bring the various agencies within a comprehensive operational framework. The program would not necessarily imply immediate pooling of funding from different agencies. Indeed, to be open to the participation of different organizations with their own specific mandates and rules, the program could allow the use of different funding methods (e.g., parallel funding, pass-through, and other mechanisms) to promote the pooling of funds. The program could also work as a tool to mobilize additional resources for the common goal of improving social protection statistics.

An exercise of this nature would require a comprehensive assessment of the social protection data situation in regional terms. This would allow gaps to be identified, and a plan to be defined toward the gradual elimination of those gaps. It can be developed gradually, starting with an agreement on a shared set of objectives and targets, moving to the creation of a working group of partners with shared interests. The global agreements around SDG Indicator 1.3.1 and respective metadata could offer a common basis for this work.

VIII. Addressing Disability through Social Protection in Asia

This chapter provides an overview of disability-inclusive social protection before elaborating on the results of the SPI disaggregation for disability expenditures presented in Chapter V. Further case studies of innovations in social protection for people with disabilities in Asia are provided throughout the chapter as well.

Introduction

For the first time, the SPI study gathered data on people with disabilities benefiting from social protection policy measures and programs. It calculated the proportion of social protection expenditure that was reaching people with disabilities. This initiative follows commitments made by ADB in 2018 at the first Global Disability Summit—cohosted by the Department for International Development of the United Kingdom, the Government of Kenya, and the International Disability Alliance—which, in turn, reflects the commitments made to address poverty and to reduce inequalities outlined in ADB's Strategy 2030.[107]

Global and regional development priorities in Asia focus on achieving the SDGs by 2030. As previously mentioned, the SDGs emphasize "leav[ing] no one behind" and refer to people with disabilities in various targets.[108] The SDGs require the disaggregation of key indicators for disability so that existing inequities are revealed, and actions are triggered to address them. The SPI disaggregation for disability status presented in Chapter V and elaborated further in this chapter hope to contribute to this work.

ADB has noted that people with disabilities in the Asia and Pacific region are among the poorest; lack access to education, social protection, health and care services, employment, and livelihood opportunities. They also face barriers in the built environment, transport and communications, and in accessing information and assistive technology.[109]

---

107 ADB. 2018. *Strategy 2030: Achieving a Prosperous, Inclusive, Resilient, and Sustainable Asia and the Pacific.* Manila.
108 The SDGs are universal and apply to all people equally. People with disabilities are explicitly mentioned 11 times in the 2030 Agenda for Sustainable Development and especially in relation to SDG 4 on education; 8 on employment; 10 on economic, social, and political inclusion; 11 on accessible cities, water, and transport; as well as 17 on data and monitoring. See United Nations. 2015. *Transforming Our World: The 2030 Agenda for Sustainable Development.* New York. A/RES/70/1.
109 ADB. 2022. *Strengthening Disability-Inclusive Development: 2021-2025 Road Map.* Manila.

Indeed, poverty and disability are widely recognized as being interrelated. Poor people are more likely to acquire disabilities because of conditions in which they live.[110] Disability is likely to make people poorer because of discrimination and inequality of access.[111]

Disability prevalence increases with age, as functioning changes and reduces. In many countries in the region, more than half of all people with disabilities are older than 60. The population of older people in the region will reach almost 1.3 billion people by 2050, tripling in size since 2010.[112] In some countries, such as the PRC, Sri Lanka, Thailand, and Viet Nam, this transition will happen very rapidly. As a result, Asia's population is on track in the next few decades to become one of the oldest in the world, and, relatedly, to have a larger percentage of people with disabilities than other parts of the world.

Governments are generally poorly prepared for this demographic transition, which will have wide social and economic consequences. Indeed, this is already evident in the low levels of social protection coverage in the region, where only 28%-30% of people with disabilities are benefiting from social protection measures, such as government-funded health care, and only 21.6% of people with severe disabilities are covered by disability benefits.[113] When only countries of the Asia and Pacific region are considered (i.e., without Central Asian countries, Armenia, Azerbaijan, and Georgia), only 9.4% of people with severe disabilities are covered by disability benefits.[114]

The data gathered for the SPI study can help discern the level of social protection expenditure in relation to people with disabilities in Asia. This effort can also help provide insights into the challenges that need to be addressed in social protection systems to prepare for the future realities of a larger proportion of people with disabilities in the region.

Challenges in Disability-Inclusive Social Protection

In keeping with CRPD, Article 28 on the right of people with disabilities to an adequate standard of living and social protection, disability-inclusive social protection means ensuring access to both general (or mainstream) social protection programs

[110] GSDRC. 2015. *Disability Inclusion*. Birmingham.
[111] UNESCAP. 2017. *Building Disability-Inclusive Societies in Asia and the Pacific: Assessing Progress of the Incheon Strategy*. Bangkok. https://www.unescap.org/publications/building-disability%E2%80%91inclusive-societies-asia-and-pacific-assessing-progress-incheon#.
[112] UNFPA Asia-Pacific Regional Office. 2020. *Addressing Population Ageing in Asia and the Pacific Region: A Life-Cycle Approach*. Bangkok. https://asiapacific.unfpa.org/sites/default/files/pub-pdf/210927_unfpa_a_life_cycle_approach_layout.pdf.
[113] ILO. World Social Protection Data Dashboards. https://www.social-protection.org/gimi/WSPDB.action?id=19 (accessed 21 September 2021).
[114] OHCHR. 2020. *Policy Guidelines for Inclusive Sustainable Development Goals: No Poverty*. Geneva.

that aim to reduce poverty or provide adequate income in old age as well as to disability-targeted (or disability-specific) programs where being recognized as having a disability is the main criterion for accessing the program. Disability-targeted programs can include both contributory and noncontributory cash benefits or pensions; other services; and support such as personal assistance, assistive devices and technology, and caregiver allowances.

The added costs of disability can also cause significant inequities; social protection programs that take these costs into account are better able to lift people with disabilities out of poverty (footnote 114). In 2018, the United Nations Department of Economic and Social Affairs compiled estimates of the additional costs of disability. It showed that these extra costs associated with "any disability" as a percentage of average income ranged from 8% to 43%. In Australia, for example, the extra costs of a moderate disability are 30% of an average income; for a "severe disability," these are 40% of an average income.[115] Note that many poverty-targeted social protection programs do not take into account the additional costs of a disability when calculating eligibility for these programs; indeed, people with disabilities are often excluded, although they face higher risks of living below established poverty thresholds due to the added costs.

Other common barriers to accessing social protection programs for people with disabilities can include constrained physical access to offices and to service providers where benefits are administered; lack of information about programs and application requirements; and stigma and discrimination by social assistance personnel. Many people with disabilities—especially those who were born with disabilities—have little or no education, and their literacy levels can be low compared with those of people without disabilities. Thus, they may have difficulty navigating complex application procedures or compliance conditions.[116] People with disabilities often have lower access to financial and banking services, mobile phones, and other important instruments of distributing social assistance as part of social protection programs as well.[117]

Providing information in accessible formats, ensuring eligibility criteria do not exclude people with disabilities, guaranteeing physically accessible administration offices for benefits, and creating inclusive data management systems and accessible payment methods can all contribute to facilitating the access of people with disabilities to social protection programs (Box 13).

---

[115] UNDESA. 2019. *Disability and Development Report.* New York. pp. 37-38.
[116] UNESCAP. 2021. *How to Design Disability-Inclusive Social Protection.* Bangkok.
[117] V. Barca, M. Hebber, and A. Côte. 2021. *SPACE Inclusive Information Systems for Social Protection: Intentionally Integrating Gender and Disability.* Washington, DC: Georgetown Institute for Women, Peace and Security.

Box 13: **Disability Cards in Thailand**

Disability registration in Thailand gives a disability card to people with disabilities, which enables them to access welfare benefits and government support under the People with Disabilities Empowerment Act (2007), such as medical services, educational opportunities, employment promotion measures, assistive devices, various accommodations, and a universal monthly disability allowance for life.

In 2017, 3.08% of the population registered as having a disability. This represented 56.00% of people with disabilities (if the prevalence rate is 5.50%, as per a 2017 National Statistics Office survey). This percentage represented a much higher coverage rate of people with disabilities than the regional average of 21.60% cited by the International Labour Organization (ILO) or 9.40% for the Asia and Pacific region (without Central Asia or Eastern Europe) cited by the Office of the United Nations High Commission for Human Rights (OHCHR).

Sources: NSO. 2017. *The 2017 Disability Survey*. Bangkok; ILO. 2021. *World Social Protection Report 2020-22*. Geneva. p. 146; and OHCHR. 2020. *Policy Guidelines for Inclusive Sustainable Development Goals: No Poverty*. Geneva. p. 8.

The goals of disability-targeted programs depend on the political and social context in a given country. In many, support for people with disabilities is closely associated with compensation for not being able to work. In this context, disability assessments are linked to the assessment of one's capacity to work. In others, support for enabling daily functioning and maximizing the ability to live independently drive the design of disability-targeted programs. In Viet Nam, for example, eligibility is based on assessing the level of support needed to undertake daily functions such as washing, dressing, and eating.[118]

In Thailand, the universal noncontributory disability allowance is designed to compensate for the additional costs of disability; however, it is not means-tested, so it cannot be taken away when people with disabilities become employed or when they reach pension age.[119] Yet in some countries, the entry into employment of people with disabilities is disincentivized, as disability-specific benefits are means-tested and can be taken away if income increases.

Social services and independent living services are an integral part of a disability-inclusive social protection system and maximize the inclusion of people with disabilities in mainstream services, including education, employment, and social participation. Figure 34 illustrates how access to mainstream cash benefits as well as disability-targeted benefits and social services—including assistive devices and rehabilitation services—provide the building blocks for social protection for people with disabilities.

---

[118] UNESCAP. 2021. *How to Design Disability-Inclusive Social Protection*. Bangkok.
[119] ADB. 2022. *Thailand: Social Protection Indicator*. Manila.

Figure 34: Building Blocks of Social Protection for People with Disabilities

INCOME SECURITY: minimum income from old-age pension, disability pension, or mainstream guaranteed minimum income program

COVERAGE OF DISABILITY-RELATED COSTS, INCLUDING SUPPORT SERVICES and access to the required support

DISABILITY/INCLUSION SUPPORT ALLOWANCE
Concessions (e.g., tax exemption, discounts, free transport cards)

Assistive devices, habilitation, and rehabilitation

Effective access to health care, early childhood development, education, vocational training, employment, and livelihoods

Community care and support services (family and parental support, personal assistance, long-term care, home visits)

Source: C. Knox-Vydmanov, A. Côte, F. Juergens, and D. Hiscock. 2021. Social Protection for Older People with Disabilities. Draft. https://socialprotection.org/sites/default/files/publications_files/Social%20protection%20and%20older%20persons%20with%20disabilities_For%20consultation_10%2024_.pdf.

Developing Social Protection for People with Disabilities

Defining the population of people with disabilities—and therefore defining the reference population for social protection programs that are targeting people with disabilities—is challenging in all countries in Asia. Stigma, discrimination, and complex assessment procedures or other barriers may mean that people are not motivated to register as people with disabilities. Thus, disability prevalence estimates based on registered people with disabilities can significantly undercount the number of people with disabilities in a population.

At the time of writing, all but one country in the Asia region—Timor-Leste—have either signed or ratified the CRPD.[120] This means that definitions of disability in national legislation have become increasingly aligned with the CRPD definition: "People with disabilities include those who have long-term physical, mental, intellectual or sensory impairments which in interaction with various barriers may hinder their full and effective participation in society on an equal basis with others."[121]

Identifying people with disabilities, nevertheless, remains challenging, and data that are comparable across countries are still limited. This is largely because methods vary,

---

[120]   Uzbekistan ratified it in June 2021, and Bhutan and Tajikistan have both signed but not yet ratified it.
[121]   United Nations. 2007. *Convention on the Rights of Persons with Disabilities*. New York. p. 4.

and disability is always understood in relation to perceptions of "normal functioning," and is therefore influenced by contextual factors such as age, sex, and even income group.[122] Older people may not think of themselves as having a disability, although they experience considerable difficulties in functioning because they perceive these challenges as normal for their age. Similarly, parents or caregivers who answer questions about their children may not accurately report their difficulties in functioning either because of stigma and fear of admitting difficulties, or due to differing perceptions of what is considered normal functioning at different stages of development. Furthermore, the way that questions are asked (e.g., face-to-face or by questionnaires) and the kind of questions that are asked (e.g., focused on impairments, "disability," or difficulties in functioning) can also influence the resulting disability prevalence rates.

Since the CRPD was introduced in 2006, several initiatives have been underway to address these challenges, resulting in the development of the WHO Disability Assessment Schedule 2.0 (WHO DAS 2) and Washington Group questions (WGQs).[123] The SDGs, with their focus on leaving no one behind and including SDG Target 1.3 to implement social protection systems for all, have also driven greater attention to disability-disaggregated data and statistics. SDG Indicator 1.3.1 tracks the proportion of the population covered by social protection systems disaggregated for sex, people with disabilities, children, and older people.[124]

The 2011 World Report on Disability used two global studies published in 2004—the World Health Survey (WHS) and Global Burden of Disease (GBD)—to estimate the often-quoted disability prevalence rate of 10%-15% of the world's adult population.[125] These studies, however, used different methods for determining disability.

The WHS collected data over 2 years, from 2002 to 2004, and used a methodology that allowed comparison across 59 countries representing 64% of the global adult population aged over 18 and over. The survey method was based on the International Classification of Functioning, which helped inform the rights-based model of disability reflected in the CRPD and used an approach focused on difficulties in functioning that has proven most reliable when asking questions about disabilities in surveys. The five possible responses to the questions on functioning were "no difficulty," "mild difficulty," "moderate difficulty," "severe difficulty," and "extreme difficulty." These were given scores ranging from 0—meaning "no disability"—to 100—for "complete disability." The WHS chose a threshold of 40 to denote people experiencing significant difficulties in their everyday lives, and a threshold of 50 for people experiencing very significant difficulties. Using these thresholds, the disability prevalence rates were 11.8% for people experiencing significant difficulties and 2.2% for people experiencing very significant difficulties. The WHS noted a higher prevalence of disability among the poorest wealth quintile, older people, and women (footnote 125, pp. 25-28). The WHS did not provide estimates on the prevalence of disability among children.

[122]   WHO and World Bank. 2011. *World Report on Disability*. Geneva.
[123]   WHO. 2012. *Measuring Health and Disability: Manual for WHO Disability Assessment Schedule (WHODAS 2.0)*. Geneva; and Washington Group on Disability Statistics. WG Short Set on Functioning (WG-SS). https://www.washingtongroup-disability.com/question-sets/wg-short-set-on-functioning-wg-ss/.
[124]   Global Change Data Lab. SDG-Tracker. https://sdg-tracker.org/no-poverty.
[125]   WHO and World Bank. 2011. *World Report on Disability*. Geneva.

The 2004 GBD updated the 1990 GBD by using the prevalence of diseases and injuries, their impact on functioning, and then their severity to discern the prevalence of disability in the general population. It used seven classes of functioning, ranging from I to VII, of which classes VI and VII denoted "severe disability," which is the equivalent of the disability inferred for conditions such as quadriplegia or blindness. This approach generated estimates that in 2004, 15.3% of the world's population, including children, experienced "moderate or severe disability," and 2.9% experienced "severe disability." Among children ages 0-14, this method produced estimates of 5.1% having a "moderate or severe disability," and 0.7% having "severe disability;" among those ages 15 and older, the estimates were 19.4% having a "moderate or severe disability," and 3.8% having a "severe disability."

The World Disability Report acknowledged that although the GBD estimates are reliable to some extent because of the consistency and comparability of the prevalence of specific diseases across populations in different countries, they are not entirely robust, as "it is not appropriate to infer the overall picture of disability from health conditions and impairments alone" (footnote 125, pp. 28-30). The GBD provided prevalence estimates for groups of countries clustered in different regions, and these regional prevalence rates were still used in 2021 by ILO and WHO when estimating disability prevalence rates (e.g., to calculate the coverage of people with severe disabilities by social protection programs and measures) (footnote 125, p. 20).

Using these two different methods of estimating disability prevalence, the WHS gives prevalence among adults with "very significant difficulties" in everyday functioning (i.e., a threshold score of 50 or more) of 2.2%, and "significant difficulties" (i.e., a threshold score of 40 or more) of 15.6%. The GBD indicates 3.8% for "severe disability" for the population ages 15 and above, and 15.3% for "moderate disability." The global disability prevalence estimation of 15.0% of the population, including children, is based on these two different methods of estimating disability prevalence in 2004 and using the world's population in 2010.

The GBD and WHS both indicate a much higher prevalence of disability among people ages 60 and over, since functional impairments increase with age, and they identify overall higher rates in the WHO Southeast Asia region compared with the world (Table 7). Both the WHS and GBD find a higher prevalence in lower-income countries than high-income countries.

The WGQs, based on functioning across different domains, are designed to address the challenges of estimating the population of people with disabilities in censuses or other surveys and have been increasingly used in the SPI countries for estimating disability prevalence.[126] The WGQs and WHO DAS 2 are designed for use when asking questions to and about adults.

---

[126] The Washington Group Short Set on Functioning asks if a person has "no difficulty," "some difficulty," "a lot of difficulty," or "cannot do at all" in six domains of functioning: vision, hearing, mobility, cognition (i.e., remembering and concentrating), self-care, and communicating (i.e., understanding and being understood). The Washington Group on Disability Statistics. WG Short Set on Functioning (WG-SS). https://www.washingtongroup-disability.com/question-sets/wg-short-set-on-functioning-wg-ss/.

Table 7: Disability Prevalence Rates among People Aged 60 and Over (%)

	Severe Disability Prevalence	Moderate and Severe Disability Prevalence
Global Burden of Disease		
Southeast Asia	12.6	58.8
World	10.2	46.6
High-income countries	8.5	36.8
World Health Survey		
World	7.4	38.1
Low-income countries	9.1	43.4
High-income countries	4.4	29.5

Source: WHO and World Bank. 2011. *World Report on Disability*. Geneva.

To address the challenges of asking questions about children, UNICEF and the Washington Group collaborated to develop the child functioning module for the UNICEF Multiple Indicator Cluster Surveys that are conducted periodically in many developing countries in Asia.[127] Reliable data on children with disabilities are generally challenging to collect, as parents and caregivers may hide their child's impairments during surveys. In addition, they may underestimate or overestimate their child's level of functioning when compared with other children.

Social Protection Indicator Measures for People with Disabilities

The SPI uses official government sources to identify the population of people with disabilities that should be covered by social protection measures. Sources of data include censuses and household surveys conducted by national statistics offices, administrative data from social protection information systems (and in some cases, from education or health management information systems), and disability-focused surveys or research. Table 8 sets out the disability prevalence rates reported by national consultants as well as their sources and, where known, the methods used for determining the rates. The prevalence rates are taken to apply to the entire population of a country, although some surveys cited refer only to the adult population (i.e., ages 18 and over) and others refer only to those who are ages 15 and over. The crude prevalence rates cannot be applied therefore to children or to the population ages 60 and over.

In some countries, there are multiple sources for disability-prevalence data. In Pakistan, for example, the government uses a 1998 census prevalence rate of 2.54% as the official rate on the number of people with disabilities, presumably deeming this rate more reliable than the rate from the 2017 census, which is very low at 0.48%. The National Institute of Population Studies, an official government agency,

---

[127] UNICEF. Module on Child Functioning: Questionnaires. https://data.unicef.org/resources/module-child-functioning/.

Table 8: Disability Prevalence Rates Used to Calculate the Social Protection Indicator

Country	Prevalence Rate (% of people with disabilities)	Source	Comments
Afghanistan	4.2	Afghanistan Living Conditions Survey 2016-17	Used WGQs
Armenia	6.3	Statistical Committee	Those registered with disabilities
Azerbaijan	6.4	State Statistical Committee	Disability benefits recipients
Bangladesh	6.9	Household Income and Expenditure Survey 2016-2017	Used WGQs
Bhutan	2.1	Population and Housing Census, 2017	Used WGQs
Cambodia	4.0	Cambodian Socio-Economic Survey, 2014	Used WGQs
China, People's Republic of	6.3	National Sample Survey of People with Disabilities, 2006	Medical standards used to measure visual, hearing, speech, physical, intellectual, mental, and multiple disabilities
Georgia	3.3	Social Service Agency	Those registered with disabilities
Indonesia	2.8	National Socio-Economic Survey (SUSENAS) 2018	Used WGQs
Japan	7.5	Ministry of Health, Labour and Welfare	Those registered with disabilities
Kazakhstan	3.7	Data presented in the National Plan to Ensure the Rights and Improve the Quality of Life of People with Disabilities in the Republic of Kazakhstan until 2025	Those registered with disabilities
Korea, Republic of	5.0	Ministry of Health and Welfare	Status of those registered with disabilities
Kyrgyz Republic	2.9	Ministry of Labor, Social Welfare, and Migration	Those registered with disabilities
Lao People's Democratic Republic	2.1	Lao Expenditure and Consumption Survey V, 2012-2013	
Malaysia	7.4	National Health and Morbidity Survey 2015	Used WGQs
Maldives	9.0	Bureau of Statistics	Used WGQs
Mongolia	4.0	Household Socio-Economic Survey 2018	Used WGQs
Nepal	2.1	2011 Census	Asked about disability and type
Pakistan	5.6	2017-18 Pakistan Demographic and Health Survey and population data for 2018	Used WGQs
Philippines	12.0	National Disability Prevalence Survey, 2016	Used a method based on the WHO Model Disability Survey
Singapore	6.2	Third Enabling Master Plan 2017-2021	
Sri Lanka	7.2	Census of Population and Housing, 2012	Used WGQs
Tajikistan	1.6	Agency of Social Insurance and Agency on Statistics	Registered recipients of disability benefits
Thailand	3.1	Ministry of Social Development and Human Security	Registered with disabilities following medical and social assessment

continued on next page

Table 8: *continued*

Country	Prevalence Rate (% of people with disabilities)	Source	Comments
Uzbekistan	2.2	Ministry of Health	Administrative data
Viet Nam	7.0	National Survey on People with Disabilities 2016	Used WGQs extended set
Average	5.0	12 countries used WGQs or WHO Model Disability Survey	
		10 countries used administrative data	
		2 countries used other ways of asking about disability in surveys	
		2 countries provided no information in reports on how rates were calculated	

WGQs = Washington Group questions, WHO = World Health Organization.

Source: Authors.

used WGQs in the 2017-2018 Demographic and Health Survey and found a rate of 6.2% among the whole population. The prevalence answers of "a lot of difficulty" and "cannot do at all" among children under age 14 recorded a rate of 2.0%, among working-age adults 5.0%, and 32.0% among people aged over 60.[128] The SPI uses an overall prevalence rate of 5.6%, which is derived by applying these age-disaggregated prevalence rates to the population for 2018.

In the PRC, a 2006 survey gave a disability prevalence rate of 6.34%, which indicates that there are 88.47 million people with disabilities if applied to the population in 2018.[129] The SPI uses this rate in the calculation of the reference population for the PRC. The Statistical Yearbook on Work with People with Disabilities for 2018 indicated that 35.66 million people are in the disability registration system, which is 2.6% of the population.[130] If the breakdown by age of the people registered with disabilities is applied to the overall 6.3% prevalence rate, then the prevalence rate for each age group can be estimated.

A disability-focused survey in Thailand using the WGQs found an overall prevalence rate of 5.5%, while 3.0% of the population registered for disability cards.[131] The SPI calculation uses the lower estimate.

A household income and expenditure survey conducted by the Maldives Bureau of Statistics in 2019 used the WGQs and calculated the disability prevalence rate at 9% for people who have "a lot of difficulty" or "cannot do at all" in at least one domain of functioning.[132] The SPI calculation uses this rate, although only 2% of the population were registered for disability allowances in 2018.[133] The Lao Population and Housing

---

[128] NIPS and ICF. 2019. *Pakistan Demographic and Health Survey 2017-18.* Islamabad and Rockville, MD: NIPS and ICF.

[129] ADB. 2022. *People's Republic of China: Social Protection Indicator.* Manila.

[130] National Bureau of Statistics of China. 2019. *Statistical Yearbook on Work with People with Disabilities 2018.* Beijing.

[131] NSO. 2017. *The 2017 Disability Survey.* Bangkok.

[132] Maldives Bureau of Statistics. 2019. *Household Income and Expenditure Survey 2019.* Malé.

[133] Maldives Bureau of Statistics. 2019. *Demographic Characteristics by Disability.* Malé.

Census 2015 used WGQs and found 2.77% of people have a disability, including people who reported "some difficulty" in at least one domain of functioning.[134]

Table 8 confirms that almost half of the countries participating in the SPI used WGQs in census and household surveys. While this indicates that statistics are improving, this has not yet translated into their use in designing social protection programs. If social protection systems continue to reach only those who find their way into the necessary physical office, undergo the required disability assessment, and apply successfully for disability allowances and services, then coverage will continue to be low and prevalence estimates relying on administrative data will continue to be underestimates.

Lower prevalence rates among children and higher prevalence rates among people ages 60 and over reported in SPI studies are consistent with global and regional estimates from the GBD and WHS (Table 9 and Figure 35). Significant variations among prevalence rates in different countries for the same age groups (e.g., around 33.0% of older people are those with disabilities in Pakistan and Sri Lanka, compared with 5.3% in the PRC and 2.1% in Georgia) can be accounted for by differing methods and questions used in surveys, varying cultural norms and perceptions of

Table 9: Prevalence Rates among Different Age Groups (%)

Country	Ages 0-14	Ages 15-59	Ages 60 and Above	Whole Population
Afghanistan	2.3	6.3	1.8	4.2
Bangladesh	2.9	6.7	23.6	6.9
Bhutan	0.4	1.3	13.3	2.1
China, People's Republic of	0.4	2.2	5.3	6.3
Georgia	1.1	4.5	2.1	3.3
Japan	4.0	5.6	11.6	7.5
Kazakhstan	1.6	3.9	7.9	3.7
Korea, Republic of	0.8	3.2	12.5	5.0
Malaysia	2.1	7.4	20.3	7.4
Maldives	10.6	17.5	24.7	9.0
Mongolia	1.0	4.6	12.1	4.0
Pakistan	2.0	5.0	31.5	5.6
Singapore	3.4	3.4	17.1	6.2
Sri Lanka	1.1	4.8	33.1	7.2
Thailand	0.7	2.0	11.7	3.1
Uzbekistan	1.1	2.1	7.8	2.2
Viet Nam	2.5	3.4	30.1	7.0

Note: Rates for the People's Republic of China are calculated from two sources: people with disabilities as the percentage of population based on a total prevalence of 6.34% from a 2006 survey, and the age ratios from the administrative data of people registered with disabilities reported in the Statistical Year Book 2019.

Source: ADB estimates, 2018, based on consultants' reports.

---

[134] Lao Statistics Bureau and UNFPA. 2020. *Disability Monograph of the Lao PDR*. Vientiane.

Figure 35: Prevalence of Disability by Age for Selected Countries

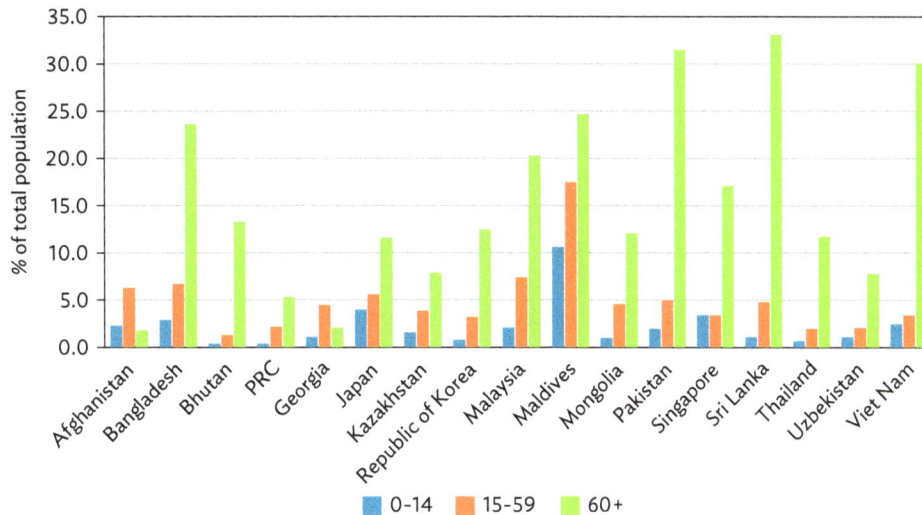

PRC = People's Republic of China.

Source: ADB estimates based on consultants' reports.

disability in distinctive contexts, as well as variable thresholds for defining disability in administrative data sets. Moreover, there are higher proportions of people in even older age ranges—such as over the age of 75 or 85—in some countries, allowing for higher disability prevalence rates.

Disability prevalence data are generally considered more reliable when WGQs and the UNICEF child functioning module are used in general population surveys or censuses and then followed up by a disability-focused survey to verify the results. A useful next step is to include WGQs in social registries and then to follow up with a disability assessment for the provision of benefits and services. These approaches require investment of resources but can provide more accurate data to support planning of services and social protection programs than only censuses or household surveys using WGQs alone, as these can only be used for screening and generating statistical estimates. The needs of people with disabilities change throughout the life cycle and cut across government sectors such as education, health, social protection, housing, employment, transport, and civic participation.

Early intervention and early childhood development can impact positively on education and employment outcomes for people with disabilities.[135] Adolescents with disabilities are significantly more likely than their peers without disabilities to not complete primary or secondary education. In Cambodia, for example,

---

135 WHO and UNICEF. 2012. *Early Childhood Development and Disability: A Discussion Paper*. Geneva: WHO; WHO, World Bank, and UNICEF. Nurturing Care for Early Childhood Development. https://nurturing-care. org/; and CBM. 2016. *Inclusion Counts: The Economic Case for Disability Inclusive Development*. Bensheim, Germany. p. 60.

only 4% of adolescents with disabilities complete secondary education, compared with 41% of adolescents without disabilities.[136] In Viet Nam, at the upper secondary level, only 40% of children with disabilities go to school compared with 76% of children without disabilities. Nearly 75% of people with disabilities aged 15 or older living in households with multidimensional poverty never attended school.[137]

In 2016, the labor force participation rate of people with disabilities in Viet Nam was 33% compared with 83% of people without disabilities, and the percentage of people with disabilities in employment was 32% compared with 82% of people without disabilities (footnote 137). Moreover, the poverty rate for adults with disabilities ages 19-40 was greater than people without disabilities of the same age.[138] Accurate data on prevalence at different ages can help ensure more targeted and effective policy responses—including social protection—that promote equity and social inclusion.

In many countries, people with disabilities cannot continue to receive disability allowances once they reach the age of retirement and are transferred to old-age pension programs. As long as people with disabilities can continue to access other services and support, such as assistive devices, social services, and reasonable accommodations, then this may not have a significant negative impact. In Thailand, for example, more than 9 in 10 older people receive a pension and, in addition, a disability allowance if they are registered with a disability card.[139] In Georgia, some older people with severe disabilities receive a disability benefit in addition to their old-age pension. However, if the move to the old-age pension represents a reduction in income or a reduction in support for the extra costs of disability, then this can have a significant impact on quality of life, dignity in old age, and the ability of people with disabilities to age actively alongside older people without disabilities.[140]

As the population ages rapidly, it will be important for governments to understand the prevalence of disability in the aging population so that they can forecast the need for different types of social services, including care services, and plan to meet the demand as it emerges. Increasingly, governments are recognizing the need to monitor disability prevalence using function-based questions in surveys or social registers as well as to follow up with disability assessments that are based on the health and social dimensions of disability (i.e., impairments and barriers to participation) to confer disability status on people.

In the example of the Philippines in Box 14, the 12% prevalence rate of severe disability is much higher than, for example, the rates returned consistently by WGQs in other countries.[141] This presents a challenge for the Government of the Philippines

---

[136] UNDESA. 2019. *Disability and Development Report*. New York, pp. 76-84.

[137] ADB. 2022. *Viet Nam: Social Protection Indicator*. Manila.

[138] UNDESA. 2019. *Disability and Development Report*. New York, pp. 34-37.

[139] C. Knox-Vydmanov. 2016. *Work, Family and Social Protection: Old Age Income Security in Bangladesh, Nepal, the Philippines, Thailand and Vietnam*. London: HelpAge International.

[140] C. Knox-Vydmanov, A. Côte, F. Juergens, and D. Hiscock. 2021. Social Protection for Older People with Disabilities. Draft. https://socialprotection.org/sites/default/files/publications_files/Social%20 protection%20and%20older%20persons%20with%20disabilities_For%20consultation_10%2024_.pdf.

[141] Under which around 6% of the population in many countries will have disabilities, with the prevalence among older people typically at around 12%-20%.

Box 14: Identifying People with Disabilities in Japan and the Philippines

In Japan, there is currently no provision for a national census to collect relevant information on people with disabilities. Instead, various surveys on people with disabilities include the Survey on People with Disabilities at Home, Survey of Social Welfare Institution, Survey on the Situation of Certification for Classification of Degree of Disability, and Patient Survey.

The number of people with disabilities in Japan greatly increased to 9.4 million in 2018 from 7.9 million in 2015. One survey recommended enhancing disability statistics; the government should consider including disability questions as part of the Comprehensive Survey of Living Conditions that will target the general population in 2022.

In 2016, the Philippine Statistics Authority conducted the National Disability Prevalence Survey using a methodology based on the World Health Organization Model Disability Survey II, finding that 12% of the population has a severe disability. A person has a severe level of disability if he/she experiences extreme difficulties in at least one of eight functioning domains (i.e., mobility, self-care, pain, cognition, interpersonal relationships, vision, sleep and energy, and affect) and has at least one of five chronic conditions that are considered to lead to disability (i.e., arthritis, diabetes, heart disease, asthma or respiratory disease, and depression or anxiety). It equated the percentage of people with a severe level of disability to the disability prevalence reported by traditional surveys.

Sources: ADB. 2022. *Japan: Social Protection Indicator:* Manila; Philippines Statistics Authority. 2016. *2016 National Disability Prevalence Survey.* Manila.

in how to interpret the data from the National Disability Prevalence Survey in terms of targeting social protection, health, education, employment, transport, and other measures to people with disabilities.

Gender and life-cycle aspects of disability prevalence also need more attention in statistics—for example, disability among women tends to increase dramatically with age, as women live longer than men. Similarly, without good data on children and young people with disabilities, it can be difficult to plan for the full range of social, educational, and employment services that are needed to support them in their families when young and into productive independent living as adults, regardless of the severity of their disability.

When calculating social protection coverage rates for people with disabilities, ILO and WHO use prevalence rates for severe disability (i.e., classes VI and VII), calculated using the GBD 2004 data for regional groups of countries that are population weighted. For countries in the SPI study, these rates show that for many countries, the prevalence rates used in the SPI calculations are considerably higher (Table 10). This means that ILO and WHO are using a conservative estimate of the population of people with disabilities as the denominator of people who should be covered by social protection measures. In fact, if the generally higher prevalence rates from administrative data and surveys are used to describe the target population as the SPI study has done, then coverage is considerably lower in the region than the 21.6% or 9.4% estimated by ILO and WHO.

Table 10: **Disability Prevalence Rates Based on Washington Group Questions and World Health Organization Regional Data (%)**

Country	Prevalence Rate Used in SPI	WHO Regional Prevalence Rate for Severe Disability
WHO Western Pacific Region		2.7
Cambodia	4.0	
China, People's Republic of	6.3	
Lao PDR	2.1	
Malaysia	7.4	
Mongolia	4.0	
Philippines	12.0	
Viet Nam	7.0	
WHO Europe Region		3.0
Armenia	6.3	
Azerbaijan	6.4	
Georgia	3.3	
Kazakhstan	3.7	
Kyrgyz Republic	2.9	
Tajikistan	1.6	
Uzbekistan	2.2	
WHO Southeast Asia Region		2.9
Bangladesh	6.9	
Bhutan	2.1	
Indonesia	2.8	
Maldives	9.0	
Nepal	2.1	
Sri Lanka	7.2	
Thailand	3.1	
WHO Eastern Mediterranean Region		2.8
Afghanistan	4.2	
Pakistan	5.6	
High-Income Countries		3.2
Japan	7.5	
Korea, Republic of	5.0	
Singapore	6.2	
Average for all countries	**5.0**	**2.9**

Lao PDR = Lao People's Democratic Republic, SPI = Social Protection Indicator, WHO = World Health Organization.

Source: ADB estimates based on consultants' reports; and WHO and World Bank. 2011. *World Report on Disability*. Geneva.

2018 Social Protection Indicator Results

The SPI for disability presented in Chapter V estimated social protection expenditures for people with disabilities, considering both expenditures of programs targeted only to people with disabilities as well as subsets of budgets of general social protection programs based on estimates of the proportion of beneficiaries who are people with disabilities. As previously stated, the SPI for disability was generally a small part of the overall SPI for all Asian countries, which is to be expected, as the population of people with disabilities is a small proportion of the overall population.

The SPI country report for the ROK is the only study to provide actual administrative data on the number of people with disabilities benefiting from general social protection programs (Box 15).[142] Otherwise, consultants used estimates based on disability prevalence or household surveys to calculate the proportion of people with disabilities benefiting from general social protection programs.

Box 15: People with Disabilities Benefiting from General and Disability-Targeted Social Protection Programs in the Republic of Korea, 2018

In the Republic of Korea, almost 2.6 million people are registered with disabilities, about 5% of the population. According to general social protection programs, 2.4 million people with disabilities benefit from health insurance (i.e., 93% of people are registered with disabilities, and 5% of all health insurance beneficiaries are people registered with disabilities). In addition, 438,000 people with disabilities benefit from the National Basic Livelihood Security System, representing 25% of all targeted beneficiaries and 17% of all people registered with disabilities.

Regarding disability-targeted programs, 365,000 people with disabilities receive a disability pension (i.e., 14.0% of adults registered with disabilities). About 19,000 children with disabilities receive the Allowance for Children with Disabilities (i.e., 36% of children registered with disabilities). Finally, 84,000 people with disabilities receive the Assistance Service for People with Severe Disabilities (i.e., 3.3% of all people registered with disabilities).

Source: ADB. 2022. *Republic of Korea: Social Protection Indicator*. Manila.

In Pakistan, for example, there were no national social assistance programs targeted to people with disabilities, although Punjab Province had a provincial program. However, a national survey indicated a high prevalence of people with disabilities (31.5%) among those ages 65 and older. If it is assumed that most or all of these older people with disabilities were receiving old-age pensions or allowances under several national pension schemes, then a greater proportion of social protection expenditures were reaching people with disabilities than if only disability-targeted programs are considered. Hence, in Pakistan, the SPI for disability ranges from 0.2% of the overall SPI if only disability-targeted programs are included to 9.5% if assumptions are made about the proportion of people with disabilities benefiting from general programs such as old-age pensions.

---

[142] See ADB. 2021. Disability and Social Protection in Asia. *ADB Briefs*. No. 203. Manila. https://www.adb.org/sites/default/files/publication/760671/adb-brief-203-disability-social-protection-asia.pdf.

Table 11 presents social protection expenditures on disability using two measures. It considers expenditures of programs targeted only to people with disabilities (i.e., the minimum disability SPI) as well as the SPI presented in Chapter V that estimated both disability-targeted expenditure and subsets of budgets of general social protection programs based on estimates of the proportion of beneficiaries who are people with disabilities (i.e., the maximum disability SPI).

Table 11 also presents the percentage of the overall SPI that was reaching people with disabilities for both the maximum and minimum estimates of the SPI. As discussed previously, in the maximum SPI for disability, the attribution of people with disabilities benefiting from general programs, can only be considered a rough estimate since it is largely based on assumptions related to disability prevalence rates.

Table 11: Disability Social Protection Indicator as a Proportion of the Overall Social Protection Indicator, 2018

Country	Overall SPI	Maximum Disability SPI	Maximum Disability SPI Divided by Overall SPI (%)	Minimum Disability SPI	Minimum Disability SPI Divided by Overall SPI (%)	Disability Prevalence Rate (%)
Afghanistan	0.3	0.1	0.3	0.00	0.0	4.2
Armenia	5.6	1.2	0.2	0.15	2.7	6.3
Azerbaijan	5.9	1.8	0.3	0.25	4.2	6.4
Bangladesh	1.2	0.1	0.1	0.03	2.5	6.9
Bhutan	1.2	0.0	0.0	0.03	2.5	2.1
Cambodia	1.0	0.1	0.1	0.02	2.0	4.0
People's Republic of China	5.8	0.2	0.0	0.03	0.5	6.3
Georgia	4.7	0.5	0.1	0.25	5.3	3.3
Indonesia	2.1	0.1	0.0	0.00	0.0	2.8
Japan	11.7	1.7	0.1	0.51	4.4	7.5
Kazakhstan	4.6	0.8	0.2	0.46	10.0	3.7
Kyrgyz Republic	5.0	0.6	0.1	0.57	11.4	2.9
Korea, Republic of	6.0	0.4	0.1	0.06	1.0	5.0
Lao PDR	0.9	0.1	0.1	0.00	0.0	2.1
Malaysia	3.7	0.8	0.2	0.33	8.9	7.4
Maldives	4.0	0.4	0.1	0.19	4.8	9.0
Mongolia	4.8	0.7	0.1	0.43	8.9	4.0
Nepal	2.7	0.0	0.0	0.03	1.1	2.1
Pakistan	2.1	0.2	0.1	0.00	0.0	5.6

continued on next page

Table 11: *continued*

Country	Overall SPI	Maximum Disability SPI	Maximum Disability SPI Divided by Overall SPI (%)	Minimum Disability SPI	Minimum Disability SPI Divided by Overall SPI (%)	Disability Prevalence Rate (%)
Philippines	3.0	0.1	0.0	0.00	0.0	12.0
Singapore	5.7	0.7	0.1	0.00	0.0	6.2
Sri Lanka	3.1	0.2	0.1	0.01	0.3	7.2
Tajikistan	4.1	0.8	0.2	0.05	1.2	1.6
Thailand	3.7	0.2	0.1	0.08	2.2	3.1
Uzbekistan	6.3	1.2	0.2	1.04	16.5	2.2
Viet Nam	4.5	0.2	0.0	0.04	0.9	7.0
Unweighted average	**4.0**	**0.5**	**12.5**	**0.17**	**4.3**	**5.0**

Lao PDR = Lao People's Democratic Republic, SPI = Social Protection Indicator.

Source: ADB estimates based on consultants' reports.

On average across the 26 countries of the region, the maximum SPI for disability was 12.5% of the overall SPI (0.5 out of 4.0) if it is assumed that people with disabilities were benefiting from general social protection programs as well as disability-specific programs. If calculated only with the programs that were targeted to people with disabilities (i.e., where 100% of beneficiaries are people with disabilities), the minimum SPI for disability was 4.3% of the overall SPI. Given the lack of disaggregated data on people with disabilities benefiting from general social assistance or social insurance programs, it is difficult to know the actual SPI for disability. It probably lies somewhere between the maximum and minimum rates presented in Table 11.

The maximum SPI in nine countries was above the regional average. In some countries, the weight of expenditure for disability in the SPI was considerably more than in others. For example, in Azerbaijan, it was around one-third of the overall SPI, and between one-fifth and one-quarter for Armenia, Malaysia, and Tajikistan.

Countries with a greater-than-average minimum SPI for disability included Uzbekistan (1.04), Kyrgyz Republic (0.57), Japan (0.51), Kazakhstan (0.46), and Mongolia (0.43). The minimum SPI for disability confirms that most countries had at least one disability-targeted program, and many had more than one under both social insurance and social assistance, where all expenditures—or at least 90% to allow for inclusion errors—can be assumed to have been spent on people with disabilities. Indonesia, the Lao PDR, the Philippines, and Singapore did not have disability-targeted programs, and Pakistan had a program in one province but no national disability-targeted program. This does not mean that people with disabilities did not benefit from other social protection programs, only that programs targeted only to people with disabilities were not identified in these countries and were not included in the minimum SPI calculation.

It should be noted that in calculating the SPI for disability, welfare assistance for people with disabilities was included for some countries—including, for example, residential and day-care services, personal assistance and caregivers' allowances, subsidies, assistive devices, and rehabilitation services—and not for others. Reasons may be that there were no such services and therefore no expenditures in the social protection program, or that such services existed but expenditures could not be distinctly identified (e.g., in the Philippines where discounts were paid through different levels and parts of government and were not captured in the SPI) or belong to other sectors (e.g., health programs may include rehabilitation services and provision of orthopedic or assistive devices in some countries, and in others, these may be included as social assistance or social insurance expenditure).

Expenditure on disability-targeted programs seemed nonexistent in the Philippines, but this was because people with disabilities were benefiting from programs that were accounted for in a different manner. Although the Philippines did not have an allowance for disability that was targeted to people with disabilities, it had many general social protection programs providing support to people with disabilities. Social insurance programs covered people in employment if they acquire disabilities and cannot continue in employment. Social assistance reached children and adults with disabilities living in low-income households that met the poverty threshold criteria for the 4Ps, which placed conditionalities on households in relation to school attendance. People with disabilities were also entitled to a disability identity card that provided a range of discounts on medicines, health services, food, and transport.

Impact of COVID-19 on Disability-Inclusive Social Protection

The SPI study is focused mainly on 2018 expenditures but also provides an overview of additional social protection measures introduced by governments in Asia in response to the COVID-19 pandemic. The pandemic has impacted social protection for people with disabilities, as they are among some of the most vulnerable groups to have been affected by the economic and health crisis. Coverage, adequacy, and accessibility of social protection measures for people with disabilities were generally low before the pandemic, as evidenced in the low SPI expenditure on disability-targeted measures and the uncertainty of the extent that people with disabilities had in accessing general social protection programs.

During the pandemic, only 44% of countries globally introduced social protection measures that explicitly mentioned people with disabilities, and the majority of these schemes were either in-kind food or hygiene packages or cash benefits.[143] Where cash benefits were often introduced specifically for people with disabilities, they tended to be expanded vertically rather than horizontally to reach more people with disabilities. This is because most countries struggled to identify people with disabilities who were not already registered as having disabilities. This further emphasizes the importance of ensuring that people with disabilities can be identified in social registers

---

[143]   C. Knox-Vydmanov, A. Côte, and V. Wodsak. 2021. *Social Protection Responses to the COVID-19 Crisis for Persons with Disabilities: Synthesis Paper*. Geneva: ILO, UNICEF, and UNPRPD.

or administrative data sets for general social protection programs so that in emergencies they can be quickly identified and supported to access suitably adapted support.

Research suggests that people with disabilities benefited from programs aimed at older people or children and from programs for informal sector workers. However, there is evidence that the barriers experienced by people with disabilities when accessing general social protection programs were also at play when accessing COVID-19 measures, and many people cannot access support to which they are entitled.[144]

Conclusions and Policy Lessons

People with disabilities are often among the poorest and most vulnerable in Asia. Disability prevalence increases with age, as functioning changes and reduces. In many countries in the region, more than half of all people with disabilities are older than age 60.

The CRPD recognizes the rights of people with disabilities to an adequate standard of living and social protection, and the Incheon Strategy is helping accelerate its implementation. Many countries in the region have signed the CRPD and Incheon Strategy and are becoming more responsive to the needs of people with disabilities. The WGQs, designed to achieve more robust statistical estimates of disability prevalence, are being used in the region as a response to monitoring CRPD implementation, resulting in better prevalence data.

Indeed, the monitoring of CRPD implementation and SDGs has helped stimulate governments to incorporate WGQs into censuses and household surveys, but there is a need to continue to strengthen these initiatives and to extend them to social registers where people are enrolled into poverty alleviation programs, employment programs, or other social protection programs to collect more data. Crude whole population prevalence rates have very limited value when applied to programs that are targeting older people or children—or even working-age adults.

Coverage of people with disabilities in general social protection programs should be tracked through administrative data and screening questions on functioning. This would mean more accurate reporting on social protection expenditures for people with disabilities.

Finally, traditionally, social protection programs for people with disabilities aim to compensate for loss of capacity to work but should also take into account the additional costs of disability and focus on supporting the inclusion and participation of people with disabilities with services, assistive devices, disability-targeted cash transfers, as well as ensuring access to mainstream social protection programs, health services, transport, education, employment, and livelihoods.

---

[144] C. Knox-Vydmanov, A. Côte, and V. Wodsak. 2021. *Social Protection Responses to the COVID-19 Crisis for Persons with Disabilities: Synthesis Paper*. Geneva: ILO, UNICEF, and UNPRPD.

IX. Anticipating the Future of Social Protection in Asia

Introduction

This chapter examines the future directions of social protection in Asia. It suggests that the content and direction of social protection in the region is likely to be shaped by a range of factors embedded in the global and regional context. These factors include demographic forces, expanding global trade in services and evolving work norms, technological change, and climate change.

Demographic forces are aging populations across the region, growing in numbers of youth transitioning into the labor force, and promising dividends in many countries. The expanding global trade in services is interacting with advancing work-from-home technologies; evolving work norms are creating new economic growth prospects as well as additional opportunities for improved social protection systems. Technological change is creating greater opportunities but also new risks, magnified by an increasingly interconnected world. The resulting economic growth is encouraging urbanization and greater formalization of economic activity, altering the landscape of vulnerabilities that social protection must now address. While the COVID-19 pandemic has demonstrated the most pointed influence over the past 2 years, climate change will dominate future patterns of severe natural, social, economic, and epidemiological shocks.

This chapter maps out five of the clearest directions for social protection in Asia, outlining how these drivers will likely shape the nature of policy responses in Asia. First, social protection systems in the region will progressively improve their coverage of vulnerable groups, adopting universal approaches. Second, these systems will link with social and infrastructure services, both improving access and integrating into more comprehensive programs that strengthen developmental outcomes. Third, in the face of climate risks, social protection systems in Asia will play a strategic role in supporting the social dimension of the transition to a green and sustainable economy and society. Fourth, these systems will support and rely on the development of inclusive digital technologies. Finally, policy makers will increasingly rely on high-quality evidence to drive good practices, growing the demand for initiatives for improved data collection and monitoring.

Developing More Inclusive Coverage of Vulnerable People

Social protection systems in Asia will improve their coverage of vulnerable groups. While historically such coverage has grown over the decades, the COVID-19 crisis has pointedly accelerated progress. While estimates do vary, global stakeholders report a dramatic increase in social protection coverage as part of the COVID-19 response.[145] Chapter VI estimates that the region's social protection responses to COVID-19 reached 1.7 billion people, about 40.0% of the global population.

The pandemic's universal impact highlights the importance of universal social protection. Countries in Asia responded by expanding an integrated mix of social insurance and social assistance. For example, Thailand initiated a noncontributory child grant in 2015 for those in formal sector employment, which has currently reached near-universal coverage thanks to accelerated expansion in response to COVID-19.[146]

Social insurance has led the social protection expansion in Asia, and continued economic growth—with its strong correlation to contributory program expansion— will likely ensure this trend into the future. As noted in Chapter IV, the region's overall SPI rose from 3.3% of GDP per capita in 2009 to 4.1% in 2018, and social protection expenditure increased from 4.6% of GDP in 2009 to 5.6% in 2018, mostly driven by increases in social insurance, particularly for health. The COVID-19 crisis emphasizes both the importance of social health insurance for protection against devastating health shocks as well as the systemic role that public health investments play in protecting the population at large.

Health insurance integration with broader social protection systems is accelerating coverage expansion in Cambodia, Indonesia, the ROK, Malaysia, Singapore, and Viet Nam, while improving joint synergies and economies of scale.[147] Pensions for older people have also expanded, as many countries in the region have achieved universal or near-universal coverage from such pensions—particularly in East Asia and post-Soviet Union transition countries—while coverage varies considerably in others, such as those in Southeast and South Asia. In addition to contributory pension expansion, countries—including the PRC, Indonesia, the Philippines, Thailand, and Viet Nam—are extending noncontributory, tax-funded provision of health coverage for poor and sometimes near-poor people. Such integration has deep roots; Indonesia's cash transfer program, PKH, coordinates with the Raskin food assistance program, scholarship provision through Bantuan Siswa Miskin, and community health protection under Jamkesmas, Indonesia's government-financed health coverage program for the poor and near-poor.[148]

---

[145] For example, the United Nations estimated a 270% increase in global social protection spending from the end of 2020 to June 2021. Other estimates are more modest. The World Bank estimated a 240% increase in global coverage and a smaller increase in spending. See United Nations. 2022. Spending on Social Protection Rose Nearly 270% with Pandemic. 7 February. *UN News.* https://bit.ly/3UCvI19 and U. Gentilini. 2021. A Game Changer for Social Development? Six Reflections on COVID-19 and the Future of Cash Transfers. 11 January. *Let's Talk Development.* World Bank Blogs. https://blogs.worldbank.org/developmenttalk/game-changer-social-protection-six-reflections-covid-19-and-future-cash-transfers.

[146] S. Jitsuchon, C. Popivanova, M. Samson, and P. Golchha. Forthcoming. The Road to Universality: The Role of Advocacy and Evidence in Realising Thailand's Child Support Grant. In *The Palgrave Handbook of Social Protection and Social Welfare in the Global South.* London: Oxford University Press.

[147] ILO. 2021. *Extending Social Health Protection: Accelerating Progress towards Universal Health Coverage in Asia and the Pacific.* Geneva. https://www.ilo.org/asia/publications/WCMS_831137/lang--en/index.htm.

[148] T. McKinley and W. Handayani. 2013. Social Protection Index Brief: Social Assistance Programs in Asia and the Pacific. *ADB Briefs.* No. 16. Manila: ADB. p. 4.

The integrated approach adopted by Indonesia reflects a comprehensive model that is influencing other countries' social protection systems across the region. The 4Ps conditional cash transfer program in the Philippines similarly aims to integrate human capital and livelihood initiatives to strengthen developmental social protection. For example, the Department of Labor and Employment is partnering with ADB, with technical support from BRAC, to implement the Padayon Sustainable Livelihoods Program, which builds on the human capital foundation of the 4Ps, with comprehensive services and support for more sustainable livelihoods.[149] Similarly, Cambodia's new family package of integrated social assistance includes maternal and child benefits, scholarship programs for primary and secondary school students, support for people with disabilities, as well as pensions for older people.

The region has also seen new and expanding social assistance programs for people with disabilities. Historically, both high-income countries like Japan, as well as middle-income countries like Azerbaijan, Georgia, Mongolia, and Uzbekistan, have provided significant social protection for people with disabilities (footnote 150). The past decade has seen other countries initiate and expand these programs. Across the region, average spending on disability-targeted programs has increased from 0.15% of GDP in 2009 to 0.23% in 2018, reflecting increases in 17 Asian countries. The COVID-19 pandemic has accelerated these trends. Sri Lanka, for example, is providing a top-up cash transfer for people receiving disability allowances, as well as for older people. Increased spending on disability benefits will likely be reinforced by the growing aging population as well.[150]

Debates are occurring over the sustainability of these expansions. The history of crisis-induced social protection expansion suggests staying power, and the likelihood of future shocks will continue to grow coverage. In response to a range of driving forces, governments and their development partners have progressively innovated and expanded core social protection programs, reaching more of the population—and demographics will continue to propel this trend. As Chapter VI notes, over the next 3 decades, the number of older people in the region will exceed 1 billion, which is more than double that population today.[151] Climate change will increase the frequency and force of shocks that intensify the demand for social protection. Globalization will create other shocks—particularly economic crises—while sharpening the potential for policy diffusion.

Urbanization will further propel coverage expansion, as global shocks illuminate gaps in urban social protection systems. Asia and the Pacific is the most rapidly urbanizing region in the world, with an average of 3% urban population growth in 2017, well

149 BRAC. Implementing Comprehensive Graduation Programming in the Philippines. The Padayon Sustainable Livelihoods Program. https://bracupgi.org/program/philippines/.
150 UNESCAP. 2021. *How to Design Disability-Inclusive Social Protection*. Bangkok. p. 40.
151 UNFPA Asia-Pacific Regional Office. 2020. *Addressing Population Ageing in Asia and the Pacific Region: A Life-Cycle Approach*. Bangkok. https://asiapacific.unfpa.org/sites/default/files/pub-pdf/210927_unfpa_a_life_cycle_approach_layout.pdf.

above the global average of 2%.[152] The COVID-19 pandemic has accelerated recognition of the importance of social protection in urban areas, particularly in terms of extending coverage to informal sector workers.

Integrating Social Protection with Social and Infrastructure Services

Social protection systems in Asia will integrate with social and infrastructure services, both improving access and linking to more comprehensive programs. Social protection's scope has long included ensuring that all people have access to vital services, particularly early childhood care and development, support services for people with disabilities and older people, and cash and service support to caregivers. Linkages with social and infrastructure services will further enable social protection's greatest developmental impacts. Demographic aging of the population is expanding the demand for care services for older people and honing the imperative for early childhood investments to drive future labor productivity. Economic growth, urbanization, and technological change will expand the demand for and supply of infrastructure services. Improved evidence documenting the efficiency and effectiveness of social protection in strengthening access and the resulting developmental impacts of vital social, economic, and information services will drive policy diffusion across the region, as lessons of global and regional experiences accelerate the adoption of good practices.

Indeed, demographic change is creating a new urgency for life-cycle social contracts. Rising dependency ratios require labor productivity to rise faster than populations age to sustain improving living standards.[153] Integrated social protection and services investments in early childhood build the foundations for future productivity as youth enter the labor force.[154] This strengthens growth that expands the economic and fiscal space for old-age benefits, compensating older people for their lifetime contributions to social protection systems. This emerging intergenerational social contract supports a stronger tax benefit system, with national development strategies integrating social protection systems with developmental social and infrastructural services that support green growth. The resulting jobs and tax revenues in turn sustain this social contract.[155]

[152]   J. L. Baker, and G. U. Gadgil, eds. 2017. East Asia and Pacific Cities: Expanding Opportunities for the Urban Poor. *Urban Development Series*. Washington, DC: World Bank. https://openknowledge.worldbank.org/bitstream/handle/10986/27614/9781464810930.pdf?sequence=13&isAllowed=y.

[153]   M. Samson. 2016. Cognitive Capital: Investing in Children to Generate Sustainable Growth. Background paper for the Third High-Level Meeting on South–South Cooperation for Child Rights in Asia and the Pacific. Kuala Lumpur. 7-8 November; and M. Samson, G. Fajth, and D. Francois. 2016. Cognitive Capital, Equity and Child Sensitive Social Protection in Asia and the Pacific. *BMJ Global Health*. 1 (Supp 2).

[154]   UNICEF. 2019. 2019 Pacific Early Childhood Development (ECD) Forum Implementing Pasifika Call to Action on ECD. Nadi, Fiji. 23-25 October. http://www.unicef.org/pacificislands/media/1771/file/2019%20Pacific%20Early%20Childhood%20Development%20(ECD)%20Forum%20Report.pdf.

[155]   UNESCAP. Social Development: Youth Empowerment. Our Work. https://www.unescap.org/our-work/social-development/youth-empowerment.

The link between social protection and services is also creating new opportunities for people with disabilities. For example, the Government of Mongolia is integrating social protection and livelihoods for people with disabilities with systems-strengthening reforms that better identify children with disabilities, improve initiatives for their support and rehabilitation, enable business and support systems to strengthen employment access for adults with disabilities, and improve frameworks for assistive technologies and inclusive design. Coaching and case-management approaches improve labor market access for people with disabilities, community-based services (e.g., personal assistant services), and enable independent living. Kazakhstan and the ROK have implemented similar integrated initiatives as well.

Integrated social protection systems also strengthen infrastructure services. Governments are increasingly recognizing that more inclusive social protection systems—by sharing the benefits of economic growth in visible and well-appreciated ways—strengthen social capital that in turn complements infrastructure investment, supporting its sustainability. National development plans in Asia as well as the strategies of regional development partners recognize the vital contribution of social and basic infrastructure services (e.g., energy, transport, water, and sanitation) as well as the connectivity within and among countries, as a robust evidence base that documents the powerful role of social protection in reinforcing social contracts between governments and people, strengthening the social capital that so effectively complements infrastructure investments.[156]

Strengthening the Social Dimension of the Transition to Green and Sustainable Livelihoods

As governments and their constituencies work to meet their climate-related commitments over the next decades, the resulting opportunities and challenges will transform Asia and the world. Social protection systems in Asia will play a strategic role in supporting the social dimension of the resulting transition to a green and sustainable economy and society. This will require an expanding role for global partnerships. Governments, international organizations, and civil society organizations recognize the accelerating pace of climate change as the greatest present and future development challenge. Environmental disasters disproportionately affect Asia, with drastic consequences for the most vulnerable people who depend more directly than any other population on the natural environment for their livelihoods. Indigenous and tribal peoples are among the most

[156] See, for example, A. Alik-Lagrange, S. K. Dreier, M. Lake, and A. Porisky. 2021. Social Protection and State–Society Relations in Environments of Low and Uneven State Capacity. *Annual Review of Political Science* 24 (1). pp. 151-74; K. Drucza. 2016. Cash Transfers in Nepal: Do They Contribute to Social Inclusion? *Oxford Development Studies.* 44 (1). pp. 49-69; HelpAge. 2021. *Theories of Social Protection on Social Cohesion and Reconciliation: Theories, Experiences and Case Studies.* London; and M. Samson. Forthcoming. Comprehensive Social Protection as an Enabler of Complex Developmental Synergies. In *The Palgrave Handbook of Social Protection and Social Welfare in the Global South.* London: Oxford University Press.

marginalized and vulnerable sectors of society in Asia and specific measures are required to address their distinct needs and enhance their access to income security and essential services.

Intensifying and accelerating climate shocks propel the urgency of shock-responsive and adaptive social protection systems, and the complexity of the crisis requires unparalleled collaboration.

Climate disasters have long interacted with other crises to compound risks and exacerbate vulnerabilities, with repeated shocks eroding resources and undermining resilience. The 2008 global financial crisis interacted with climate and epidemiological shocks across Asia, fueling a complex system of covariate shocks that intensified negative coping mechanisms and underscored the importance of comprehensive social protection systems.

Today, global and regional stakeholders are assuming greater responsibility for supporting national social protection systems. Multilateral development banks, in particular, are playing a vital role in both raising global awareness and facilitating strategic responses. For example, ADB has committed 65% of its operations to address climate change by 2024—allocating $35 billion for climate finance during this period—rising 75% by 2030 to $80 billion.[157] ADB President Masatsugu Asakawa observed, "The battle against climate change will be won or lost in Asia and the Pacific."[158]

Climate change shocks drive a convergence between social protection and emergency response systems. The region's geography—with long coastlines aggravating both sudden climate hazards as well as slow-onset phenomena such as rising sea levels and increasing temperatures—disproportionately affects the poor and creates new vulnerabilities. Strategies thus must integrate social protection systems with mechanisms to address both phenomena and hazards.[159]

The future involves social protection binding together multisector strategies that support an optimal mix of climate, development, and equity initiatives, tackling poverty while building green and sustainable prosperity. This future involves an expanding role for global and regional development partners to support comprehensive social protection investments that strengthen integrated climate and development strategies. The Government of Nepal's partnership with ADB and the World Bank on a green, resilient, and inclusive development strategy offers a glimpse into this future. A joint climate risk assessment documents how COVID-19 has compounded "the multiple challenges that vulnerable populations already face in day-to-day life, with the potential to create devastating health, social, economic and environmental crises

[157] MIGA. 2020. *Annual Report 2020*. Washington, DC. p. 3.
[158] ADB. 2021. ADB Raises 2019-2030 Climate Finance Ambition to $100 Billion. 13 October. https://www.adb.org/news/adb-raises-2019-2030-climate-finance-ambition-100-billion#:~:text=%E2%80%9CThe%20battle%20against%20climate%20change,call%20for%20increased%20climate%20finance.
[159] N. Anschell, and M. Tran. 2020. *Slow-Onset Climate Hazards in Southeast Asia: Enhancing the Role of Social Protection to Build Resilience*. Stockholm: Stockholm Environmental Institute.

that can leave a deep, long-lasting mark."[160] The collaborative effort identifies a unique opportunity to create economies that are more sustainable, inclusive and resilient [with] investments that boost jobs and economic activity; have positive impacts on human, social and natural capital; protect biodiversity and ecosystems services; boost resilience; and advance the decarbonization of countries (footnote 160).

In 2021, the Government of Nepal endorsed the Kathmandu Declaration, committing to an integrated green, resilient, and inclusive agenda with development partners, identifying an additional $4.2 billion in future finance complementing existing commitments of $3.2 billion to support sustainable tourism, renewable energy, cleaner transport and resilient roads, integrated solid waste management, sustainable forest management, watershed protection and water supply, biodiversity conservation, adaptive social protection, climate-smart agriculture, and sustainable cities.[161] Countries across Asia are adopting similar approaches and integrating them into larger national policy frameworks. The Government of Viet Nam's 2020 National Strategy for Disaster Mitigation and Management recognizes that "measures for disaster mitigation and management must be compatible with measures for poverty reduction and natural resource protection, so that development can be equitable and sustained."[162]

Similarly, the Government of Indonesia's Climate Resilience Development Policy, 2020-2045 acknowledges the direct implications of climate change for the poor and articulates climate resilience actions, with a focus on pro-poor policies. This strategy opens the door to collaborative initiatives such as the ADB-supported project, Advancing Inclusive and Resilient Urban Development Targeted at the Urban Poor, which integrates adaptive and shock-responsive social protection initiatives with investments in sustainable livelihoods, public health, housing, and community infrastructure.[163]

These strategies incorporate social protection initiatives that support livelihood opportunities for the development of environmental assets. Examples of green public works programs include a 4-year integration of climate-smart agriculture under Pakistan's Ehsaas Emergency Cash Programme; developing a circular economy model in Phu Quoc, Viet Nam; the Green Jobs Act in the Philippines, which promotes decent jobs that build climate-change resilience; and the Green Entrepreneurship Program in Indonesia for private sector initiatives.[164] The Government of India

[160] World Bank and ADB. 2021. *Climate Risk Country Profile: Cambodia*. Washington, DC and Manila. p. 4. https://openknowledge.worldbank.org/handle/10986/36380.

[161] World Bank. 2021. Government of Nepal and Development Partners Join Forces on Nepal's Green, Resilient, and Inclusive Development. Press release. 24 September. https://www.worldbank.org/en/news/press-release/2021/09/24/government-of-nepal-and-development-partners-join-forces-on-nepal-s-green-resilient-and-inclusive-development.

[162] S. Vaziralli. 2021. *Building Climate-Responsive Social Protection*. London: International Growth Centre.

[163] ADB. 2022. *Building Resilience of the Urban Poor in Indonesia*. Manila.

[164] DFAT, AWP. 2021. *Towards a Circular Island Economy—Duong Dong Freshwater Wildlife Conservation Park, Phu Quoc Case Study Report: Valuing the Benefits of Nature-Based Solutions for Integrated Urban Flood Management in the Greater Mekong Region*. Canberra; IFAD. 2020. *Pakistan: Proposed Loan and Grant for the Gwadar-Lasbela Livelihoods Support Project II*. Rome. https://webapps.ifad.org/members/eb/129/docs/EB-2020-129-R-18.pdf; ILO. *Pakistan: Green Livelihoods of Rural Populations for Climate Resilience*. https://www.ilo.org/global/topics/green-jobs/projects/asia/WCMS_466526/lang--en/index.htm.

and International Institute for Environment and Development have also launched a climate information digital tool to improve climate risk management under the Mahatma Gandhi National Rural Employment Guarantee Act.[165]

Social protection aims to build broad-based resilience by strengthening human capital development, improving social risk management, protecting human security, and reinforcing trust and social cohesion. All of these impacts build the foundation required for a transition to a green and sustainable economy and society. In addition, social protection supports green fiscal reforms. For example, the Government of Indonesia's unconditional cash transfer initiative, PKH, supported a successful strategy in overcoming social and political opposition to a fuel-subsidy reform.[166]

Utilizing Inclusive Digital Technologies

Social protection provides direct benefits to vulnerable people to give them tools and resources to access vital digital resources, while also supporting—with its system investments—the extension of information and communication technology infrastructure to include them in the information web. Just as social cash transfers have proven over the past few decades to be key to making markets and governments work better for the poor and vulnerable, the future will demonstrate the transformative power of social and economic development to previously marginalized groups.

Social protection systems in Asia will both support and rely on the development of inclusive digital technologies. Technological progress has driven a range of transformative changes both socially and economically. For social protection, these technologies have lowered the cost and expanded the coverage of digital infrastructure, enabling innovations not possible before. While social protection systems have progressively adopted electronic innovations in registration and payment mechanisms over the previous 3 decades, the COVID-19 pandemic rapidly accelerated such digitalization across Asia. It demonstrated the power of inclusive digital technologies in both enabling rapid and effective social protection responses as well building resilience across multiple domains.

Digital technologies have better enabled governments and their development partners to respond to the pandemic and to more effectively and rapidly deliver social protection benefits to millions of people. The crisis highlighted the costs of outdated, incomplete, or absent social registries across the region. Pandemic-related public health measures multiplied the costs of physical payment and

[165] IIED. 2021. Launch of the CRISP-M Tool. 13 October. https://www.iied.org/launch-crisp-m-tool.
[166] C. Arndt, S. Jones, and F. Tarp. 2015. Assessing Foreign Aid's Long-Run Contribution to Growth and Development. *World Development*. 69. pp. 6-18; M. Samson, P. Golchha, and K. Stephan. 2018. Social Protection Systems Background Paper: Indonesia. Cape Town: EPRI; OECD. 2019. *Update on Recent Progress in Reform of Inefficient Fossil-Fuel Subsidies that Encourage Wasteful Consumption 2021*. Paris; and World Bank. 2020. *Energy Subsidy Reform Facility: Generates Knowledge to Support Governments to Design and Implement Sustainable Energy Subsidy Reforms While Safeguarding the Welfare of the Poor.* Washington, DC.

benefit delivery systems. In response, governments accelerated the pace of digitalization in registration and payment systems. Across developing countries, at least 155 programs in 58 countries have leveraged digital payments for the delivery of at least one of their new or expanded social assistance programs in response to COVID-19.[167]

Chapter VI highlights how COVID-19 has accelerated digital transformation in Asia, increasing the reliance of essential functions, including education, financial inclusion, work, social protection, and social services on digital delivery. Pakistan's Ehsaas Emergency Cash Programme glimpses the future: public–private partnerships supporting substantial investments in information technology infrastructure and digital innovations to strengthen delivery, including a biometric payment system, demand-side SMS-based platform, and advanced data analysis tools. Similarly, the pandemic accelerated the Government of Cambodia's plans to develop a digital on-demand component for its IDPoor social registry, and technological advancements have expanded the reach of its social protection programs to urban areas. The pandemic also spurred the Government of the Philippines to update its Listahanan social registry and introduced digital innovations in the second round of COVID-19 cash transfers.

These innovations are strengthening the core functionality of permanent and reliable social protection systems. By lowering the delivery costs to governments, as well as private costs to beneficiaries to access benefits, these innovations provide financial, economic, and social returns that propel their development and ensure their sustainability. A powerful impetus for their future expansion and sustainability results from the ways in which social protection's digital systems support comprehensive information and communication technology infrastructure, with feedback effects supporting broad-based resilience in multiple sectors including health, education, livelihoods, and market access. The pandemic has also demonstrated the vital role for inclusive digital technologies in supporting emergency remote learning, telehealth, adaptive livelihoods and work-from-home opportunities, e-markets and e-government, and other vital spheres for which resilience requires virtual connectivity.

These experiences and resulting lessons on the enabling potential of these technologies will likely become more important as Asia addresses the future shocks of climate change. Reviewing the evidence, IMF concluded that digital payment technologies "can further contribute to inclusive growth by bringing financial accounts to the unbanked, empowering women financially, and helping small and medium enterprises grow within the formal sector."[168] The World Bank found that "countries that decided to use digital payments are likely to achieve a more

---

[167]   U. Gentilini, M. Almenfi, I. Orton, and P. Dale. 2020. *Social Protection and Jobs Responses to COVID-19: A Real-Time Review of Country Measures.* Washington, DC: World Bank. https://openknowledge.worldbank. org/handle/10986/33635.

[168]   D. Prady, H. Tourpe, S. Davidovic, and S. Nunhuck. 2020. Beyond the COVID-19 Crisis: A Framework for Sustainable Government-to-Person Mobile Money Transfers. *IMF Working Papers.* No. 2020/198. Washington, DC: IMF.

efficient delivery of their social assistance payments."[169] These positive results are likely to sustain the considerable momentum for inclusive digital technologies well into the future.

However, Chapter VI also identifies the associated risk of exclusion for those with limited access to digital technology and low digital literacy, which often affects the most vulnerable groups most severely. The consequences are not limited to immediate exclusion—they can also create a reverberating inequality shock, as children without access to remote learning return to school much farther behind those students who had access to high-quality internet-based e-learning resources. Digital technologies also pose the risk of adverse inclusion, as technologies create opportunities for unscrupulous operators to reach vulnerable people through new channels that may lack the necessary consumer protections and regulatory oversight.[170]

Developing Monitoring, Data Collection, and Evidence for More Effective Social Protection Systems

Policy makers in Asia will increasingly rely on initiatives for monitoring, data collection, and evidence-building technologies. Globalization and technological progress interact with the dynamics of policy diffusion to increase policy-maker demand for better evidence, advancing interest in improved information systems. The COVID-19 crisis has sharpened the urgency of adapting innovative approaches to data collection and monitoring and thus motivated the development of new technologies. Innovations include monitoring technologies that harness big data, satellite imagery, and other nontraditional data sources and analytical engines driven by artificial intelligence.

The growing digitalization of social protection systems both creates demand for and better enables data-driven monitoring and evidence building. In 2018, OECD commissioned researchers to harness Cambodia's IDPoor database to create analytical data sets to support the analysis of poverty dynamics. The data that previously only enabled more effective and efficient system operations (e.g., targeting) now provide an unparalleled longitudinal census of the drivers of poverty and vulnerability, enabling policy evaluations and planning of more comprehensive interventions.[171]

The COVID-19 pandemic has elevated the importance of these efforts. In 2020, the Joint SDG Fund in Indonesia began supporting the government to link the

[169] U. Gentilini et al. 2021. *Social Protection and Jobs Responses to COVID-19: A Real-Time Review of Country Measures*. Washington, DC: World Bank. p. 22.

[170] M. Samson. 2019. Opportunities and Challenges for Social Protection's Linkages with Financial Inclusion. *EPRI Policy Briefs*. Cape Town: EPRI.

[171] M. Samson, P. Golchha, and K. Stephan. 2016. Cambodia's IDPoor System and the Potential for Poverty Dynamics Analysis. *EPRI Technical Briefs*. Cape Town: EPRI.

nation's Integrated Social Welfare Database to the One Data Indonesia initiative. Maliki, director, Alleviating Poverty and Development of Social Welfare, National Development Planning Agency, highlighted the potential of this flagship initiative to strengthen socioeconomic programs.[172] The nation's SDG review recognized how the process to achieve the objectives of the One Data Indonesia initiative will provide an opportunity for evidence-based policy using standardized, interoperable, and updated data to strengthen transparency and accountability of the government.[173] Digital technologies will offer opportunities as governments continue to advance evidence-based approaches to integrated policy development.

Increased development partner collaboration will continue to strengthen regional evidence bases and to share cross-country lessons. The United Nations has supported the advance of evidence-informing social protection policy development. UNICEF has commissioned impact assessments of social protection programs in India, Nepal, the Philippines, Thailand, and other countries and has hosted regional events to share lessons. ILO has supported a range of evidence initiatives and diagnostic tools for strengthening national capacity for social protection as well.

ADB also invests in products such as the SPI, a unique source of regional social protection data supporting social protection policy development. Chapter VII highlights the scope for improving regional evidence systems, highlighting gaps in countries updating key social protection information. This underscores the potential contribution of initiatives, such as the ILO Social Security Inquiry, to strengthen evidence building.

The regional focus on evidence building and data complements a growing regional focus on building capacity for social protection policy development. The United Nations, with bilateral development partners, has supported initiatives to institutionalize national training programs for social protection in Viet Nam, linking international and national research institutes.[174] Similarly, Bangladesh's Ministry of Finance, with support from international research institutes in Thailand and South Africa, has trained cadres of government officials in social protection policies and programs.[175] ADB has provided support to governments in Mongolia, Nepal, and Viet Nam to strengthen the capacity of government agencies to monitor and to assess social protection in Mongolia, Nepal, and Viet Nam.[176]

[172] Joint SDG Fund. 2021. Socioeconomic Registration and Information System for the Elderly (SILANI) in Support of Social Protection System Reform. 10 August. https://www.jointsdgfund.org/article/socioeconomic-registration-and-information-system-elderly-silani-support-social-protection.

[173] Government of Indonesia, National Development Planning Agency. 2021. *Indonesia's Voluntary National Review 2021*. Jakarta. http://sustainabledevelopment.un.org/content/documents/280892021_VNR_Report_Indonesia.pdf.

[174] UNDP. 2017. Project Document: Viet Nam—Supporting the Improvement of Social Assistance System in Viet Nam, Period 2017-2020 (SAP Phase II). New York. p. 2.

[175] Socialprotection.org. Strengthening Public Financial Management for Social Protection (SPFMSP). https://socialprotection.org/connect/stakeholders/strengthening-public-financial-management-social-protection-spfmsp; and EPRI. 2019. *South–South Capacity Building in Bangladesh: Status Report*. Cape Town.

[176] ADB. 2018. *Completion Report: Assessing and Monitoring Social Protection Programs in Asia and the Pacific*. Manila. https://www.adb.org/sites/default/files/project-documents/47215/47215-001-tcr-en.pdf.

Conclusions

A cascading and interacting confluence of global and regional forces—many of them magnified by the COVID-19 pandemic—are reshaping the future of social protection in Asia and the rest of the world. The trends analyzed in this chapter are not evolving independently—they reinforce and feedback, creating a complex challenge for governments, development partners, and nonstate actors.

The first trend—the increasing coverage of social protection systems—reflects the reality of the universal shocks that the region faces over the next decades. The COVID-19 pandemic represents a crisis for everyone—even those who never encountered the virus. Chapter VI highlights how new risk profiles compounded by COVID-19 and other shocks could reinforce intergenerational poverty and lead to deterioration in education, health, and other development indicators. More than any global event, the policy response (including public health measures) to the pandemic has accelerated and intensified the economic and social impacts of the crisis. Never before have governments responded with more universal social protection responses—providing financial support to countries that were flailing.

The second trend expands the potential of the first. Social protection encompasses more than financial benefits—it integrates access to vital social and infrastructure services to create synergies and to multiply impact. Social protection itself represents a social service, but it incorporates a responsibility to ensure that everyone— particularly the most vulnerable—can access other vital benefits required to sustain well-being and to realize opportunities. These include health, education, and livelihoods but also infrastructure-dependent services including energy, transport, information, and communications.

Future shocks, including climate change, will similarly affect people across the income spectrum, sometimes in catastrophic ways. The resulting global consensus for universal social protection has consolidated the foundation for future development partnership, which is vital for building a new model of development, climate, and equity strategies that enable a transition to a green and sustainable economy and society. This highlights the importance of the fourth trend, since inclusive digital technologies can strengthen resilience across many domains.

Perhaps the most important development is the fifth—policy makers are demanding the data-driven evidence and capacities required to improve social protection systems. This trend increases the agency of governments and their development partners to overcome the difficulties and to realize the opportunities that the future has in store.

The five trends all interact to propel policy makers to reshape future social protection systems, with an urgency accentuated by the threat of climate change. The momentum of increasing coverage reflects the commitments by governments and their development partners to deliver the benefits that people not only need but that also enable inclusive social development and equitable economic growth. The increasing focus on integrating social and infrastructure services multiply these impacts, particularly in the face of climate change, which requires—now more than ever—integrated and comprehensive protection systems to shape the social dimension of a transition to a green and sustainable society and economy. Inclusive digital technologies—while posing substantial risk—do offer enormous promise to strengthen shock-responsiveness and build resilience in health, education, livelihoods, and other sectors. Governments and their development partners are channeling these forces with choices that are shaping the transition, investing in data-driven policy innovations, and relying more on the global public good that the social protection evidence base represents.

Appendixes

Table A1: Social Protection Indicator by Developing Member Country, 2018
(% of GDP per capita)

Country	Overall SPI	Social Insurance	Social Assistance	Labor Market Programs
Afghanistan	0.3	0.1	0.2	0.0
Armenia	5.6	4.1	1.5	0.0
Azerbaijan	5.9	4.5	1.3	0.1
Bangladesh	1.2	0.4	0.6	0.2
Bhutan	1.2	0.8	0.3	0.1
Cambodia	1.0	0.8	0.1	0.1
China, People's Republic of	5.8	4.8	0.6	0.4
Georgia	4.7	0.2	4.5	0.0
Indonesia	2.1	1.1	0.9	0.1
Japan	11.7	10.7	1.0	0.0
Kazakhstan	4.6	3.5	1.0	0.1
Korea, Republic of	6.0	4.6	1.2	0.2
Kyrgyz Republic	5.0	3.9	1.1	0.0
Lao PDR	0.9	0.8	0.1	0.0
Malaysia	3.7	3.6	0.1	...
Maldives	4.0	2.6	1.4	...
Mongolia	4.8	3.7	1.1	0.0
Nepal	2.7	1.9	0.8	0.0
Pakistan	2.1	1.7	0.3	0.1
Philippines	3.0	2.0	1.0	0.0
Singapore	5.7	4.6	0.8	0.3
Sri Lanka	3.1	2.5	0.6	0.0
Tajikistan	4.1	3.6	0.5	0.0
Thailand	3.7	3.0	0.7	0.0
Uzbekistan	6.3	5.2	1.0	0.1
Viet Nam	4.5	4.0	0.4	0.1
Unweighted Average	**4.0**	**3.0**	**0.9**	**0.1**

0.0 = less than 0.1, ... = data not available, Lao PDR = Lao People's Democratic Republic, SPI = Social Protection Indicator.

Source: ADB estimates based on consultants' country reports.

Table A2: Social Protection Indicator by Category and by Income Group, 2018
(% of GDP per capita)

	Overall	Social Insurance	Social Assistance	Labor Market Programs
High-Income	**7.8**	**6.6**	**1.0**	**0.2**
Japan	11.7	10.7	1.0	0.0
Korea, Republic of	6.0	4.6	1.2	0.2
Singapore	5.7	4.6	0.8	0.3
Upper Middle-Income	**4.8**	**3.3**	**1.4**	**0.1**
Armenia	5.6	4.1	1.5	0.0
Azerbaijan	5.9	4.5	1.3	0.1
Georgia	4.7	0.2	4.5	0.0
Kazakhstan	4.6	3.5	1.0	0.1
Malaysia	3.7	3.6	0.1	...
Maldives	4.0	2.6	1.4	...
China, People's Republic of	5.8	4.8	0.6	0.4
Thailand	3.7	3.0	0.7	0.0
Lower Middle-Income	**3.0**	**2.3**	**0.6**	**0.1**
Bangladesh	1.2	0.4	0.6	0.2
Bhutan	1.2	0.8	0.3	0.1
Cambodia	1.0	0.8	0.1	0.1
Indonesia	2.1	1.1	0.9	0.1
Kyrgyz Republic	5.0	3.9	1.1	0.0
Lao PDR	0.9	0.8	0.1	0.0
Mongolia	4.8	3.7	1.1	0.0
Nepal	2.7	1.9	0.8	0.0
Pakistan	2.1	1.7	0.3	0.1
Philippines	3.0	2.0	1.0	0.0
Sri Lanka	3.1	2.5	0.6	0.0
Tajikistan	4.1	3.6	0.5	0.0
Uzbekistan	6.3	5.2	1.0	0.1
Viet Nam	4.5	4.0	0.4	0.1
Unweighted Asia Average	**4.1**	**3.1**	**0.9**	**0.1**

0.0 = less than 0.1, ... = data not available, Lao PDR = Lao People's Democratic Republic, SPI = Social Protection Indicator.

Source: ADB estimates based on consultants' country reports.

Table A3: Social Protection Indicator by Category and Income Group, 2009-2018
(% of GDP per capita)

	2009				2012				2015				2018			
	SPI	SI	SA	LMP	SPI	SI	SA	LMP	SPI	SI	SA	LMP	SPI	SI	SA	LMP
High-Income	**6.2**	**5.4**	**0.7**	**0.1**	**7.7**	**6.3**	**1.2**	**0.2**	**7.9**	**6.6**	**1.1**	**0.1**	**7.8**	**6.6**	**1.0**	**0.2**
Japan	10.4	9.2	1.0	0.2	11.7	10.5	1.1	0.1	12.1	11.0	1.1	0.0	11.7	10.7	1.0	0.0
Korea, Republic of	4.1	3.2	0.8	0.1	5.1	4.0	1.0	0.1	5.3	4.1	1.1	0.1	6.0	4.6	1.2	0.2
Singapore	4.2	3.9	0.2	0.1	6.3	4.4	1.6	0.3	6.2	4.8	1.1	0.3	5.7	4.6	0.8	0.3
Upper Middle-Income	**3.7**	**2.3**	**1.3**	**0.0**	**4.5**	**2.8**	**1.7**	**0.0**	**4.9**	**3.2**	**1.7**	**0.0**	**4.8**	**3.3**	**1.4**	**0.1**
Armenia	2.1	0.8	1.3	0.0	4.9	3.4	1.5	0.0	5.5	3.8	1.6	0.1	5.6	4.1	1.5	0.0
Azerbaijan	4.9	3.6	1.3	0.0	6.2	4.3	1.9	0.0	7.9	5.8	2.1	0.0	5.9	4.5	1.3	0.1
Georgia	5.2	1.3	3.9	0.0	4.9	0.1	4.8	0.0	5.6	0.2	5.4	0.0	4.7	0.2	4.5	0.0
Kazakhstan	...	...	...	...	...	...	...	...	...	...	...	...	4.6	3.5	1.0	0.1
Malaysia	3.9	3.6	0.3	0.0	4.2	3.8	0.4	0.0	4.0	3.9	0.1	0.0	3.7	3.6	0.1	0.0
Maldives	3.1	1.5	1.6	0.0	4.2	2.6	1.6	0.0	4.2	2.4	1.8	0.0	4.0	2.6	1.4	0.0
China, People's Republic of	3.5	3.0	0.4	0.1	4.3	3.7	0.5	0.1	4.6	4.1	0.4	0.1	5.8	4.8	0.6	0.4
Thailand	3.0	2.4	0.5	0.1	2.9	1.9	1.0	0.0	2.8	2.2	0.6	0.0	3.7	3.0	0.7	0.0
Lower Middle-Income	**2.5**	**1.6**	**0.8**	**0.1**	**2.9**	**2.1**	**0.8**	**0.1**	**3.0**	**2.3**	**0.6**	**0.1**	**3.0**	**2.3**	**0.6**	**0.1**
Bangladesh	0.9	0.2	0.3	0.4	1.1	0.4	0.4	0.3	1.1	0.5	0.4	0.2	1.2	0.4	0.6	0.2
Bhutan	0.8	0.3	0.5	0.0	0.8	0.6	0.2	0.0	0.7	0.4	0.2	0.1	1.2	0.8	0.3	0.1
Cambodia	0.5	0.1	0.3	0.1	1.2	0.3	0.9	0.0	0.6	0.1	0.4	0.1	1.0	0.8	0.1	0.1
Indonesia	1.3	0.4	0.9	0.0	1.2	0.4	0.8	0.0	2.1	1.4	0.6	0.1	2.1	1.1	0.9	0.1
Kyrgyz Republic	3.8	1.4	2.4	0.0	5.7	4.4	1.3	0.0	5.5	4.3	1.1	0.1	5.0	3.9	1.1	0.0
Lao PDR	0.6	0.4	0.2	0.0	0.6	0.5	0.1	0.0	0.6	0.5	0.1	0.0	0.9	0.8	0.1	0.0
Mongolia	5.1	3.4	1.6	0.1	4.8	2.3	2.5	0.0	5.2	3.8	1.3	0.1	4.8	3.7	1.1	0.0
Nepal	1.7	1.0	0.7	0.0	1.7	0.9	0.7	0.1	2.7	1.6	1.0	0.1	2.7	1.9	0.8	0.0
Pakistan	1.1	0.9	0.2	0.0	1.4	1.1	0.2	0.0	1.7	1.4	0.3	0.0	2.1	1.7	0.3	0.1
Philippines	2.1	1.7	0.3	0.1	2.2	1.5	0.6	0.1	2.6	1.8	0.8	0.0	3.0	2.0	1.0	0.0
Sri Lanka	2.9	2.5	0.3	0.1	2.7	2.3	0.4	0.0	3.2	2.5	0.6	0.1	3.1	2.5	0.6	0.0
Tajikistan	1.0	0.6	0.3	0.1	3.8	3.3	0.5	0.0	4.0	3.4	0.6	0.0	4.1	3.6	0.5	0.0
Uzbekistan	8.8	6.3	2.5	0.0	9.3	7.5	1.8	0.0	8.1	6.9	1.2	0.0	6.3	5.2	1.0	0.1
Viet Nam	3.9	3.3	0.5	0.1	4.0	3.3	0.6	0.1	4.1	3.6	0.4	0.1	4.5	4.0	0.4	0.1
Unweighted Asia Average	**3.3**	**2.3**	**0.9**	**0.1**	**4.0**	**2.8**	**1.1**	**0.1**	**4.2**	**3.1**	**1.0**	**0.1**	**4.1**	**3.1**	**0.9**	**0.1**

0.0 = less than 0.1, ... = data not available, Lao PDR = Lao People's Democratic Republic, LMP = labor market program, SA = social assistance, SI = social insurance, SPI = Social Protection Indicator.

Source: ADB estimates based on consultants' country reports.

Table A4: SPI Depth (% of GDP per capita) and SPI Breadth (% of total target beneficiaries) by Income Group and Category, 2018

	Overall Depth	Social Insurance	Social Assistance	Labor Market Programs	Overall Breadth	Social Insurance	Social Assistance	Labor Market Programs
High-Income	**6.7**	**7.6**	**7.4**	**2.2**	**114.9**	**87.9**	**21.1**	**6.0**
Japan	9.1	9.0	12.3	0.9	128.3	119.1	7.8	1.4
Korea, Republic of	5.5	5.3	8.1	2.6	110.3	89.3	14.4	6.6
Singapore	5.4	8.4	1.9	3.1	106.2	55.2	41.0	10.0
Upper Middle-Income	**13.1**	**21.9**	**6.0**	**6.7**	**64.6**	**36.7**	**26.3**	**2.1**
Armenia	11.1	23.0	4.7	9.8	50.1	17.6	32.4	0.1
Azerbaijan	17.1	25.8	9.0	3.4	34.8	17.5	15.2	2.1
Georgia	5.3	31.5	5.1	5.5	89.1	0.6	88.4	0.1
Kazakhstan	13.4	22.7	5.4	7.4	34.6	15.8	17.9	0.9
Malaysia	43.5	58.7	2.9	...	8.5	6.2	2.3	...
Maldives	5.9	4.5	14.6	...	68.1	58.8	9.3	...
China, People's Republic of	6.1	6.2	4.0	13.9	95.6	77.5	15.2	2.9
Thailand	2.7	3.0	2.4	0.1	135.9	99.7	29.9	6.4
Lower Middle-Income	**8.0**	**35.8**	**3.4**	**7.4**	**55.9**	**31.7**	**25.8**	**0.7**
Bangladesh	3.7	116.3	2.0	5.7	33.5	0.4	29.3	3.8
Bhutan	11.8	80.6	3.7	16.0	9.8	1.0	8.5	0.3
Cambodia	5.0	53.8	0.6	21.4	19.4	1.5	17.6	0.3
Indonesia	1.6	2.0	1.3	4.0	129.0	57.0	72.0	0.0
Kyrgyz Republic	8.8	9.2	7.5	3.4	56.9	42.6	14.1	0.2
Lao PDR	1.3	1.2	4.6	0.2	66.2	64.9	0.9	0.4
Mongolia	4.3	5.3	2.7	0.7	111.9	69.9	39.9	2.1
Nepal	9.4	39.6	3.4	1.0	29.1	4.9	24.2	0.0
Pakistan	6.6	81.7	1.1	19.9	32.6	2.2	30.1	0.3
Philippines	2.5	2.1	4.5	4.5	119.1	95.3	23.3	0.5
Sri Lanka	4.8	18.9	1.2	4.3	65.0	13.3	51.5	0.2
Tajikistan	20.9	35.3	5.5	4.6	19.5	10.1	9.2	0.2
Uzbekistan	26.9	49.9	8.2	6.7	23.3	10.5	11.6	1.2
Viet Nam	4.5	5.8	1.3	11.2	100.2	70.0	29.6	0.6
Unweighted Asia Average	**9.2**	**36.9**	**4.6**	**6.4**	**65.2**	**38.5**	**25.1**	**1.7**

0.0 = less than 0.1, ... = data not available, Lao PDR = Lao People's Democratic Republic, SPI = Social Protection Indicator.

Source: ADB estimates based on consultants' country reports.

Table A5: Depth of Social Protection Benefits by Income Group and Category, 2009–2018
(% of GDP per capita)

	Overall				Social Insurance				Social Assistance				Labor Market Programs			
	2009	2012	2015	2018	2009	2012	2015	2018	2009	2012	2015	2018	2009	2012	2015	2018
High-Income	**7.5**	**8.9**	**8.5**	**6.7**	**9.2**	**10.1**	**8.6**	**7.6**	**6.4**	**9.1**	**9.0**	**7.4**	**1.4**	**2.8**	**3.1**	**2.2**
Japan	11.5	13.6	14.4	9.1	13.1	13.8	14.6	9.0	10.2	13.8	12.7	12.3	1.7	3.8	4.2	0.9
Korea, Republic of	5.6	4.4	5.2	5.5	5.5	4.2	4.8	5.3	8.4	7.4	8.8	8.1	1.5	1.6	1.6	2.6
Singapore	5.3	8.8	6.0	5.4	9.0	12.3	6.5	8.4	0.7	6.1	5.4	1.9	1.1	3.0	3.4	3.1
Upper Middle-Income	**11.3**	**9.1**	**14.7**	**13.1**	**21.8**	**23.8**	**25.5**	**21.8**	**9.0**	**8.8**	**7.1**	**6.1**	**4.3**	**1.5**	**1.6**	**4.7**
Armenia	6.5	15.5	14.6	11.1	4.4	26.2	27.0	23.0	8.7	8.3	7.1	4.7	12.0	3.4	7.1	9.8
Azerbaijan	15.6	16.8	20.2	17.1	26.3	23.2	31.5	25.8	7.4	10.5	10.8	9.0	0.8	1.7	0.2	3.4
China, People's Republic of	4.5	4.5	5.3	6.1	4.5	4.9	6.1	6.2	4.6	2.6	2.2	4.0	3.9	4.5	4.1	13.9
Georgia	10.9	8.7	5.6	5.3	5.6	1.0	36.7	31.5	15.7	10.0	5.4	5.1	0.0	0.0	0.0	5.5
Malaysia	27.3	9.1	48.7	43.5	94.1	83.5	70.9	58.7	3.7	1.1	4.6	2.9	0.3	1.2	...	...
Maldives	10.8	6.0	6.0	5.9	6.9	4.0	4.1	4.5	21.8	29.1	17.4	14.6	13.2	...	...	...
Thailand	3.6	3.3	2.2	2.7	5.0	2.9	2.3	3.0	7.3	4.7	2.5	2.4	0.2	0.0	0.1	0.1
Lower Middle-Income	**8.3**	**8.8**	**9.0**	**8.0**	**30.0**	**35.6**	**34.3**	**35.5**	**4.6**	**3.9**	**3.6**	**3.4**	**6.8**	**7.0**	**8.1**	**7.4**
Bangladesh	9.7	7.8	6.3	3.7	123.1	209.1	176.9	111.8	6.2	4.3	2.5	2.0	9.1	5.7	7.5	5.7
Bhutan	8.9	12.5	11.5	11.8	54.8	44.6	43.5	80.6	6.6	4.2	3.8	3.7	0.5	12.1	25.8	16.0
Cambodia	2.3	2.7	1.3	5.0	6.0	4.4	1.0	53.8	1.5	2.4	1.3	0.6	6.7	2.0	14.9	21.4
Indonesia	5.4	1.5	2.3	1.6	3.4	1.1	2.7	2.0	3.9	1.8	1.8	1.3	14.6	2.9	2.5	4.0

continued on next page

Table A5: continued

	Overall				Social Insurance				Social Assistance				Labor Market Programs			
	2009	2012	2015	2018	2009	2012	2015	2018	2009	2012	2015	2018	2009	2012	2015	2018
Kyrgyz Republic	4.9	10.0	9.7	8.8	3.2	10.3	10.0	9.2	6.8	9.1	8.7	7.5	6.1	3.8	5.0	3.4
Lao PDR	2.5	3.6	2.3	1.3	9.4	6.6	2.5	1.2	1.1	1.1	2.3	4.6	0.1	9.0	0.1	0.2
Mongolia	6.8	4.6	4.6	4.3	7.9	5.5	5.5	5.3	5.7	4.1	3.3	2.7	3.5	1.1	1.2	0.7
Nepal	11.1	7.8	11.1	9.4	50.3	36.6	45.0	39.6	6.8	3.9	5.2	3.4	1.0	4.0	9.5	1.0
Pakistan	14.7	4.6	9.1	6.6	18.1	26.7	42.7	81.7	8.4	0.9	2.2	1.1	20.4	8.2	20.3	19.9
Philippines	6.7	2.3	2.2	2.5	26.4	2.0	2.1	2.1	1.2	2.9	2.4	4.5	4.8	20.1	2.2	4.5
Sri Lanka	5.8	5.9	5.0	4.8	44.0	25.9	32.0	18.9	0.6	1.0	1.2	1.2	2.3	2.1	2.4	4.3
Tajikistan	5.3	19.1	20.9	20.9	7.2	37.8	40.2	35.3	3.6	4.3	5.8	5.5	3.2	3.4	3.0	4.6
Uzbekistan	26.0	36.3	34.8	26.9	58.6	82.6	70.1	49.9	10.7	10.9	8.7	8.2	2.7	2.8	5.5	6.7
Viet Nam	5.6	5.0	4.8	4.5	8.2	5.3	6.4	5.8	1.5	3.2	1.5	1.3	20.8	21.1	14.0	11.2
Unweighted Asia Average	**9.1**	**8.9**	**10.6**	**9.3**	**24.8**	**28.1**	**28.5**	**28.2**	**6.4**	**6.2**	**5.3**	**4.7**	**5.4**	**5.3**	**6.1**	**6.5**

0.0 = less than 0.1, ... = data not available, GDP = gross domestic product, Lao PDR = Lao People's Democratic Republic, SPI = Social Protection Indicator.

Source: ADB estimates based on consultants' country reports.

Table A6: Breadth of Social Protection Coverage by Income Group and Category, 2009–2018
(% of total target beneficiaries)

	Overall				Social Insurance				Social Assistance				Labor Market Programs			
	2009	2012	2015	2018	2009	2012	2015	2018	2009	2012	2015	2018	2009	2012	2015	2018
High-Income	**81.2**	**90.8**	**96.8**	**114.9**	**57.6**	**69.6**	**78.3**	**87.9**	**16.1**	**15.4**	**13.6**	**21.1**	**7.5**	**5.8**	**4.8**	**6.0**
Japan	90.4	86.1	84.4	128.3	70.4	76.8	75.4	119.1	10.1	7.8	8.3	7.8	9.9	1.5	0.8	1.4
Korea, Republic of	73.1	114.9	102.6	110.3	58.8	96.3	85.4	89.3	9.5	12.7	13.0	14.4	4.8	5.9	4.2	6.6
Singapore	80.2	71.5	103.3	106.2	43.7	35.6	74.2	55.2	28.8	25.7	19.5	41.0	7.7	10.1	9.5	10.0
Upper Middle-Income	**45.2**	**60.5**	**67.0**	**70.3**	**29.3**	**36.6**	**37.2**	**40.7**	**10.9**	**23.3**	**28.3**	**27.8**	**5.0**	**0.7**	**1.5**	**1.7**
Armenia	32.5	31.8	37.6	50.1	17.0	12.9	14.1	17.6	15.3	18.7	23.1	32.4	0.2	0.2	0.3	0.1
Azerbaijan	31.4	36.8	39.1	34.8	13.7	18.4	18.3	17.5	17.2	18.3	19.4	15.2	0.4	0.2	1.4	2.1
Georgia	47.4	56.1	101.2	89.1	22.3	12.2	0.6	0.6	25.1	43.9	100.6	88.4	0.0	0.0	0.0	0.1
Malaysia	14.2	45.8	8.3	8.5	3.9	4.5	5.5	6.2	6.7	38.9	2.8	2.3	3.7	2.4	…	…
Maldives	28.3	70.7	70.7	68.1	20.7	65.2	60.6	58.8	7.3	5.5	10.1	9.3	0.2	…	…	…
China, People's Republic of	79.3	95.1	86.8	95.6	67.2	75.5	67.8	77.5	9.4	17.6	16.9	15.2	2.7	2.1	2.1	2.9
Thailand	83.6	87.2	125.1	145.7	48.2	67.2	93.5	106.8	7.8	20.0	25.1	32.0	27.7	0.0	6.5	6.9
Lower Middle-Income	**36.7**	**45.5**	**50.3**	**58.4**	**14.3**	**21.7**	**26.5**	**31.7**	**20.2**	**22.8**	**22.8**	**26.0**	**2.2**	**1.0**	**1.0**	**0.7**
Bangladesh	8.9	13.6	17.8	33.5	0.2	0.2	0.3	0.4	4.6	8.0	14.3	29.3	4.2	5.4	3.2	3.8
Bhutan	9.2	6.8	6.4	9.8	0.5	1.4	1.0	1.0	8.4	5.2	5.0	8.5	0.4	0.2	0.4	0.3
Cambodia	22.4	43.2	42.5	19.4	2.2	6.9	9.0	1.5	19.0	34.6	33.2	17.6	1.3	1.7	0.2	0.3
Indonesia	23.8	77.0	90.4	129.0	5.3	33.2	51.2	57.0	15.0	42.9	35.1	72.0	3.5	0.9	4.1	0.0
Kyrgyz Republic	77.2	57.7	56.7	56.9	41.0	43.4	43.2	42.6	36.0	14.0	13.2	14.1	0.3	0.2	0.3	0.2

continued on next page

Table A6: *continued*

	Overall				Social Insurance				Social Assistance				Labor Market Programs			
	2009	2012	2015	2018	2009	2012	2015	2018	2009	2012	2015	2018	2009	2012	2015	2018
Lao PDR	25.2	16.5	26.9	66.2	4.6	7.5	22.2	64.9	18.5	9.0	2.9	0.9	2.1	0.0	1.9	0.4
Mongolia	75.2	103.6	112.4	111.9	42.6	42.7	69.9	69.9	27.6	59.2	40.8	39.9	5.0	1.7	1.7	2.1
Nepal	15.4	21.2	23.8	29.1	1.9	2.5	3.5	4.9	10.4	18.0	20.0	24.2	3.1	0.6	0.3	0.0
Pakistan	8.0	30.1	19.2	32.4	5.0	4.2	3.2	2.1	2.8	25.6	15.8	30.0	0.2	0.3	0.1	0.3
Philippines	31.7	97.1	117.6	119.1	6.5	74.4	84.9	95.3	22.4	22.1	32.2	23.3	2.8	0.5	0.5	0.5
Sri Lanka	50.0	45.4	63.0	65.0	5.8	9.0	7.9	13.3	40.5	35.5	54.7	51.5	3.7	1.0	0.4	0.2
Tajikistan	18.5	19.8	19.0	19.5	8.8	8.8	8.4	10.1	9.5	10.6	10.1	9.2	0.2	0.5	0.6	0.2
Uzbekistan	33.9	25.6	23.3	23.3	10.8	9.1	9.9	10.5	22.9	16.5	13.3	11.6	0.2	0.0	0.0	1.2
Viet Nam	69.3	79.7	85.2	100.2	40.0	61.1	56.7	70.0	28.7	18.0	28.0	29.6	0.6	0.7	0.5	0.6
Unweighted Asia Average	**42.9**	**55.6**	**61.0**	**67.0**	**22.5**	**32.0**	**36.1**	**41.0**	**16.8**	**22.0**	**23.2**	**25.7**	**3.5**	**1.6**	**1.8**	**1.8**

0.0 = less than 0.1, ... = data not available, Lao PDR = Lao People's Democratic Republic, SPI = Social Protection Indicator.

Source: ADB estimates based on consultants' country reports.

Table A7: Poverty Dimensions of Social Protection by Income Group, 2009–2018
(% of GDP per capita)

	2009		2012		2015		2018	
	SPI Poor	SPI Nonpoor	SPI Poor	SPI Nonpoor	SPI Poor	SPI Nonpoor	SPI Poor	SPI Nonpoor
High-Income	**1.7**	**4.5**	**2.4**	**5.3**	**2.1**	**5.8**	**2.2**	**5.6**
Japan	3.3	7.1	3.5	8.2	3.5	8.6	3.5	8.2
Korea, Republic of	0.9	3.2	1.1	4.0	1.2	4.1	1.3	4.7
Singapore	1.0	3.2	2.6	3.7	1.6	4.6	1.8	3.9
Upper Middle-Income	**0.7**	**2.9**	**1.0**	**3.5**	**1.2**	**3.8**	**0.8**	**3.9**
Armenia	0.5	1.6	1.7	3.2	1.9	3.6	1.7	3.9
Azerbaijan	1.1	3.8	0.8	5.4	0.9	7.0	0.7	5.2
Georgia	1.4	3.8	2.4	2.5	2.8	2.8	1.6	3.1
Kazakhstan	...	...	...	...	...	...	0.4	4.2
Malaysia	0.4	3.5	0.5	3.7	0.3	3.7	0.4	3.3
Maldives	0.6	2.5	0.7	3.5	1.7	2.5	0.4	3.6
China, People's Republic of	0.3	3.2	0.4	3.9	0.3	4.3	0.8	5.0
Thailand	0.8	2.2	0.3	2.6	0.3	2.5	0.2	3.5
Lower Middle-Income	**0.4**	**1.9**	**0.7**	**2.2**	**0.6**	**2.3**	**0.7**	**2.2**
Bangladesh	0.3	0.6	0.3	0.8	0.3	0.8	0.2	1.0
Bhutan	0.1	0.7	0.1	0.7	0.2	0.5	0.3	0.9
Cambodia	0.2	0.3	0.4	0.8	0.3	0.3	0.2	0.8
Indonesia	0.1	1.2	0.2	1.0	0.7	1.4	0.6	1.5
Kyrgyz Republic	1.1	2.7	0.9	4.8	0.9	4.6	1.3	3.7

continued on next page

Table A7: *continued*

	2009		2012		2015		2018	
	SPI Poor	SPI Nonpoor	SPI Poor	SPI Nonpoor	SPI Poor	SPI Nonpoor	SPI Poor	SPI Nonpoor
Lao PDR	0.1	0.5	0.1	0.5	0.0	0.6	0.1	0.8
Mongolia	0.7	4.4	1.3	3.5	0.8	4.4	1.1	3.7
Nepal	0.2	1.5	0.3	1.4	0.4	2.3	0.3	2.4
Pakistan	0.1	1.0	0.2	1.2	0.2	1.5	0.3	1.8
Philippines	0.4	1.7	0.5	1.7	0.7	1.9	1.0	2.0
Sri Lanka	0.3	2.6	0.3	2.4	0.5	2.7	0.6	2.5
Tajikistan	0.2	0.8	0.4	3.4	0.5	3.5	0.5	3.6
Uzbekistan	1.6	7.2	3.5	5.8	2.9	5.2	2.1	4.2
Viet Nam	0.5	3.4	0.5	3.5	0.4	3.7	0.3	4.2
Unweighted Average	**0.7**	**2.6**	**1.0**	**3.0**	**1.0**	**3.2**	**0.9**	**3.2**

0.0 = less than 0.1, ... = data not available, GDP = gross domestic product, Lao PDR = Lao People's Democratic Republic, SPI = Social Protection Indicator.

Source: ADB estimates based on consultants' country reports.

Table A8: Gender Dimensions of Social Protection by Income Group, 2009-2018
(% of GDP per capita)

	2009		2012		2015		2018	
	Women	Men	Women	Men	Women	Men	Women	Men
High-Income	**2.8**	**3.4**	**3.4**	**4.3**	**3.4**	**4.5**	**3.5**	**4.3**
Japan	4.8	5.6	5.5	6.2	5.7	6.4	5.9	5.8
Korea, Republic of	1.8	2.3	2.3	2.8	2.4	2.9	2.4	3.6
Singapore	1.8	2.4	2.5	3.8	2.1	4.1	2.3	3.4
Upper Middle-Income	**1.5**	**2.1**	**2.0**	**2.5**	**2.3**	**2.7**	**2.4**	**2.3**
Armenia	0.9	1.2	2.1	2.8	2.9	2.6	3.0	2.6
Azerbaijan	1.8	3.1	2.3	3.9	2.9	5.0	3.2	2.7
Georgia	2.3	2.9	2.2	2.7	2.7	2.9	2.8	1.9
Kazakhstan	...	...	...	...	...	...	3.1	1.5
Malaysia	1.6	2.3	2.0	2.2	1.8	2.2	1.7	2.0
Maldives	1.3	1.8	1.9	2.3	1.9	2.3	1.9	2.1
China, People's Republic of	1.6	1.9	2.0	2.3	2.3	2.3	2.5	3.3
Thailand	1.2	1.8	1.3	1.6	1.4	1.4	1.9	1.8
Lower Middle-Income	**1.0**	**1.4**	**1.3**	**1.6**	**1.5**	**1.5**	**1.5**	**1.5**
Bangladesh	0.4	0.4	0.4	0.7	0.4	0.7	0.5	0.7
Bhutan	0.4	0.5	0.2	0.6	0.1	0.6	0.2	1.0
Cambodia	0.2	0.3	0.5	0.7	0.3	0.2	0.5	0.5
Indonesia	0.6	0.7	0.5	0.7	1.0	1.1	1.0	1.1
Kyrgyz Republic	1.4	2.4	2.4	3.3	3.2	2.3	3.2	1.8
Lao PDR	0.2	0.4	0.2	0.4	0.2	0.4	0.4	0.5
Mongolia	1.9	3.2	2.2	2.6	2.5	2.7	2.3	2.5
Nepal	0.5	1.2	0.7	1.0	1.0	1.7	1.0	1.7
Pakistan	0.2	0.9	0.1	1.3	0.1	1.6	0.3	1.8
Philippines	1.0	1.1	0.9	1.3	1.1	1.5	1.5	1.5
Sri Lanka	1.4	1.5	1.2	1.5	1.5	1.7	1.5	1.6
Tajikistan	0.4	0.6	2.1	1.7	2.5	1.5	2.5	1.6
Uzbekistan	4.0	4.8	4.4	4.9	5.1	3.0	4.0	2.3
Viet Nam	1.8	2.1	1.9	2.1	1.9	2.2	2.2	2.3
Unweighted Average	**1.4**	**1.9**	**1.7**	**2.2**	**2.0**	**2.2**	**2.0**	**2.1**

0.0 = less than 0.1, ... = data not available, GDP = gross domestic product, Lao PDR = Lao People's Democratic Republic, SPI = Social Protection Indicator.

Source: ADB estimates based on consultants' country reports.

Table A9: Disability Dimensions of Social Protection by Income Group, 2018
(% of GDP per capita)

	SPI for People with Disabilities	SPI for People without Disabilities
High-Income	**0.9**	**6.9**
Japan	1.7	10.0
Korea, Republic of	0.4	5.6
Singapore	0.7	5.0
Upper Middle-Income	**0.7**	**4.0**
Armenia	1.2	4.4
Azerbaijan	1.8	4.1
Georgia	0.5	4.2
Kazakhstan	0.8	3.8
Malaysia	0.8	2.9
Maldives	0.4	3.6
China, People's Republic of	0.2	5.6
Thailand	0.2	3.5
Lower Middle-Income	**0.3**	**2.7**
Bangladesh	0.1	1.1
Bhutan	0.0	1.2
Cambodia	0.1	0.9
Indonesia	0.1	2.0
Kyrgyz Republic	0.6	4.4
Lao PDR	0.1	0.8
Mongolia	0.7	4.1
Nepal	0.0	2.7
Pakistan	0.5	1.6
Philippines	0.1	2.9
Sri Lanka	0.2	2.9
Tajikistan	0.8	3.3
Uzbekistan	1.2	5.1
Viet Nam	0.2	4.3
Unweighted Average	**0.5**	**3.5**

0.0 = less than 0.1, … = data not available, GDP = gross domestic product, Lao PDR = Lao People's Democratic Republic, SPI = Social Protection Indicator.

Source: ADB estimates based on consultants' country reports.

Table A10: Share of Social Protection Expenditures to Gross Domestic Product by
Country and Category, 2018

Country	Share of Total Social Protection Expenditures to GDP	Share of Social Insurance Expenditures to GDP	Share of Social Assistance Expenditures to GDP	Share of Labor Market Programs Expenditures to GDP
Afghanistan	0.4	0.1	0.2	0.0
Armenia	6.0	4.3	1.6	0.0
Azerbaijan	5.9	4.4	1.3	0.1
Bangladesh	1.3	0.5	0.6	0.2
Bhutan	1.1	0.7	0.3	0.1
Cambodia	1.1	1.0	0.1	0.1
China, People's Republic of	9.2	7.6	1.0	0.6
Georgia	7.2	0.3	6.9	0.0
Indonesia	2.1	1.2	0.9	0.0
Japan	20.5	18.8	1.7	0.0
Kazakhstan	4.8	3.7	1.0	0.1
Kyrgyz Republic	9.2	7.2	2.0	0.0
Korea, Republic of	9.6	7.4	1.8	0.3
Lao People's Democratic Republic	1.1	1.0	0.1	0.0
Malaysia	3.6	3.5	0.1	0.0
Maldives	4.6	3.1	1.6	0.0
Mongolia	8.5	6.6	1.9	0.0
Nepal	3.2	2.3	1.0	0.0
Pakistan	2.5	2.0	0.4	0.1
Philippines	3.1	2.0	1.1	0.0
Singapore	4.6	3.8	0.6	0.3
Sri Lanka	2.8	2.2	0.6	0.0
Tajikistan	4.0	3.5	0.5	0.0
Thailand	5.3	4.2	1.0	0.0
Uzbekistan	6.0	5.0	0.9	0.1
Viet Nam	6.7	6.0	0.6	0.1
Asia Average	**5.2**	**3.9**	**1.1**	**0.1**

0.0 = less than 0.1, GDP = gross domestic product.

Source. ADB estimates based on consultants' country reports.

Table A11: Share of Social Protection Expenditures to Gross Domestic Product by Income Group, 2009-2018

	2009	2012	2015	2018
High-Income	**10.2**	**11.4**	**11.6**	**11.6**
Japan	19.2	22.1	21.1	20.5
Korea, Republic of	7.9	7.5	8.4	9.6
Singapore	3.5	4.7	5.3	4.6
Upper Middle-Income	**4.4**	**5.6**	**6.1**	**6.0**
Armenia	2.2	6.5	7.3	6.0
Azerbaijan	6.1	6.4	7.6	5.9
China, People's Republic of	5.4	6.5	7.7	9.2
Georgia	6.4	6.4	6.8	7.2
Malaysia	3.7	3.8	4.2	3.6
Maldives	3.3	5.2	5.0	4.6
Thailand	3.5	4.4	4.1	5.3
Lower Middle-Income	**3.6**	**4.1**	**3.8**	**3.8**
Bangladesh	1.2	1.3	1.2	1.3
Bhutan	1.0	0.9	0.8	1.1
Cambodia	1.0	1.2	0.8	1.1
Indonesia	1.2	1.2	2.1	2.1
Kyrgyz Republic	8.0	11.6	10.3	9.2
Lao People's Democratic Republic	0.9	0.7	0.8	1.1
Mongolia	9.6	13.2	8.8	8.5
Nepal	2.1	2.2	2.6	3.2
Pakistan	1.3	1.4	1.9	2.5
Philippines	2.5	2.6	2.9	3.1
Sri Lanka	3.0	2.6	3.2	2.8
Tajikistan	3.5	4.1	4.0	4.0
Uzbekistan	10.2	9.9	7.9	6.0
Viet Nam	4.7	5.0	6.3	6.7
Average	**4.6**	**5.5**	**5.5**	**5.4**

Source: ADB estimates based on consultants' country reports.

Table A12: Social Protection Expenditures, Social Insurance, by Income Group and Subcategory, 2009–2018 (% share of GDP)

	Overall Social Insurance				Pension				Health Insurance			Unemployment Benefit				Disability				Sickness				Other Social Insurance			
	2009	2012	2015	2018	2009	2012	2015	2018	2012	2015	2018	2009	2012	2015	2018	2009	2012	2015	2018	2009	2012	2015	2018	2009	2012	2015	2018
High-Income	**8.8**	**9.7**	**10.0**	**10.0**	**3.6**	**4.7**	**4.3**	**4.2**	**3.9**	**3.8**	**4.0**	**0.2**	**0.2**	**0.1**	**0.2**	**0.0**	**0.0**	**0.0**	**0.1**	**0.0**	**0.0**	**0.0**	**0.0**	**1.8**	**0.9**	**1.7**	**1.5**
Japan	17.0	19.9	19.4	18.8	8.9	11.3	10.8	10.1	8.3	8.3	8.1	0.3	0.2	0.1	0.1	0.0	0.0	0.0	0.3	0.0	0.0	0.0	0.0	1.7	0.2	0.1	0.1
Korea, Republic of	6.2	5.9	6.5	7.4	2.0	2.0	2.2	2.5	2.7	2.8	3.2	0.4	0.3	0.3	0.4	0.0	0.0	0.0	0.0	0.0	0.0	0.0	0.0	1.0	0.9	1.2	1.2
Singapore	3.2	3.3	4.1	3.8	0.0	0.9	0.0	0.0	0.6	0.4	0.7	0.0	0.0	0.0	0.0	0.0	0.0	0.0	0.0	0.0	0.0	0.0	0.0	2.7	1.7	3.7	3.0
Upper Middle-Income	**3.2**	**3.9**	**4.0**	**3.9**	**2.1**	**2.6**	**2.5**	**2.7**	**0.8**	**0.8**	**0.8**	**0.0**	**0.0**	**0.0**	**0.0**	**0.0**	**0.0**	**0.0**	**0.0**	**0.0**	**0.0**	**0.0**	**0.0**	**0.6**	**0.5**	**0.6**	**0.4**
Armenia	0.8	4.5	5.1	4.3	0.5	4.2	4.9	4.1	0.0	0.0	0.0	0.1	0.1	0.0	0.0	0.0	0.0	0.0	0.0	0.0	0.0	0.0	0.0	0.1	0.2	0.2	0.2
Azerbaijan	4.5	4.4	5.6	4.4	4.1	4.2	5.4	4.3	0.0	0.0	0.0	0.0	0.0	0.0	0.0	0.0	0.0	0.0	0.0	0.0	0.0	0.0	0.0	0.3	0.1	0.2	0.1
Georgia	4.9	3.5	0.4	0.3	4.1	3.5	0.3	0.3	0.0	0.0	0.0	0.0	0.0	0.0	0.0	0.0	0.0	0.0	0.0	0.0	0.0	0.0	0.0	0.0	0.0	0.0	0.0
Kazakhstan	...	...	...	3.7	...	...	...	3.4	...	0.0	0.0	...	...	...	0.0	...	...	...	0.0	...	...	...	0.0	...	...	...	0.3
Malaysia	3.4	3.4	4.1	3.5	2.0	1.8	1.8	1.9	0.0	0.0	0.0	0.0	0.0	0.0	0.0	0.0	0.0	0.0	0.1	0.0	0.0	0.0	0.0	1.4	1.5	2.2	1.4
Maldives	1.6	3.2	2.9	3.1	0.4	0.8	0.5	0.4	2.4	2.4	2.6	0.0	0.0	0.0	0.0	0.0	0.0	0.0	0.0	0.0	0.0	0.0	0.0	0.8	0.0	0.0	0.0
China, People's Republic of	4.6	5.7	6.9	7.6	2.2	2.7	3.3	5.4	1.5	1.8	2.0	0.1	0.1	0.1	0.1	0.0	0.0	0.0	0.0	0.0	0.0	0.0	0.0	1.2	1.4	1.7	0.2
Thailand	2.8	2.9	3.1	4.2	1.6	1.2	1.4	1.7	1.6	1.6	1.8	0.1	0.0	0.0	0.0	0.0	0.0	0.0	0.0	0.0	0.0	0.0	0.0	0.1	0.1	0.1	0.7
Lower Middle-Income	**2.1**	**2.7**	**2.8**	**2.9**	**1.7**	**2.3**	**2.3**	**2.3**	**0.2**	**0.3**	**0.3**	**0.0**	**0.0**	**0.0**	**0.0**	**0.0**	**0.0**	**0.0**	**0.1**	**0.0**	**0.0**	**0.0**	**0.0**	**0.2**	**0.1**	**0.2**	**0.2**
Bangladesh	0.3	0.5	0.6	0.5	0.3	0.5	0.6	0.4	0.0	0.0	0.0	0.0	0.0	0.0	0.0	0.0	0.0	0.0	0.0	0.0	0.0	0.0	0.0	0.0	0.0	0.0	0.0
Bhutan	0.3	0.6	0.4	0.7	0.1	0.6	0.4	0.7	0.0	0.0	0.0	0.0	0.0	0.0	0.0	0.0	0.0	0.0	0.0	0.0	0.0	0.0	0.0	0.2	0.0	0.0	0.0

continued on next page

Table A12: continued

	Overall Social Insurance				Pension				Health Insurance				Unemployment Benefit				Disability				Sickness				Other Social Insurance			
	2009	2012	2015	2018	2009	2012	2015	2018	2009	2012	2015	2018	2009	2012	2015	2018	2009	2012	2015	2018	2009	2012	2015	2018	2009	2012	2015	2018
Cambodia	0.3	0.3	0.4	1.0	0.2	0.1	0.3	0.7	0.0	0.0	0.0	0.2	0.0	0.0	0.0	0.0	0.0	0.0	0.0	0.0	0.0	0.0	0.0	0.0	0.0	0.2	0.0	0.0
Indonesia	0.4	0.4	1.4	1.2	0.1	0.1	0.9	0.8	0.1	0.1	0.5	0.3	0.0	0.0	0.0	0.0	0.0	0.0	0.0	0.0	0.0	0.0	0.0	0.0	0.2	0.2	0.0	0.0
Kyrgyz Republic	2.8	9.0	8.1	7.2	2.4	8.6	7.3	5.8	0.4	0.4	0.4	0.4	0.0	0.0	0.0	0.0	0.0	0.0	0.0	1.0	0.0	0.0	0.0	0.0	0.0	0.0	0.4	0.0
Lao PDR	0.6	0.6	0.7	1.0	0.0	0.3	0.6	0.5	0.3	0.3	0.1	0.5	0.0	0.0	0.0	0.0	0.0	0.0	0.0	0.0	0.0	0.0	0.0	0.0	0.0	0.0	0.0	0.0
Mongolia	6.3	6.5	6.5	6.6	5.0	5.1	5.1	5.1	0.8	0.8	0.8	1.0	0.1	0.0	0.1	0.1	0.0	0.0	0.0	0.0	0.0	0.0	0.0	0.0	0.3	0.5	0.5	0.4
Nepal	1.2	1.3	1.6	2.3	1.1	1.1	1.2	1.8	0.0	0.0	0.0	0.1	0.0	0.0	0.0	0.0	0.0	0.0	0.0	0.0	0.0	0.0	0.0	0.0	0.1	0.1	0.4	0.4
Pakistan	1.0	1.2	1.5	2.0	1.0	1.1	1.5	2.0	0.0	0.0	0.0	0.0	0.0	0.0	0.0	0.0	0.0	0.0	0.0	0.0	0.0	0.0	0.0	0.0	0.0	0.0	0.0	0.0
Philippines	2.0	1.7	2.0	2.0	1.1	1.1	1.1	1.1	0.5	0.5	0.7	0.7	0.0	0.0	0.0	0.0	0.0	0.0	0.0	0.0	0.0	0.0	0.0	0.0	0.4	0.1	0.1	0.2
Sri Lanka	2.6	2.3	2.6	2.2	2.6	2.2	2.6	2.1	0.0	0.0	0.0	0.0	0.0	0.0	0.0	0.0	0.0	0.0	0.0	0.0	0.0	0.0	0.0	0.0	0.0	0.0	0.0	0.0
Tajikistan	3.1	3.5	3.4	3.5	2.5	3.3	3.2	3.2	0.0	0.0	0.0	0.0	0.0	0.0	0.0	0.0	0.0	0.0	0.0	0.0	0.0	0.0	0.0	0.0	0.6	0.2	0.2	0.2
Uzbekistan	7.3	8.0	6.8	5.0	7.1	7.9	6.8	4.4	0.0	0.0	0.0	0.0	0.0	0.0	0.0	0.0	0.0	0.0	0.0	0.6	0.0	0.0	0.0	0.0	0.2	0.1	0.0	0.1
Viet Nam	4.0	4.1	5.5	6.0	2.7	2.5	3.5	3.2	0.9	0.9	1.2	1.6	0.0	0.1	0.1	0.2	0.0	0.0	0.0	0.1	0.0	0.0	0.0	0.0	0.5	0.6	0.8	1.0
Unweighted Average	**3.1**	**3.9**	**4.0**	**3.9**	**2.0**	**2.7**	**2.6**	**2.5**	**0.8**	**0.8**	**0.8**	**0.9**	**0.0**	**0.0**	**0.0**	**0.0**	**0.0**	**0.0**	**0.0**	**0.1**	**0.0**	**0.0**	**0.0**	**0.0**	**0.5**	**0.3**	**0.5**	**0.4**

0.0 = less than 0.1, … = data not available, GDP = gross domestic product, Lao PDR = Lao People's Democratic Republic, SPI = Social Protection Indicator.

Source: ADB estimates based on consultants' country reports.

Table A13: Social Protection Expenditures, Social Assistance, by Income Group and Subcategory, 2009-2018
(% share of GDP)

	Overall Social Assistance				Assistance for Older People				Health Assistance				Child Protection				Disability				Other Social Assistance			
	2009	2012	2015	2018	2009	2012	2015	2018	2009	2012	2015	2018	2009	2012	2015	2018	2009	2012	2015	2018	2009	2012	2015	2018
High-Income	**1.2**	**1.5**	**1.5**	**1.4**	**0.4**	**0.2**	**0.2**	**0.3**	**0.2**	**0.1**	**0.1**	**0.1**	**0.2**	**0.4**	**0.3**	**0.3**	**0.1**	**0.0**	**0.2**	**0.2**	**0.4**	**0.8**	**0.6**	**0.4**
Japan	1.9	2.0	1.7	1.7	0.7	0.0	0.0	0.0	0.0	0.0	0.0	0.0	0.4	0.9	0.5	0.5	0.2	0.0	0.4	0.6	0.6	1.1	0.8	0.7
Korea, Republic of	1.5	1.4	1.8	1.8	0.3	0.3	0.6	0.7	0.4	0.4	0.4	0.4	0.3	0.4	0.4	0.5	0.0	0.0	0.0	0.1	0.4	0.3	0.3	0.2
Singapore	0.2	1.2	0.9	0.6	0.0	0.2	0.1	0.2	0.0	0.0	0.0	0.0	0.0	0.0	0.0	0.0	0.0	0.0	0.0	0.0	0.1	0.9	0.8	0.4
Upper Middle-Income	**1.1**	**1.6**	**2.1**	**1.8**	**0.2**	**0.3**	**0.9**	**0.7**	**0.1**	**0.2**	**0.2**	**0.3**	**0.1**	**0.3**	**0.2**	**0.1**	**0.0**	**0.0**	**0.2**	**0.2**	**0.7**	**0.9**	**0.7**	**0.5**
Armenia	1.4	2.1	2.2	1.6	0.1	0.0	0.0	0.0	0.0	0.1	0.3	0.3	0.3	0.3	0.4	0.3	0.0	0.0	0.0	0.1	1.1	1.6	1.4	0.9
Azerbaijan	1.6	2.0	2.0	1.3	0.0	0.0	0.0	0.1	0.2	0.1	0.4	0.1	0.1	0.1	0.1	0.1	0.0	0.0	0.2	0.2	1.4	1.7	1.3	0.9
Georgia	1.5	2.9	6.5	6.9	0.0	0.0	4.1	3.6	0.0	1.2	0.5	1.9	0.0	0.0	0.0	0.0	0.0	0.0	0.5	0.4	1.5	1.7	1.3	0.9
Kazakhstan	..	..	..	1.0	..	..	..	0.0	..	..	..	0.0	..	..	..	0.2	..	..	..	0.5	..	..	..	0.4
Malaysia	0.2	0.4	0.1	0.1	0.0	0.3	0.0	0.0	0.0	0.0	0.0	0.0	0.1	0.0	0.0	0.0	0.0	0.0	0.0	0.0	0.1	0.0	0.0	0.0
Maldives	1.7	2.0	2.1	1.6	1.4	1.3	1.6	1.2	0.2	0.0	0.0	0.1	0.1	0.2	0.1	0.1	0.0	0.0	0.3	0.2	0.1	0.4	0.1	0.0
China, People's Republic of	0.7	0.7	0.6	1.0	0.0	0.0	0.0	0.0	0.0	0.0	0.0	0.0	0.2	0.2	0.1	0.1	0.0	0.0	0.1	0.1	0.4	0.5	0.4	0.7
Thailand	0.7	1.4	0.9	1.0	0.2	0.4	0.5	0.4	0.0	0.0	0.1	0.0	0.2	0.9	0.4	0.3	0.0	0.0	0.1	0.1	0.2	0.1	0.0	0.2
Lower Middle-Income	**1.6**	**1.2**	**0.8**	**0.8**	**0.2**	**0.1**	**0.1**	**0.1**	**0.0**	**0.1**	**0.1**	**0.1**	**0.4**	**0.3**	**0.3**	**0.2**	**0.0**	**0.0**	**0.0**	**0.1**	**0.9**	**0.7**	**0.3**	**0.3**
Bangladesh	0.4	0.5	0.4	0.6	0.1	0.1	0.1	0.1	0.0	0.0	0.0	0.0	0.1	0.2	0.1	0.1	0.0	0.0	0.0	0.0	0.2	0.2	0.2	0.3
Bhutan	0.7	0.2	0.2	0.3	0.0	0.0	0.0	0.0	0.0	0.0	0.0	0.0	0.7	0.2	0.2	0.3	0.0	0.0	0.0	0.0	0.0	0.0	0.0	0.0
Cambodia	0.6	0.9	0.4	0.1	0.0	0.0	0.0	0.0	0.2	0.1	0.1	0.0	0.2	0.2	0.2	0.0	0.0	0.0	0.0	0.0	0.2	0.6	0.1	0.0

continued on next page

Table A13: *continued*

	Overall Social Assistance				Assistance for Older People				Health Assistance				Child Protection				Disability				Other Social Assistance			
	2009	2012	2015	2018	2009	2012	2015	2018	2009	2012	2015	2018	2009	2012	2015	2018	2009	2012	2015	2018	2009	2012	2015	2018
Indonesia	0.8	0.8	0.6	0.9	0.0	0.0	0.0	0.0	0.1	0.1	0.0	0.2	0.4	0.4	0.4	0.4	0.0	0.0	0.0	0.0	0.3	0.3	0.2	0.3
Kyrgyz Republic	5.2	2.6	2.1	2.0	0.0	0.1	0.0	0.1	0.0	0.0	0.1	0.1	0.5	0.7	0.7	1.2	0.0	0.0	0.0	0.0	4.7	1.8	1.3	0.6
Lao PDR	0.3	0.1	0.1	0.1	0.1	0.1	0.0	0.0	0.0	0.0	0.0	0.0	0.0	0.0	0.0	0.0	0.0	0.0	0.0	0.0	0.2	0.0	0.0	0.0
Mongolia	3.0	6.7	2.3	1.9	0.6	0.6	0.5	0.2	0.0	0.0	0.0	0.0	0.4	0.1	1.1	0.6	0.1	0.0	0.0	0.3	1.9	6.0	0.6	0.8
Nepal	0.9	0.9	1.0	1.0	0.4	0.3	0.3	0.4	0.0	0.1	0.0	0.1	0.2	0.2	0.2	0.2	0.0	0.0	0.0	0.0	0.2	0.4	0.5	0.3
Pakistan	0.3	0.2	0.4	0.4	0.0	0.0	0.0	0.0	0.0	0.0	0.0	0.0	0.0	0.0	0.0	0.0	0.0	0.0	0.0	0.0	0.3	0.2	0.4	0.3
Philippines	0.3	0.8	0.9	1.1	0.0	0.0	0.0	0.1	0.0	0.1	0.1	0.0	0.2	0.4	0.0	0.0	0.0	0.0	0.0	0.0	0.1	0.3	0.7	0.9
Sri Lanka	0.3	0.3	0.6	0.6	0.0	0.0	0.1	0.1	0.0	0.0	0.0	0.0	0.2	0.2	0.1	0.1	0.0	0.0	0.0	0.0	0.0	0.2	0.4	0.3
Tajikistan	0.4	0.5	0.6	0.5	0.0	0.0	0.0	0.3	0.0	0.0	0.0	0.0	0.1	0.0	0.0	0.0	0.0	0.0	0.0	0.0	0.3	0.4	0.5	0.1
Uzbekistan	2.8	1.9	1.1	0.9	0.1	0.0	0.0	0.0	0.0	0.0	0.0	0.0	2.0	1.4	0.6	0.4	0.0	0.0	0.3	0.4	0.7	0.5	0.2	0.1
Viet Nam	0.5	0.7	0.6	0.6	0.1	0.1	0.1	0.1	0.2	0.4	0.4	0.3	0.0	0.0	0.0	0.0	0.0	0.0	0.1	0.1	0.3	0.1	0.0	0.1
Unweighted Average	**1.4**	**1.3**	**1.2**	**1.1**	**0.2**	**0.2**	**0.3**	**0.3**	**0.1**	**0.1**	**0.1**	**0.1**	**0.3**	**0.3**	**0.2**	**0.2**	**0.0**	**0.0**	**0.1**	**0.1**	**0.8**	**0.8**	**0.5**	**0.4**

0.0 = less than 0.1, ... = data not available, GDP = gross domestic product, Lao PDR = Lao People's Democratic Republic, SPI = Social Protection Indicator.

Source: ADB estimates based on consultants' country reports.

Table A14: Social Protection Expenditures, Labor Market Programs, by Income Group and Subcategory, 2009–2018
(% of GDP)

	Overall Labor Market Programs				Food/Cash for Work				Trainings				For People with Disabilities			
	2009	2012	2015	2018	2009	2012	2015	2018	2009	2012	2015	2018	2009	2012	2015	2018
High-Income	**0.2**	**0.2**	**0.1**	**0.2**	**0.0**	**0.1**	**0.0**	**0.0**	**0.2**	**0.0**	**0.1**	**0.1**	**0.0**	**0.0**	**0.0**	**0.1**
Japan	0.3	0.1	0.1	0.0	0.0	0.1	0.0	0.0	0.3	0.0	0.0	0.0	0.0	0.0	0.0	0.0
Korea, Republic of	0.1	0.1	0.1	0.3	0.0	0.0	0.0	0.0	0.1	0.1	0.1	0.1	0.0	0.0	0.0	0.1
Singapore	0.1	0.2	0.3	0.3	0.0	0.2	0.0	0.0	0.1	0.0	0.3	0.3	0.0	0.0	0.0	0.0
Upper Middle-Income	**0.0**	**0.0**	**0.0**	**0.1**	**0.0**	**0.0**	**0.0**	**0.1**	**0.0**	**0.0**	**0.0**	**0.0**	**0.0**	**0.0**	**0.0**	**0.0**
Armenia	0.0	0.0	0.0	0.0	0.0	0.0	0.0	0.0	0.0	0.0	0.0	0.0	0.0	0.0	0.0	0.0
Azerbaijan	0.0	0.0	0.0	0.1	0.0	0.0	0.0	0.0	0.0	0.0	0.0	0.1	0.0	0.0	0.0	0.0
Georgia	0.0	0.0	0.0	0.0	0.0	0.0	0.0	0.0	0.0	0.0	0.0	0.0	0.0	0.0	0.0	0.0
Kazakhstan	...	...	...	0.1	...	...	...	0.0	...	...	...	0.0	...	0.0	0.0	0.0
Malaysia	0.0	0.0	0.0	0.0	0.0	0.0	0.0	0.0	0.0	0.0	0.0	0.0	0.0	0.0	0.0	0.0
Maldives	0.0	0.0	0.0	0.0	0.0	0.0	0.0	0.0	0.0	0.0	0.0	0.0	0.0	0.0	0.0	0.0
China, People's Republic of	0.2	0.1	0.1	0.6	0.0	0.1	0.0	0.5	0.2	0.0	0.1	0.1	0.0	0.0	0.0	0.0
Thailand	0.1	0.0	0.0	0.0	0.0	0.0	0.0	0.0	0.1	0.0	0.0	0.0	0.0	0.0	0.0	0.0
Lower Middle-Income	**0.1**	**0.1**	**0.1**	**0.0**	**0.0**	**0.1**	**0.0**	**0.0**	**0.1**	**0.0**	**0.0**	**0.0**	**0.0**	**0.0**	**0.0**	**0.0**
Bangladesh	0.5	0.4	0.3	0.2	0.3	0.4	0.3	0.2	0.2	0.0	0.0	0.0	0.0	0.0	0.0	0.0
Bhutan	0.0	0.0	0.1	0.1	0.0	0.0	0.0	0.0	0.0	0.0	0.1	0.1	0.0	0.0	0.0	0.0
Cambodia	0.2	0.0	0.0	0.1	0.2	0.0	0.0	0.0	0.0	0.0	0.0	0.1	0.0	0.0	0.0	0.0
Indonesia	0.0	0.0	0.1	0.0	0.0	0.0	0.0	0.0	0.0	0.0	0.1	0.0	0.0	0.0	0.0	0.0
Kyrgyz Republic	0.0	0.0	0.0	0.0	0.0	0.0	0.0	0.0	0.0	0.0	0.0	0.0	0.0	0.0	0.0	0.0

continued on next page

Table A14: *continued*

	Overall Labor Market Programs				Food/Cash for Work				Trainings				For People with Disabilities			
	2009	2012	2015	2018	2009	2012	2015	2018	2009	2012	2015	2018	2009	2012	2015	2018
Lao PDR	0.0	0.0	0.0	0.0	0.0	0.0	0.0	0.0	0.0	0.0	0.0	0.0	0.0	0.0	0.0	0.0
Mongolia	0.3	0.1	0.0	0.0	0.0	0.0	0.0	0.0	0.3	0.0	0.0	0.0	0.0	0.0	0.0	0.0
Nepal	0.0	0.0	0.0	0.0	0.0	0.0	0.0	0.0	0.0	0.0	0.0	0.0	0.0	0.0	0.0	0.0
Pakistan	0.0	0.0	0.0	0.1	0.0	0.0	0.0	0.0	0.0	0.0	0.0	0.1	0.0	0.0	0.0	0.0
Philippines	0.2	0.1	0.0	0.0	0.0	0.1	0.0	0.0	0.2	0.0	0.0	0.0	0.0	0.0	0.0	0.0
Sri Lanka	0.1	0.0	0.0	0.0	0.1	0.0	0.0	0.0	0.0	0.0	0.0	0.0	0.0	0.0	0.0	0.0
Tajikistan	0.0	0.0	0.0	0.0	0.0	0.0	0.0	0.0	0.0	0.0	0.0	0.0	0.0	0.0	0.0	0.0
Uzbekistan	0.0	0.0	0.0	0.1	0.0	0.0	0.0	0.1	0.0	0.0	0.0	0.0	0.0	0.0	0.0	0.0
Viet Nam	0.1	0.2	0.1	0.1	0.0	0.1	0.0	0.0	0.1	0.1	0.1	0.1	0.1	0.0	0.0	0.0
Unweighted Average	**0.1**	**0.1**	**0.1**	**0.1**	**0.0**	**0.1**	**0.0**	**0.0**	**0.1**	**0.0**	**0.0**	**0.0**	**0.0**	**0.0**	**0.0**	**0.0**

0.0 = less than 0.1, ... = data not available, GDP = gross domestic product, Lao PDR = Lao People's Democratic Republic, SPI = Social Protection Indicator.

Source: ADB estimates based on consultants' country reports.

Table A15: **Distribution of Social Protection Expenditures, Social Insurance,
by Income Group and Subcategory, 2018**
(%)

	Share of Social Insurance to Total Expenditures	Pension	Health Insurance	Unemployment Benefit	Disability	Sickness	Other Social Insurance
High-Income	**83.45**	**29.13**	**35.27**	**2.06**	**0.69**	**0.00**	**32.86**
Japan	91.68	53.90	43.18	0.56	1.64	0.00	0.72
Korea, Republic of	77.87	33.48	43.69	5.61	0.43	0.00	16.79
Singapore	80.79	0.00	18.93	0.00	0.00	0.00	81.07
Upper Middle-Income	**69.65**	**68.83**	**19.48**	**0.60**	**0.57**	**0.10**	**10.42**
Armenia	72.74	95.39	0.00	0.00	0.00	0.82	3.79
Azerbaijan	75.79	95.93	0.56	0.94	0.00	0.00	2.56
China, People's Republic of	82.55	70.55	25.93	1.33	0.00	0.00	2.19
Georgia	3.89	89.22	0.00	0.00	0.00	0.00	10.78
Kazakhstan	77.64	91.74	0.00	0.16	0.54	0.00	7.57
Malaysia	98.16	54.58	0.14	1.40	3.87	0.00	40.01
Maldives	65.91	13.55	86.45	0.00	0.00	0.00	0.00
Thailand	80.49	39.67	42.75	1.01	0.14	0.00	16.43
Lower Middle-Income	**75.42**	**79.43**	**13.40**	**0.38**	**2.20**	**0.15**	**4.45**
Bangladesh	34.94	97.09	0.00	0.00	2.91	0.00	0.00
Bhutan	68.28	99.81	0.00	0.00	0.00	0.00	0.19
Cambodia	88.68	76.29	21.65	0.00	0.00	2.06	0.00
Indonesia	55.42	69.97	28.51	0.00	0.00	0.00	1.53
Kyrgyz Republic	78.61	80.25	5.65	0.00	14.10	0.00	0.00
Lao PDR	95.11	48.58	50.90	0.52	0.00	0.00	0.00
Mongolia	77.19	77.05	14.72	1.61	0.00	0.00	6.62
Nepal	70.11	78.53	3.07	0.00	0.00	0.00	18.40
Pakistan	82.17	99.75	0.07	0.00	0.00	0.00	0.18
Philippines	65.03	54.54	33.51	0.03	2.00	0.00	9.92
Sri Lanka	79.71	97.24	2.14	0.00	0.00	0.00	0.62
Tajikistan	87.33	93.46	0.00	0.30	0.00	0.00	0.24
Uzbekistan	83.57	87.07	0.00	0.01	11.74	0.00	1.18
Viet Nam	89.68	52.38	27.33	2.88	0.00	0.00	17.41
Asia Average	**72.98**	**71.15**	**17.28**	**0.63**	**1.44**	**0.11**	**9.39**

0.00 = less than 0.001, ... = data not available, Lao PDR = Lao People's Democratic Republic, SPI = Social Protection Indicator.

Source: ADB estimates based on consultants' country reports.

Table A16: **Distribution of Social Protection Expenditures, Social Assistance, by Income Group and Subcategory, 2018**
(%)

	Share of Social Assistance to Total Expenditures	Assistance for Older People	Health Assistance	Child Protection	Disability Assistance	Other Social Assistance
High-Income	**13.74**	**22.70**	**9.11**	**17.29**	**12.56**	**38.34**
Japan	8.22	0.00	0.00	27.14	33.91	38.95
Korea, Republic of	19.31	36.26	22.33	24.72	3.76	12.93
Singapore	13.69	31.83	5.01	0.00	0.00	63.15
Upper Middle-Income	**29.12**	**29.86**	**8.37**	**12.14**	**14.48**	**35.15**
Armenia	27.17	0.64	20.33	18.39	6.50	54.14
Azerbaijan	23.02	4.34	7.93	7.04	11.27	69.42
China, People's Republic of	10.51	5.05	4.57	14.13	5.16	71.09
Georgia	96.04	52.01	28.09	0.52	6.13	13.26
Kazakhstan	20.93	0.01	0.65	15.50	47.73	36.11
Malaysia	1.84	60.21	0.00	8.38	15.18	16.23
Maldives	34.09	76.76	5.42	4.16	13.64	0.02
Thailand	19.37	39.86	0.00	29.01	10.20	20.93
Lower Middle-Income	**21.99**	**18.07**	**7.64**	**29.93**	**8.95**	**35.41**
Bangladesh	47.17	15.07	3.63	19.90	6.00	55.40
Bhutan	27.00	2.36	0.00	97.62	0.00	0.02
Cambodia	4.99	0.00	0.00	67.85	32.15	0.00
Indonesia	44.52	0.10	23.06	42.41	0.22	34.21
Kyrgyz Republic	21.24	3.12	3.80	62.03	0.02	31.03
Lao PDR	4.82	70.39	1.37	0.00	0.00	28.23
Mongolia	22.51	8.97	0.00	33.58	17.50	39.95
Nepal	29.89	42.22	6.80	20.56	4.05	26.38
Pakistan	14.96	0.01	9.70	0.99	1.38	87.93
Philippines	34.24	9.36	2.30	1.65	0.00	86.69
Sri Lanka	20.09	12.02	3.13	22.66	1.91	60.28
Tajikistan	12.39	70.37	0.00	4.83	1.62	23.18
Uzbekistan	15.14	1.27	3.46	41.70	41.84	11.73
Viet Nam	8.92	17.67	49.66	3.27	18.64	10.77
Asia Average	**24.67**	**21.53**	**7.74**	**21.99**	**12.66**	**36.07**

0.00 = less than 0.001, ... = data not available, Lao PDR = Lao People's Democratic Republic, SPI = Social Protection Indicator.

Source: ADB estimates based on consultants' country reports.

Table A17: Distribution of Social Protection Expenditures, Labor Market Programs, by Income Group and Subcategory, 2018
(%)

	Share of Labor Marker Programs to Total Expenditures	Food/Cash for Work	Trainings	For People with Disabilities
High-Income	**2.82**	**6.25**	**70.83**	**22.92**
Japan	0.11	9.15	77.42	13.44
Korea, Republic of	2.82	9.59	35.07	55.34
Singapore	5.52	0.00	100.00	0.00
Upper Middle-Income	**1.23**	**22.54**	**69.67**	**7.79**
Armenia	0.09	0.00	55.44	44.56
Azerbaijan	1.19	0.00	100.00	0.00
China, People's Republic of	6.93	84.23	14.64	1.13
Georgia	0.07	0.00	99.07	0.93
Kazakhstan	1.43	50.98	48.89	0.12
Malaysia	...	...	...	...
Maldives	...	...	...	...
Thailand	0.14	0.00	100.00	0.00
Lower Middle-Income	**2.59**	**37.71**	**59.08**	**3.21**
Bangladesh	17.89	100.00	0.00	0.00
Bhutan	4.72	0.00	100.00	0.00
Cambodia	6.33	0.00	100.00	0.00
Indonesia	0.06	0.00	100.00	0.00
Kyrgyz Republic	0.15	56.47	43.53	0.00
Lao PDR	0.1	0.00	100.00	0.00
Mongolia	0.30	36.76	19.77	43.47
Nepal	0.00	100.00	0.00	0.00
Pakistan	2.87	0.00	100.00	0.00
Philippines	0.73	11.91	88.09	0.00
Sri Lanka	0.20	67.26	31.33	1.40
Tajikistan	0.28	13.76	86.24	0.00
Uzbekistan	1.29	95.86	4.14	0.00
Viet Nam	1.40	45.99	54.01	0.00
Asia Average	**2.35**	**28.42**	**64.90**	**6.68**

0.00 = less than 0.001, ... = data not available, Lao PDR = Lao People's Democratic Republic, SPI = Social Protection Indicator.

Source: ADB estimates based on consultants' country reports.

Table A18: Trends on Social Protection Expenditure, 2009–2018

	SPI (% of GDP per capita)				Expenditure (% of GDP)			
	Average for 24 Countries	High-Income	Upper Middle-Income	Lower Middle-Income	Average for 24 Countries	High-Income	Upper Middle-Income	Lower Middle-Income
2009	3.3	6.2	3.7	2.5	4.6	10.2	4.4	3.6
2012	4.0	7.7	4.5	2.9	5.5	11.4	5.6	4.1
2015	4.2	7.9	4.9	3.0	5.5	11.6	6.1	3.8
2018	4.1	7.8	4.8	3.0	5.4	11.6	6.0	3.8

GDP = gross domestic product, SPI = Social Protection Indicator.

Source: ADB estimates based on consultants' country reports.

www.ingramcontent.com/pod-product-compliance
Lightning Source LLC
Chambersburg PA
CBHW041432270326
41935CB00025B/1858